Capitalism, Crisis and Democracy

Historical Materialism Book Series

VOLUME 392

The titles published in this series are listed at *brill.com/hm*

Capitalism, Crisis and Democracy

Theory and Conflict in Portugal's Dawn of Decline

By

Jonas Van Vossole

BRILL

ISSN 1570-1522
ISBN 978-90-04-76622-8
ISBN 978-90-04-76623-5 (PDF)
DOI https://doi.org/10.1163/9789004766235

Library of Congress Control Number: 2026942978

Brill and Koninklijke Brill BV are part of De Gruyter Brill.
www.degruyterbrill.com

Questions about General Product Safety Regulation: productsafety@degruyterbrill.com

Dedicated to Marcela Uchôa, without whose insistence, love, and inspiration this book would never have materialised, and to Alice and Aurora – whose new lives solidified my hope to continue striving for a better future.

Contents

Introduction

Nearly 15 years have passed since the onset of the democratic crisis that followed the 2008 global financial crisis. In the years since, liberal democracies have undergone a tumultuous series of changes and crises: from the collapse of democratic legitimacy and the rise of the Occupy movements, through the period of exception of the Covid-19 pandemic, to the global surge of far-right populism.

Fifteen years ago, these contemporary developments would have seemed improbable, to say the least. At the time, liberal democracy and depoliticised technocracy were hegemonic. Today, far-right parties dominate much of the public discourse. Radical right-wing leaders openly attack LGBT+ rights, higher education institutions face direct threats, and immigration policies have become increasingly harsh, marked by deportations, state violence, and the resurgence of overt racism. In many countries, the rule of law has been suspended to advance right-wing agendas. Internationally, the standing of international law has deteriorated into little more than symbolic rhetoric, particularly in the wake of the wars in Ukraine and Gaza.

A superficial historical comparison with the 1930s reveals – despite significant differences – some troubling similarities. Then, too, a period of relative stability during the liberal capitalist 'roaring twenties' dominated by liberal democratic governance was followed by a financial crash and a prolonged economic crisis that destabilised liberal democracy. Although the left appeared poised to offer an alternative to capitalism, leftist parties ultimately inscribed themselves within the liberal bourgeois order – whether out of ideological alignment or geopolitical pragmatism. The result was a radicalisation of the right, which paradoxically succeeded in presenting itself as anti-systemic, gaining momentum and ultimately seizing power.

The contemporary Portuguese context offers a particularly striking and instructive case study in how a seemingly stable and progressive liberal democracy can be rocked by political upheaval. At the same time, it illustrates – at least from the perspective put forward in this book – the extent to which these changes have been shaped by the actions, or inaction, of the left.

The most recent Portuguese parliamentary elections in May 2025 confirmed the meteoric rise of the far-right party Chega, which has gone from holding no seats to 58 in just four years. Meanwhile, traditional left-wing parties have suffered repeated electoral defeats: the once dominant Socialist Party has fallen to third place, behind Chega, and the Communist Party and Left Bloc are nearing political oblivion, holding only four seats combined. While the global zeit-

 | HTTPS://DOI.ORG/10.1163/9789004766235-002

geist, personified by figures like Donald Trump, is often cited as an explanation for the ongoing crisis and democratic decline, it is increasingly clear that a more nuanced analysis is needed – one that interrogates both left-wing political strategies and the internal dynamics of liberal democracy itself.

Over the past centuries, a wide range of often contradicting intellectual schools have tried to theorise democracy. Reviews often analysed and categorised different democratic theories in closed and separate theoretical and ideological models, which most often failed to explain the origins of those differences, let alone offer a perspective about how to overcome the differences between these schools. These scientific reviews have usually represented democratic models as an evolution. At the end of this evolution – in true Fukuyama-style – liberal democracy appeared as the hegemonic principle of governance. Paradoxically, in this very same 'post-political' or 'post-democratic' world, democracy was reduced to 'low-intensity democracy', in which management took the place of politics and democratic sovereignty became increasingly curtailed through neoliberal policies and globalisation.[1] While democratic participation declined, neoliberal ideology remained uncontested and an elitist, formal legitimation sufficed to ensure governance stability.[2] Much of the current state of democratic theory reflects this hegemony by detaching democracy from the organisation of the political economy. A liberal kernel can be found in almost all important contemporary democratic schools, from the democratic elitism of Schumpeter and Przeworski and the positivist empiricism of Huntington to critical schools of Habermas's and Benhabib's deliberativism and Mouffe's agonistic democracy.[3]

Due to its semi-peripheral position, and the crisis it went through, Portugal is an excellent case-study to understand the contradictions and struggles that exist behind the concept of democracy.[4] In contrast to many peripheral countries, Portugal has known 40 years of a relatively stable parliamentary democracy, in which a democratic hegemony could develop. In contrast to the richer, imperialist countries of the core, however, the country has less economic room of manoeuvre to pacify and therefore submerge subjacent social and political conflicts.

From its democratisation in 1974 onwards, ideological struggles about the meaning of democracy involved continuous processes of reinterpretation and

1 Gills and Rocamora 1992; Santos and Avritzer 2005.
2 Santos 2005.
3 Schumpeter 1976; Przeworski 1999; Huntington 1991; Habermas and Benhabib 1996; Mouffe 2013.
4 Santos 2016b, pp. 42–5.

rewriting of historical events. In the initial years, many political entities fought over the legitimacy of different forms of governance (electoral, participatory, constitutional, local or national), including the church, the military command hierarchy and the MFA (left-wing Armed Forces Movement), the PS (*Partido Socialista* – Socialist Party), the PCP (*Partido Comunista Português* – Portuguese Communist Party), the radical left and the right-wing parties.[5] This conflict inspired the renowned Portuguese sociologist Boaventura de Sousa Santos's concept of demodiversity – 'The peaceful or conflicting coexistence [...] of different models and practices of democracy'.[6] This concept was developed not only as a historical description, but also as a means of emancipation, an inspiration of alternatives against the situation of liberal hegemony he called a 'democratic monoculture'. During the next decades, the diversity gave way to a hegemonic re-articulation around an elitist constitutional representative democracy within the European Union. The European project brought the possibility to enter the globalised 'civilised' world and to establish a modern liberal democratic state with a modern judicial system, new markets and a national infrastructure – a task the Portuguese elites were never able to develop before.[7]

And then came the crisis. The socio-economic crises of the 1930s and 1970s coincided with a disruption of the liberal, rationalist conceptualisation of democracy and led to renewed debates about democracy.[8] Just as Habermas theorised the legitimation crisis of the 'late-capitalist' social-democratic welfare state as the emergence of a range of different narratives or 'contradicting legitimacy claims' on democracy, the Euro crisis and European austerity policies raised questions of democracy and legitimacy.[9] While the democratic deficit of European governance structures is not a new problem, the crisis exacerbated these, leading some authors to warn about the dangers of what would be considered a 'democracy without choices', or 'a bloodless *coup d'etat*' in the eurozone.[10]

During the research for this book, many other insightful and valuable contributions have been published by researchers and intellectuals. Some scholars have analysed the social protest movements in Portugal during the austerity period from descriptive, comparative, and anthropological perspectives. Britta

5 Santos 1985.
6 Santos 2005, p. lxiii; Santos and Mendes 2017, p. 70. Our translation. In the original: '*A coexistência pacífica ou conflitual ... de diferentes modelos e práticas democráticas*'.
7 Santos 2012.
8 Avritzer 2002; Santos and Avritzer 2005.
9 Habermas 1975a Scharpf 2012; Schmidt 2013.
10 Magnette 2003; Bosco and Verney 2012; McGiffen 2011; Magnette 2003.

Baumgarten, an academic and activist who made significant contributions by helping to synthesise and systematise these analyses, deserves special mention.[11] Her passing in 2018 was a great loss. Equally deserving of recognition is André Freire, whose work on the *Geringonça* provided a foundation for the discussion of the phenomenon in the final chapters of this book. He was also a member of the jury for the doctoral research that underpins this work and sadly passed away unexpectedly in 2024. Among others are the auto-analysis of the *Acampada de Coimbra*, the work of Accornero and Pinto, Costa, Camargo, Soeiro, Fonseca, Estanque, Estanque, Costa and Soeiro, Fonseca and Estanque, and the book *Protest, youth and precariousness: the unfinished fight against austerity in Portugal*, by Carmo and Simões, to which I had the opportunity to contribute.[12] Some have proposed the experiences brought by the anti-austerity protests as democratic alternatives to neoliberal capitalism. Examples include the work on performativity in the Occupy movement by Judith Butler, the possibility for a left populist articulation in the work of Chantal Mouffe, and the participative experiences in the work of Boaventura de Sousa Santos.[13] Others have done excellent work in political economy and ideological criticism, problematising neoliberal capitalism and deconstructing the discourse of austerity. In the specific case of Portugal, one could for example refer to the analysis of austerity in Reis, Rodrigues, Santos and Teles and Costa and Caldas, as well as the deconstruction of neoliberal discourse by Soeiro, Cardina and Serra.[14]

The title of this book – *Capitalism, Crisis and Democracy* – is a subtle nod to Joseph Schumpeter's *Capitalism, Socialism and Democracy*. Written in the aftermath of World War II, Schumpeter's work defended market-driven, parliamentary representative democracy grounded in competition, at a moment when he believed liberal capitalism was on the verge of disappearing. This book, by contrast, aims to do the opposite: it seeks to integrate many of the previously mentioned insights and contributions – from austerity-ridden Portugal and beyond – into a systemic critique of the crisis of representative liberal democracy at a time when no credible alternative to capitalism appears to be on the horizon. We approach this task from a Marxist-inspired perspective. As we aim

11 Baumgarten 2013.

12 Alípio, Norega, Bras, Gomes and Moya 2013; Accornero and Pinto (2015a), Costa (2019), Camargo (2014), Soeiro (2014), Fonseca (2016), Estanque (2014), Estanque, Costa and Soeiro (2013), Fonseca and Estanque (2018), and the book *Protest, youth and precariousness: the unfinished fight against austerity in Portugal*, by Carmo and Simões (2020).

13 Butler 2011; Mouffe 2018.

14 Reis, Rodrigues, Santos and Teles 2013; Costa and Caldas 2014; Soeiro, Cardina and Serra 2013.

to demonstrate throughout the book, Marxism offers a particularly fitting analytical framework for several key reasons: 1) Historical Materialism: The historical materialist methodology of Marxism enables us to understand the present within the broader context of historical and ongoing struggles and power relations. It situates specific phenomena within a universal theory that accounts for dynamics of class, periphery, legitimacy, political economy, and crisis – all of which play a decisive role in the current democratic crisis. 2) Crisis Theory of Capitalism: Marxism is the preeminent theoretical framework for analysing social phenomena within the context of capitalist political economy. As a critical and crisis-oriented theory of capitalism, its relevance becomes especially clear when that economy enters a period of deep crisis. 3) Ontological Politicisation: Marxism is grounded in an ontological commitment to politicisation – through the central category of class – which is indispensable in a global context marked by the depoliticisation of the past three decades of neoliberal hegemony. Unlike the 'original' conservative-nationalist politicisation found in Carl Schmitt, Marxism offers a vision of universal social emancipation. 4) Unity of Theory and Practice: Marxism fundamentally connects analysis and scientific inquiry to historical and political practice. As Marx famously stated in his eleventh thesis on Feuerbach: 'Philosophers have only interpreted the world in various ways; the point is to change it'.[15]

Within the contemporary crisis of democracy, the theorist's task is not only to empirically analyse the crisis and its expression in different moments and discourses in their contemporary and historical context. The theorist needs to condense historical experiences and debates about strategies and tactics into political knowledge that can be used to build alternatives for fundamental change. The aim of this book is not only to expose how the crisis of democracy is an expression of social struggles, but also to arrive at strategies on how to obtain an alternative notion of democracy, warning about the pitfalls of co-optation and ideological confusion.

This book begins with a description of democracy in Portugal, its history, institutions, traditions and political economy. The following two chapters delineate a general theoretical and philosophical framework of the two interacting concepts: crisis and democracy. First comes an analysis of the role of the crisis in the construction of knowledge in the social sciences and how it permits the development of a critical and political approach to the subject. Then follows an analysis of the history of democratic theory, the crisis

15 *Die Philosophen haben die Welt nur verschieden interpretiert; es kömmt darauf an, sie zu verändern.* Marx 1998.

of democratic participation and the different alternatives that critical theory has developed in recent decades to come to a political framework of analysis that can be applied to the crisis of democratic legitimacy in Portugal. In the second half of this book, two chapters are devoted to the empirical analysis of democratic discourses during the Portuguese crisis, drawing on interviews with key actors involved in social conflicts. These chapters examine the neoliberal and formal democratic narratives used to legitimise austerity policies and contrast them with the perspectives of protesters who rejected the prevailing democratic order and sought to articulate alternative visions of democracy. We explore the contradictions and overlaps between the discourses, practices, and democratic strategies of elites and protesters, the role of electoral cycles in reshaping relationships between social movements, trade unions, and political parties, as well as the limitations of the proposed alternatives. The final section of the book offers conclusions in light of recent developments.

CHAPTER 1

Democracy in Portugal: Context and Crisis

During the summer of 2011, the euro crisis hit the Portuguese economy hard and protests rocked the country. As a young activist and academic, like many young people, I participated in many of these protests. Inspired by the Spanish *indignados*' movement, hundreds of thousands mobilised against austerity and demanded 'Real Democracy Now!' The crisis involved a sentiment of loss and fragility regarding democracy. It was also a time full of hope and plans for other alternative forms of democracy. This research is an attempt to give voice and legitimacy to these mobilisations.

How does the crisis affect democracy in Portugal? The question seemed like a good start to this research. I could have chosen a purely empirical and comparative approach – as many political scientists have done in the past decades. Soon, however, I came across some fundamental problems: Is this investigation universal or only applicable to Portugal? If we ask how the crisis affects democracy, what parameters can we use to measure the crisis and democracy in order to find correlations? Can we use quantitative statistics? How do we define crisis? How do we define democracy? What is lost if we use one definition or another? What is the historical and political context and effect of using one definition or another? And what is the role of the scientist and social activist in all these issues? Assuming that an analysis cannot be carried out in the void, in this chapter we begin to outline an indispensable historical and economic context of Portuguese democracy and its crisis that will serve as the basis for the rest of our endeavour.

1 The Making of Portuguese Democracy

Where do we start with the historical context of Portuguese democracy? We probably shouldn't go back to ancient Greek influence in southern Iberia, from the 5th century BCE. But we could return to the phenomenon of communal management of '*baldios*' – common lands, administered by local communities – which dates back to medieval times, and survives to this day, being inscribed in the Constitution and often serving as an example of participatory management and democratic practices in Portugal.[1] Another starting point

1 Brouwer 1995; Serra 2019.

 | HTTPS://DOI.ORG/10.1163/9789004766235-003

could be the influence of French republicanism and anticlericalism through the Napoleonic invasions in the first decades of the 19th century, the ensuing civil war over constitutionalism, or the ideas and events that led to the republican revolution of 5 October 1910.[2]

As our generation knows, the making of Portuguese democracy – not coincidentally also the title of Kenneth Maxwell's work on the Carnation Revolution – was, however, mainly influenced by the events of the Revolution of April 1974.[3] The Carnation Revolution not only had great international importance, as it marked the beginning of what Huntington would call the third wave of democratisation and the transitions to liberal democracy in the countries of Southern Europe – Portugal, Spain and Greece.[4] To this day, this period strongly influences the institutional and discursive scenario of democracy in Portugal. An analysis of the current crisis of democracy must therefore begin with a historical understanding of this democratic transition.

1.1 The Collapse of Fascism

Portugal was governed by a right-wing authoritarian dictatorship – often labelled fascist – between 1926 and 1974. The *'Estado Novo'*, as the regime called itself, was led by António de Oliveira Salazar from 1932 to 1968. For health reasons, Salazar was succeeded by Marcelo Caetano. The regime entered a deep crisis in 1969, a period marked by working-class uprisings and student protests. According to Boaventura de Sousa Santos, the crisis is a consequence of a combination of class struggles, the internal divisions of the elites and the internal logics of the *'Estado Novo'*.[5] During its first three decades, the dictatorship relied on the hegemony of the agrarian bourgeoisie, whose economic interests aligned with those of other social classes. However, after World War II, Portugal's integration into European industrial reconstruction – initially through the Marshall Plan and later via the *'planos de fomento'* in the 1960s, which modernised the country's industrial sector[6] – along with the militarisation prompted by the colonial wars, forced the government to shift its economic policies. As a result, agrarian hegemony began to decline in the early 1960s.

The opening to international capital and the effects of massive emigration – and with migrants bringing back the fruits of their labour – ended up

2 Catroga 2010.
3 Maxwell 1997.
4 Huntington 1991.
5 Santos 2016b, pp. 17–21.
6 Rollo 1994; 2007.

bringing an influx of foreign exchange that created an economic boom in the 1960s and accelerated the process of industrialisation. The industrial and financial bourgeoisie – made up of large industrial groups in partnership with foreign capital – gained influence while the influence of the agrarian bourgeoisie declined. For the former, the colonies were too small, and they preferred to look to European markets in search of expansion. At the same time, the organised working class roared and demanded higher wages.[7]

With the replacement of Salazar by Marcelo Caetano, the regime seemed to open up a little from 1969 onwards – the so-called period of *Marcelism* tried to appease the industrial-financial bourgeoisie and opened doors for the 'liberal wing' of the official opposition in the National Assembly. At the same time, the regime attempted concessions to the working class, granting more autonomy to unions and some social security. But the concessions were fragile and insufficient; reforms collided with the rigidity of the State. The unequal growth of industrial monopoly capital made the central role of the corporatist State in mediating between different economic sectors obsolete.[8] The new conflicts that emerged were met with fascist authoritarianism and state repression, and the state was unable to deal with the new conditions of capital concentration and the end of colonialism – which eventually led to a crisis of legitimacy:

> In the case of Portugal, the legitimation crisis resided in the state's incapacity to institutionalise the relations between capital and labour in concordance with the changing power relations that the economic development and emigration had provoked during the sixties. It also resided in the state's incapacity to catch up with the new expanding sector of the petite bourgeoisie, discontent with political paralysis, the mediocrity of cultural life and the lack of civic and political liberties.[9]

Colonialism had been the basis of the regime, but the economic importance of the colonies for Portuguese industry was declining. Only a few family monopol-

---

7 Santos 2016b, pp. 17–21.

8 Ibid.

9 Santos 2016b, p. 21. Our translation. In the original: '*En el caso portugués, la crisis de legitimación residió en la incapacidad del Estado para institucionalizar las relaciones entre capital y el trabajo en consonancia con las alteraciones en la correlación de las fuerzas sociales que el desarrollo económico y la emigración de la década de los sesenta habían provocado. Residió también en la incapacidad del Estado para captar al sector en expansión de la nueva pequeña burguesía descontenta con la parálisis política, la mediocridad de la vida cultural y la ausencia de libertades cívicas y políticas*'.

ies profited, and by the end of the 1960s more than half of Portuguese exports were directed to European markets, while African colonies accounted for less than a quarter. Furthermore, although the agrarian bourgeoisie had important compensations in the underdeveloped colonies, the products of modern industry were destined for the more developed economies. The advanced sectors of the Portuguese economy would have preferred a neocolonial relationship with the colonies, in which direct control was replaced by indirect control, but the Portuguese state was too weak to support this.[10]

Foreign debt became a problem and as conscription stole young recruits from the job market, labour became scarce and more expensive, increasing inflation. Unpopular wars demoralised the population and soldiers and worsened economic problems.[11] At the international level, the Yom Kippur war[12] in 1973 and the oil crisis that followed worsened the international economic and political environment.

Everything depended on the military apparatus. But as no military solution was possible and the war was unwinnable, a stalemate was reached that would politicise the military. It would lay the groundwork for a polarisation between the old loyalists of the 'rheumatic brigade' and the newly created Armed Forces Movement (*Movimento das Forças Armadas*, MFA), made up of junior officers and captains influenced by highly politicised students who forced recruitment turned into disgruntled officers. Losing its last pillar of support – the military apparatus, including General Spínola – the regime collapsed.[13]

1.2 The Revolutionary Period

On Thursday, 25 April 1974, the broadcast of the emblematic song '*Grândola, Vila Morena*' announced a military uprising led by a group of young democratic and anti-fascist Army officers, led by Major Otelo Saraiva de Carvalho. The 'April Captains', as they became known, put an end to the regime with extraordinary speed in a relatively bloodless coup – only six people died, five of them due to fire from the fascist secret police. The captains and junior officers of the armed forces were fed up with the war and had been influenced by the university protests and left-wing ideology of the late 1960s.[14] Rather than a revolution,

10 Santos 2016b, pp. 23–5.
11 Chilcote 2010, pp. 90–91.
12 Maxwell (1997, pp. 54–5) explains how the Yom Kippur war between the Arab states and Israel led to an isolation of the Caetano's regime versus the USA.
13 Santos 2016b, pp. 23–5.
14 Chilcote 2010, p. 90; Maxwell 1997, p. 60; Santos 2016b, p. 48.

the process began as a purely military coup with progressive content. Neither the Socialist nor the Communist parties played a decisive role in it. The MFA programme focused on the 3 Ds: Democratisation, Development, and Decolonisation. The majority of the population quickly identified with the coup, and the masses ratified it, literally embracing the rebel soldiers.[15] The MFA demanded the elimination of fascist elements from the State, democratic elections for a Constituent Assembly that implemented parliamentary democracy, political pluralism, union autonomy, and an economic policy to combat monopolies and guarantee more redistributive justice.[16] The original MFA programme was modest;[17] however, it was instrumental for the left.[18] The condemnation by the fascist regime of all opposition as 'communist' created a confusion that made the former most persecuted villains the new heroes.[19] The modesty of the MFA programme reflected strong charismatic personalities and leadership, ideological divisions within the ranks, contrasting social class origins and affiliation within the officer corps, and a dispersion of power within the MFA.[20] Among the different forces within the MFA, we can distinguish those that sympathised with Spínola, those around Vasco Gonçalves (the so-called *Gonçalvistas*, who identified with the PCP and its model of socialist transition), the Group of Nine, around Melo Antunes, who mixed clear counter-revolutionary positions with others that defended a continuous social-democratic transformation, and a populist revolutionary current around Otelo Saraiva de Carvalho.[21]

The uprising overthrew the oldest dictatorship in Europe, but initially it did not have revolutionary connotations.[22] It meant a rupture with the one-party state, the political police, political courts, paramilitary militias, political repression and censorship. But while many people linked to the former fascist regime were fired, most institutions remained in place, including the police, the military, and the church.[23] General Spínola, who had been critical of the regime's colonial policy but represented the military hierarchy and the interests of the financial bourgeoisie, took office as president. The first government – which would remain in power between 15 May and 10 July, was led by Adelino da

15 Antunes 1985, p. 48; Chilcote 2010, pp. 92–3; Santos 1985, p. 29.
16 Antunes 1985, pp. 48–9; Maxwell 1997, pp. 56–7; Santos 2016b, p. 48.
17 Due to the influence of General Spínola, references to fascism and to decolonisation were removed from the final version of the programme (Maxwell 1997, p. 58).
18 Chilcote 2010, p. 97.
19 Maxwell 1997, p. 62.
20 Chilcote 2010, p. 122.
21 Chilcote 2010, p. 125.
22 Maxwell 1997, p. 60.
23 Santos 2016b, p. 48.

Palma Carlos and was composed of members of the MFA and party representatives from left to right.[24] Although the PCP Labour Minister implemented a minimum wage, the policies were quite centre-right and focused on establishing a liberal democracy and integration in the European Economic Community.[25]

The Portuguese Communist Party, led by Álvaro Cunhal, was the largest party when the dictatorship fell. For decades he had organised clandestine resistance on a large scale and had a strong base in the industrial working class of urban centres and rural workers in the south of the country. As a result of its clandestine activities, the party was very centralised and had a general distrust of any spontaneous popular mobilisation.[26] Revolutionary legality and popular power were opposed as 'adventurism' by the PCP; the party seemed to suffer from an insurrectionary vertigo.[27] From the moment the large industries were nationalised in March 1975, and popular support guaranteed the influence of the MFA's left wing in the government, its policy was largely concentrated in the state. During the revolutionary period, the PCP maintained a policy of containing workers' demands and demonstrated loyalty to the different governments in which it participated.[28] The PCP's policies led to a division on the left. Popular unrest in the summer of 1975 was met with laws – passed by both the PS and PCP on 16 August – restricting the right to strike and seeking to control protesting workers.[29]

Unlike the PCP, the Socialist Party (PS), led by Mário Soares, was a newly created and heterogeneous party. Mário Soares had been a young organiser of the PCP, but moved away from that party and was one of the co-founders of *Acção Socialista Portuguesa* in 1964. The PS, as a party, was eventually created by the Portuguese diaspora on 19 April 1973 in Bad Münstereifel, West Germany, with the help of the German Social Democratic Party (*Sozialdemokratische Partei Deutschlands*, SPD) led by Willy Brandt. It strongly favoured parliamentary democracy. During the revolutionary period, the party transformed into a broad coalition of political forces opposing the PCP.[30] At the height of the cold

24 Maxwell 1997, p. 64.
25 Chilcote 2010, pp. 95–6.
26 Maxwell 1997, p. 133.
27 Louçã 1985; Santos 1984, p. 24, and 2016b, p. 50.
28 Varela 2010, p. 2.
29 On 28 August, the PCP and the MFA criticised a strike at Lisbon Airport, organised by the MES, demanding better working conditions. COPCON occupied Lisbon Airport and imposed martial law. While the Communist Party pushed for a democratic and national revolution as a prelude to future socialism, the radical left group wanted socialism immediately (Chilcote 2010, pp. 96, 99).
30 Santos 2016b, p. 50.

war, the PS and Mário Soares would obtain the full support of the United States of America to keep the communists in a minority position in the provisional governments.[31] In the period after the revolution, many placed hopes in a transition to socialism based on a collaboration between communists and socialists. But the centrist inclination of the PS leadership and its anti-communism made the PS lean more towards the PPD than towards the PCP. The PS preferred a liberalisation of the regime under the leadership of the national bourgeoisie.[32] Relations between the PS and the PCP would deteriorate qualitatively due to the union confederation issue in January 1975. The PCP and the MFA mobilised for a single union confederation representing a unified working class. Mário Soares' PS, the PPD, and the church wanted free union elections.[33] At the time, this conflict was presented as an opposition between revolutionary vanguard socialism and a broad-based democratic route to socialism.[34]

The Popular Democratic Party (PPD), precursor of the later Social Democratic Party (PSD), was only founded after the fall of the fascist regime, on 6 May 1974, by Francisco Sá Carneiro, Francisco Pinto Balsemão, and Joaquim Magalhães Mota. It was made up of former members of the liberal wing of the National Assembly, the dictatorship's parliamentary structure. The elections held in 1969 resulted in the victory of the regime party, *União Nacional*, which won 100 percent of the seats.[35] Francisco Sá Carneiro had been elected on this UN's ticket, but shortly afterwards he declared himself 'independent of Caetano's government'. The PPD called itself social democratic and intended to compete for the 'political centre'. It had a strong influence from lawyers and law professors whose main objective was the maintenance of order and law in the transition to democracy.

The 25 April coup transformed the regime's long-lasting crisis, which had worsened since 1969, into the biggest explosion of the popular movement in Europe since the end of the Second World War. The revolutionary period that followed the military coup – the 'Revolutionary Process in Course' (PREC), between 25 April 1974 and 25 November 1975 – was marked by massive social struggles, agrarian reform, and nationalisations, driven from below. These transformed the coup into a revolution and prevented it from resolving the crisis of hegemony of the fascist regime in favour of the industrial-financial bourgeoisie.[36] While the Spinolists and the MFA were divided over the colo-

31 Maxwell 1997, p. 95.
32 Chilcote 2010, p. 84.
33 Vasconcelos 2019, p. 20.
34 Maxwell 1997, p. 109.
35 Chilcote 2010.
36 Santos 2016b, pp. 26–7.

nial question, labour struggles definitively divided them. The right-wing PPD accused the PCP of organising the strikes and being disloyal to the government, but the MFA refused to repress the strikes.

It was in the context of internal struggles over social and colonial issues in the First Provisional Government that the so-called 'people–MFA alliance' emerged.[37] After the coup, the MFA gradually assumed responsibility for the social demands of popular movements.[38] The 'people-MFA alliance' is the result of a social explosion that called for a military presence in collective life for multifaceted and pacifying tasks and a new form of direct democracy. This participatory role of the military ranged from repairing roads or showing films to creating new forms of social and political organisation, such as popular assemblies and neighbours' committees, etc. On 8 July 1974, on the initiative of the MFA, Continent Operational Command (*Comando Operacional do Continente*, COPCON) was created, headed by Otelo Saraiva de Carvalho to restore civil order in the chaos and resolve disputes between the MFA and popular movements. COPCON would end up bringing together the most radical wing of the MFA and being the main link between popular struggles and the military.[39] COPCON had a notable influence on housing issues and the occupation of buildings for popular housing, for example.[40]

Amid the process of radicalisation of the military, Spínola tried to regain the initiative in a speech on 10 September 1974. In this speech, he appealed for the support of the 'silent majority' against extremism and totalitarianism and pressed for a demonstration to take the capital on 28 September. Spínola, however, underestimated the popular support of the left. The attempted coup against the provisional government led by the MFA brought together the left. Barricades were erected at the entrances to Lisbon with the participation of civilians and military personnel, and Spínola's attempt ended with the general's dismissal and exile on 30 September 1974.[41] The defeat of Spinola's self-coup forced the bourgeoisie and right-wing forces into a defensive position. Meanwhile, the progressive MFA – less aligned with the monopolists behind Spínola – was further strengthened by the mobilisation of popular movements. Within the heterogeneous MFA itself, popular support neutralised its right and radicalised its left.[42]

37 Varela 2013.
38 Santos 1985, p. 29.
39 Chilcote 2010, p. 98.
40 Santos 1985, p. 29.
41 Chilcote 2010, p. 99.
42 Santos 2016b, pp. 26–7, 48.

The real beginning of a revolutionary crisis was the consequence of a second right-wing coup attempt again led by Spínola on 11 March 1975 – the so-called 'reactionary *intentona*'.[43] Its failure led to further radicalisation that would bring the industrial-financial bourgeoisie as a class to the brink of collapse. While the country was experiencing a massive capital flight and capitalists abandoned or disorganised production, this situation was responded to by nationalisations, cooperatives, and workers' control.[44] Members of the former oligarchy, such as the Espírito Santo and Melo families, were arrested and imprisoned in the former International and State Defence Police (*Polícia Internacional e de Defesa do Estado*, PIDE) stronghold of Caxias due to their alleged cooperation with Spínola's coup attempt.[45] The State nationalised banking, insurance, and all large industrial groups – including CUF, *Companhia União Fabril*, which was the largest Portuguese conglomerate for decades. The rest of the economy should remain private.

The nationalisations of March 1975 directly affected 250 companies, but due to the monopoly positions of the Portuguese bourgeoisie, these companies were themselves owners of more than 2,000 other companies. Nationalisations affected finance, energy, transport, chemistry, beer, oil refineries, and shipbuilding. The State decided to rationalise banking and business organisations and concentrated them, founding companies such as CIMPOR in the cement sector, UNICER in beverages, PORTUCEL in forestry, EDP in energy and Petrogal in the oil industry.[46] In the southern region of Alentejo and Ribatejo, the lands of large landowners were occupied and expropriated. In large urban centres, neighbourhood committees were created to organise the occupation of buildings to resolve the housing issue. Workers' committees took over the management of abandoned companies. Commercial, agricultural, and industrial cooperatives and popular clinics were created. Led by the MFA, the government and some social movements organised cultural dynamisation and a literacy campaign in the most underdeveloped regions of the country.[47]

The first elections for the Constituent Assembly on 25 April 1975 – which gave the PS a relative majority and were disappointing for the PCP, which obtained only 12.5 percent – did not prevent popular mobilisation. The state went through a revolutionary crisis until 25 November. This so-called 'Hot Summer' (*Verão Quente*) left the country on the brink of civil war. In some respects,

43 Maxwell 1997, p. 110.
44 Santos 2016b, p. 52.
45 Maxwell 1997, p. 110.
46 Costa, Fazenda, Honório, Louçã and Rosas 2010, p. 268.
47 Santos 2016b, p. 49.

the situation could have been compared to the situation of dual power[48] during the Russian Revolution,[49] which pitted the legality of the provisional government against the bottom-up popular legitimacy of the soviets[50] between February and October 1917. This duality of powers, between the State and the popular councils, expressed a moment of transition in which one of the powers would eventually have to disappear. Instead of duality of powers, Boaventura de Sousa Santos characterised the Portuguese situation as one of 'dual impotence', since none of the social forces were prepared or had the capacity to take power and impose their hegemony. Instead, we had a struggle for political power within the State between the Socialist Party – which defended social-democratic capitalism – and the Communist Party – which supposedly defended workers-oriented politics and proposed a bureaucratically planned economy.[51] During this revolutionary period, the left was faced with different dilemmas: centralised command versus participatory democracy at the local level, authoritarianism versus pluralism, discipline versus spontaneism.[52]

This stalemate situation ended on 25 November 1975, with another military coup that neutralised the radical left of the MFA. The Bonapartist coup that put an end to the revolutionary crisis was possible thanks to popular demobilisation and the institutionalisation and containment of the PCP. The left had been weakened by internal factionalism, the deterioration of discipline in military units and the worsening of the economic situation. The right gained increasing support from the conservative petty bourgeoisie of the North who rose up against the revolutionary events in Lisbon.[53] The new counter-coup, the third attempt, led by Ramalho Eanes, was the culmination of a period of near anarchy and failure of the sixth provisional government, led by the moderate Pinheiro de Azevedo, in maintaining control over the media, the armed forces, and the labour movement. Ramalho Eanes would consolidate his power

48 Trotsky (2001, p. 224) defines dual power as 'a situation in which the class which is called to realize a new social system, although not yet master of the country, has concentrated in its hands a significant part of state power, while the official apparatus of the government is still in the hands of the old lords'.

49 The comparison went so far that Kissinger named Mário Soares 'the Portuguese Kerensky' (Maxwell 1997, p. 95), and Huntington (1991, p. 4) branded Spínola's coup attempt in March 1975 as Portuguese 'Kornilov-conspiracy'.

50 The soviets were workers' and soldiers councils which were guided by the principles of the 1871 Paris Commune: substituting the police and military by the armed workers and peasants, substituting the bureaucracy of the state by elected and deposable workers' representatives.

51 Santos 1985, p. 27; 2016b, pp. 27–32.

52 Chilcote 2010, p. 121.

53 Maxwell 1997, p. 132.

over the moderate wing of the military and the counter-coup would neutralise COPCON and the MFA. Eanes would be president and Mário Soares of the PS would lead the first constitutional government.[54] The counter-coup closed the path to socialism and led Portugal to a European democratic model and capitalist restoration.[55] In the end, the moderates won, or as Mário Soares was quick to paraphrase the French writer André Malraux: 'For the first time in history, the Mensheviks managed to defeat the Bolsheviks'.[56]

In April 1976, the Constituent Assembly, elected in 1975, approved a new constitution. It is one of the most progressive on the European continent. The preamble assured 'the primacy of the democratic rule of law, paving the way for a socialist society, respecting the will of the Portuguese people, with a view to building a freer, more just and more fraternal country'.[57] Still, it reflects the change in the balance of forces after the defeat of the radical left on 25 November 1975.[58] The text not only confirms all the civic, political, and cultural rights found in most constitutions, but also enshrines many of the social achievements of the revolutionary period: the irreversibility of nationalisations, agrarian reform, the different forms of democratic participation parallel to parliamentary democracy, and social rights of relatively broad scope, such as the rights to free education, housing, free healthcare, etc.[59] In the following years, the document would provide a unifying meeting point for progressive forces in Portugal.[60]

From 1976 onwards, democratic legality was no longer challenged by revolutionary legality. With the support of all parties, excluding the communists, General Ramalho Eanes was elected the first constitutional president and took office in June 1976.[61] The bourgeoisie as a whole did not assume a leadership role. Instead, a new cross-class Bonapartist power bloc emerged that, at least temporarily, respected some of the popular achievements of the revolutionary period. Nationalisations and agrarian reform – which moderated workers – were included in the legal democratic order. The working class was granted a

54 Chilcote 2010, pp. 98, 103.
55 Santos 2016b, p. 53.
56 Vasconcelos 2019, p. 19. Our translation. In the original: *'Pela primeira vez na História, os Socialistas Portugueses demonstraram que os Mencheviques são capazes de vencer os Bolcheviques'.*
57 Portugal 1976.
58 Maxwell 1997, p. 159.
59 Santos 2016b, p. 53.
60 Antunes 1985, p. 52.
61 Maxwell 1997, p. 160.

strong social position that could only very slowly be dismantled.[62] The share of wages in national income rose from 43.7 percent of GDP in 1973 to 57.6 percent in 1975.[63]

1.3 European Integration and Parliamentary Democracy

The share of wages in national income, which had increased to 57.6 percent of Gross Domestic Product (GDP) in 1976, ended up decreasing to 44 percent of GDP in 1978 and to 42.3 percent in 1983.[64] Wage gains in the revolutionary period opened a market for consumer durables such as televisions and washing machines, which average Portuguese families had not previously been able to access. The rise in wages and imports, however, had a detrimental effect on the trade balance and external debt. Consequently, the country requested financial assistance from the International Monetary Fund (IMF) for the first time in 1978. The agreed structural adjustment programme would restrict domestic consumption and aim to promote exports. Its implementation would not be easy, due to the existence of progressive laws, the still strong position of the Communist Party, and the unions. It could have discredited the dominant political discourse and meant a return to the revolutionary period. The situation was resolved by the organised absence of the state and the creation of a disparity between the constitution and the law, on one hand, and social and political practices, on the other. The working class was strong enough to prevent the dismantling of social laws, but too weak to impose their practical application. Fordist-type laws and institutions were thus combined with informal practices of primitive accumulation. There were common situations of workers with wages delayed for months, fears of unemployment, the persistent use of child labour in the north of the country, the common practice of employing people with salaries below the minimum wage, the flourishing of the parallel economy, etc.[65]

The decade that followed the revolution was marked by the reconstitution of capital in Portugal. The process of reconstituting agrarian capital was relatively easy and began in 1977: land was returned to the former large landowners, or they were compensated for their losses. In the end, only 18 percent of the land had been effectively expropriated and the agrarian working class was relatively weak. Agricultural workers did not have much power in the PCP or the trade

62 Santos 2016b, pp. 33–34.
63 Santos 2016b, p. 52.
64 Santos 2016b, p. 55.
65 Santos 2016b, pp. 53–6.

union confederation, which was more focused on the urban working class. The recomposition of industrial capital was more difficult. The main industries were nationalised during the revolutionary process and their reprivatisation was not easy. State-owned companies were the sector with the greatest union representation and most advanced social rights. These companies were in fact the only ones where Fordist labour legislation actually applied. The unions would not give up on them easily and privatisations did not fit well with the PS discourse. Nationalisations also fostered relationships of clientelism and populism within and between these companies and the public. Management positions were distributed according to political loyalties, and new investments and services from these companies were used for electoral purposes. The individual and partisan interests of many political decision makers thus proved to be obstacles to privatisation. Finally, capital, technology, and its personnel were not prepared for the new free market international economic environment, particularly because several of the nationalised sectors were already uncompetitive and undervalued at the time of their nationalisation.[66]

The rationalisation and concentration of companies, facilitated by their nationalisation, would ultimately provide a strategic advantage for the economic groups that regained their ownership in the next decade. The Portuguese bourgeoisie, with its international ties of dependence, never constituted a leadership for the country. The reconstitution of capital meant a return to rentier capitalism, protected by the state, based on financial and reproductive logics.[67] Social and economic normalisation from the late 1970s onwards and European integration from 1986 onwards would make this reconstitution possible. At the same time, the underground economy would be slowly restricted by the same process.[68] The victories of the right in 1979 and 1980 and the formation of alliances between PS and PSD created the possibilities for constitutional changes that opened the doors to reprivatisations. The constitutional revision of 1982–3 opened the finance, insurance, fertilisers, and cement sectors to the private sector.[69] From 1985 onwards, with the ten years of government of the right-wing PSD headed by Aníbal Cavaco Silva, privatisations became an ideological objective, in addition to having the purpose of cleaning up public finances. The 1989 constitutional agreement with the PS finally made possible the privatisa-

66 Santos 2016b, pp. 60–1.
67 Costa et al. 2010, p. 268.
68 Santos 2016b.
69 Costa et al. 2010, p. 269.

tions[70] that would lay the foundations for a new monopoly sector.[71] In 1995, when António Guterres's PS government took power, 22 of the 30 largest companies in Portugal had been partially or fully privatised.[72] The following PS and PSD governments kept privatising the rest of the state property. Under Guterres,[73] total public revenues from privatisations reached the equivalent of 25 percent of national debt.[74] The weight of public companies decreased from 21.5 percent to 8.4 percent of GDP between 2000 and 2010.[75] At the end of the cycle, large private capital groups such as Espírito Santo, Mello, Champalimaud, Amorim, and Sonae were reconstituted. If we compare fortunes and properties between 1910 and 2010, a considerable part of economic interest groups persisted into contemporary fortunes, surviving wars and revolutions. After all, the contemporary owners of Portugal are the same families from the entire last century.[76]

Portugal finally completed the legal process of European integration in 1986. Integration was facilitated by the close relationship between Mitterrand and Mário Soares, who was the Portuguese Prime Minister in 1976–1978 and again in 1983–1985.[77] Portugal joined the European Community for political and economic reasons. The new political elites of the PS and PSD saw Europe as a beacon of political stability, as well as an opportunity to regain international respectability after decades of authoritarian rule. On the economic level, they sought industrial and agricultural modernisation.[78] In the same year that Portugal joined, Europe took a qualitative step towards becoming the main political instrument of neoliberal reforms. That year, French socialist Mitterrand finally gave in to Thatcher's political influence on European fiscal policies,

70 In 1989, not only Unicer breweries and Aliança insurances, but also the majority of the big Portuguese banks, including Totta, BES and BPA, were privatised. This privatised financial sector would, together with the dominant political elites, be the new backbone of the Portuguese bourgeoisie, the European integration based market-doctrines and the vanguard in the new privatisations of the 1990s (Reis et al. 2013, pp. 33–5).

71 Santos 2016b, p. 61.

72 Costa et al. 2010, pp. 266–77.

73 António Guterres is a former Portuguese prime minister and the current general secretary of the United Nations.

74 Costa et al. 2010, p. 283. Costa compares this process of nationalisations and privatisations with a similar process at the start of the XIX century when properties of the church and royal family had been nationalised and afterwards privatised to solve public debt (Costa et al. 2010, p. 279).

75 Reis et al. 2013, p. 35.

76 Costa et al. 2010, p. 342.

77 Dinan 2004, p. 189.

78 Dinan 2004, p. 184.

which the latter had imposed as a condition for further European enlargement.[79] Political and economic constraints would become the guidelines for all new EU members. Although officially political restrictions included democratic demands, such as free and fair elections and transparency, integration had perverse consequences for democracy in the acceding countries.[80] The integration process increased the gap between the state and citizens, stripping power from national parliaments in favour of the executives. Furthermore, the neoliberal consensus hindered debates and undermined the basic functions of political parties.[81]

The first period of European integration after the Second World War was a neo-Keynesian project of reconstruction under the umbrella of the United States, based on economic planning, public investment, Fordist industry, and strong welfare states.[82] Portugal joined the European communities in 1986, the year of the Single European Act, which launched the single European market, under the leadership of Jacques Delors. This prepared the Maastricht Treaty and the monetary unification promoted by Helmut Kohl and François Mitterrand.[83] Free market ideology and monetarism would become the guiding principles of this second period of integration that would culminate in the Euro.[84] The neoliberal model brought about by the Single European Act and Maastricht was fundamentally incompatible with the welfare state model, but the extraordinary influx of foreign capital into peripheral countries led to economic growth and low unemployment. The social consequences of its incompatibility would only be felt later.[85]

Portugal joined the European communities in a favourable international context, after having successfully exited the IMF's structural adjustment programme (which recovered the economy through a controlled devaluation of the escudo). The precipitous fall in oil prices boosted the economy since 1984, the increase in foreign investment and European structural funds boosted public investment, and its main trading partners experienced steady growth in demand at a time when trade barriers were torn down by the single market. Unemployment decreased from 9.3 percent in 1986 to 3.9 percent in 1992. The processes of liberalisation, privatisation, and deregulation imposed by

79 Dinan 2004, p. 189.
80 Orbie 2008, p. 27.
81 De Ridder, Schrijvers and Vos 2008, p. 251.
82 Reis et al. 2013, pp. 30–1.
83 Dinan 2004, p. 7.
84 Reis et al. 2013, pp. 30–1.
85 Pureza 2015a, p. 10; Reis et al. 2013.

European integration played a crucial role in the reconstitution of capital and the transformation of capital accumulation in Portugal.[86]

Fighting inflation was one of the convergence criteria for a monetary union policy.[87] These deflationary policies created the first period of slow growth and recession between 1991 and 1995. From 1993 onwards, there was a convergence of interest rates towards the low averages existing in the core European countries that by expanding internal demand and investment benefited both the private and the public sectors. The dominant explanation was that: 'the country is reaping the fruits of the modernisation of the financial system'.[88] Keeping the country at or close to Maastricht Treaty standards until 1998 (3 percent deficit, 60 percent public debt) prepared it to be one of the founding countries of the Euro, which at the time was seen as a great success.[89]

However, at the turn of the millennium, three factors would strongly affect Portugal's position in the newly created European single currency area, or eurozone. The first was an increasingly strong euro in relation to the dollar and other currencies, which affected Portuguese exports and its balance of trade. The second was the trade agreements with China, starting in 2001, which seriously affected industries such as textiles and footwear. A third factor was the expansion of the European Union into Eastern Europe. All these factors were due to the interests of core EU countries, and particularly Germany, which saw lucrative opportunities for its capital and possibilities to relocate industries to countries with cheap labour while maintaining control of value chains. But all three seriously affected Portugal's competitiveness, exports, and ability to attract productive industrial investment.[90] At the same time, no measures were taken to absorb asymmetric shocks in the eurozone; no European budget was created, nor a banking union, nor the creation of the European Central Bank (ECB) as lender of last resort.[91] Furthermore, in Portugal, some political forces saw the euro as an opportunity to forge a disciplinary mechanism to guarantee neoliberal ruptures in economic policy and impose, quickly and externally, a model of competitiveness on a global scale.[92]

Portugal has traditionally had high aggregate levels of public support for EU membership.[93] From the mid-1970s until 1992, political support for Europe was

86 Reis et al. 2013, pp. 31–32.
87 Reis et al. 2013, p. 36.
88 Reis et al. 2013, p. 25. Our translation. In the original: *o país colhia os frutos da chamada 'modernização do sistema financeiro'*.
89 Reis et al. 2013, p. 37.
90 Reis et al. 2013, pp. 40–1.
91 Reis et al. 2013, p. 26.
92 Reis et al. 2013, p. 36.
93 Lobo and Magalhães 2011, p. 81.

monopolised by the two main pro-European establishment parties, the PS and the PSD, which have alternated in the leadership of all governments since the end of the PREC. Euroscepticism could only be found at the extremes of the party system.[94] According to Lobo and Magalhães, euroscepticism at the party level was influenced by two factors: ideology and strategy. At the ideological level, we find economic arguments expressed by the left that criticise integration as a market-oriented capitalist project – 'a Trojan horse of international capitalism' – and the emphasis on the 'decline of economic sovereignty and its consequences for social losers'.[95]

The political argument criticising the loss of formal political sovereignty was expressed mainly by the Social Democratic Centre–People's Party (*Centro Democrático Social–Partido Popular*, CDS), the most right-wing party in the Portuguese parliament, in the 1995 elections. It ran a successful Eurosceptic campaign following the Maastricht Treaty, being more Eurosceptic than the PCP, but more based on strategic aspects of seeking votes and positions than because of ideological principles. Later, the party minimised and softened the importance of these issues in its programme, in order to be an acceptable partner for sharing power with the PSD.[96]

On the left, the PCP always had a very critical position in relation to the EU. Portugal's accession to the EEC was a conscious movement by the country's elite directed against the communist threat. With the collapse of the Soviet bloc as an alternative model to liberal democracy, growing popular support for European integration, and its participation in direct elections to the European Parliament from 1988 onwards, the PCP was forced to significantly moderate its resistance to Europe and defend less Eurosceptic positions.[97] The party only returned to more Eurosceptic positions in periods of economic crisis and from the moment it had a competitor – the *Bloco de Esquerda* in 1999 – which defended Eurosceptic propositions based on criticisms of neoliberalism.[98]

A similar strengthening of the Eurosceptic position was therefore to be expected in the midst of the euro crisis. As we will see later, Euroscepticism certainly exists on the left since the intervention of the Troika. There was a consensus on the left, supported by a growing number of leading international economists and academics that European institutions were at least partially, if

94 Lobo and Magalhães 2011; Freire 2006, p. 384.
95 Lobo and Magalhães 2011, pp. 85–90.
96 Lobo and Magalhães 2011; Freire 2006, p. 384.
97 Lobo and Magalhães 2011; Freire 2006, p. 384.
98 Lobo and Magalhães 2011.

not entirely responsible for the economic and social crisis that began in 2011.[99] As a result, all political movements to the left of the PS – which tried to avoid Troika involvement for as long as possible – excluded themselves from any talks with the European institutions in the negotiations on the response to the crisis.

1.4 Pre-crisis State of Democracy

Since the revolution, Portugal has evolved into a semi-presidential constitutional democracy.[100,101] Although other authors have characterised the regime as parliamentary, Amorim Neto and Lobo's analysis of Portuguese politics between 1976 and 2006 concludes that the President of the Republic maintains crucial constitutional powers that make him relevant, despite these having been restricted by the reform of the constitutional law of 1982. The functions of the president include the appointment and dismissal of governments, setting the agenda, the power to dissolve parliament, influence on ministerial appointments, and the power to subject bills to prior review on their constitutionality and ultimately veto them.[102] Portugal has evolved from a presidential-parliamentary variety to a premier-presidentialism in which the president shares executive power with a prime minister and his cabinet. The unique interaction between the two different types of semi-presidentialism and a changing multi-party system has given rise to a wide range of flexible government formulas – presidential initiative governments, single-party minority governments, majority coalitions, near-majority or majority single-party governments, and periods of cohabitation – which ultimately guaranteed the consolidation of Portuguese democracy as we know it.[103] Presidential elections are contested under a run-off majority system, with a strong tendency towards personalisation, although many candidates receive official party support. The system forces parties to form coalitions in a bipolar logic: the presidential elections saw left-wing and right-wing parties form separate ideological blocs.[104]

Portuguese parliamentary democracy is marked by a stable party system that emerged during the revolutionary period. Legislative power is based on

99 De Grauwe 2010; Krugman 2012a, and 2012b; Stiglitz 2017.

100 Freire 2006; Amorim Neto and Lobo 2009.

101 Duverger (1980, p. 187) defined semi-presidential regimes as being based on an effective sharing of power between two bodies of executive power: the President and the government, led by the prime minister.

102 Amorim Neto and Lobo 2009, p. 235.

103 Amorim Neto and Lobo 2009, p. 250.

104 Freire 2006, p. 389.

a single chamber of 230 representatives elected in 22 multi-party constituencies. Although parliament is based on proportional representation, Portuguese democracy has always tended towards majoritarianism.[105] National legislative elections, held every four years, ultimately determine which parties form the government and who becomes prime minister, sharing executive power with the president.[106] Since 1976, four parties have continuously represented almost 90 percent of the electorate, with a general tendency for voting to focus on two centrist 'catch-all' parties: the centre-left Socialist Party (*Partido Socialista*, PS) and the centre-right Social Democratic Party (PSD, *Partido Social Democrata*, PSD). At the same time, the Portuguese Communist Party (PCP, *Partido Comunista Português*, PCP), which normally participates in elections under the CDU banner, and the conservative Social Democratic Centre (*Centro Democrático Social*, CDS) became the main parties in the system. Since 1999, a fifth party has joined these four: the *Bloco de Esquerda*, or Left Bloc.[107,108]

The three main parties comprised the so-called *arco da governação* (arc of governance). The PS, PSD and CDS formed governments between democratisation and the euro crisis. Traditionally, they depended on clientelism networks and state support to establish relationships with civil society and havepoorly defined ideological profiles, according to Freire.[109] The right-left divide is traditionally based on socioeconomic issues, sometimes combined with religious ones, such as the issue of abortion and state support for private Catholic education.[110]

Despite the high levels of mass mobilisation, protest and political engagement that characterised the democratic transition in the 1970s, the level of contemporary political participation – including voting in elections, as well as recourse to conventional and unconventional forms of political action and

105 Lijphart (2012, p. 7) defines majoritarianism – the rule of parliamentary majorities – based upon competitive and uncoordinated pluralism – by contrasting it with consensus democracies which are coordinated and compromise-oriented and tend to protect minorities. The general trend towards majoritarianism was contradicted by the 2015 elections, which produced a government based on parliamentary compromises that did not include the party with the most votes.

106 Freire 2006, p. 376.

107 Freire 2006, p. 373.

108 The crisis has eventually led to a further fragmentation of the Portuguese political landscape. In 2019 another four parties had parliamentary representatives: the animal-rights party PAN, the centre-left party *Livre*, the right-wing libertarian *Iniciativa Liberal* and the extreme-right party *Chega*.

109 Freire 2006, p. 373.

110 Freire 2006, p. 385. The crisis and the intervention of the Troika placed the main dividing line between left and right essentially around the scope of the welfare state.

Anos	Eleitores		
	Total	Votantes	Abstenção
— 1975	100,0	91,5	8,5
1976	100,0	83,3	16,7
1979	100,0	87,1	12,9
— 1980	100,0	84,8	15,2
1983	100,0	77,8	22,2
1985	100,0	74,3	25,7
1987	100,0	71,5	28,5
1991	100,0	67,4	32,6
1995	100,0	66,2	33,8
1999	100,0	61,0	39,0
2002	100,0	61,6	38,4
2005	100,0	64,4	35,6
2009	100,0	59,7	40,3
2011	100,0	58,1	41,9
2015	100,0	55,9	44,1
2019	100,0	48,6	51,4

Fontes/Entidades: SGMAI, PORDATA
Última actualização: 2019-10-25

TABLE 1
Votes and abstention in legislative elections
Source: Pordata, 2019.

civic activism – has been relatively low. Turnout in legislative elections has consistently declined since the revolutionary period.[111] It declined from averages well above 80 percent in the 1970s, to 60 percent around 2000, to less than 50 percent in the most recent elections.[112] While decreasing political participation is a general trend in the whole European continent, Portugal went from being one of the Western nations with the highest participation to being below the average of western European democracies without mandatory voting. Portugal represents the sharpest decline among the Organisation for Economic Cooperation and Development (OECD) countries.[113] According to Magalhães, the Portuguese situation is more a case of 'democratic disaffection' rather than 'democratic dissatisfaction':[114] feelings of estrangement from politics have tended to breed political passivity instead of growing discontent and political activism within an accepted democratic framework.

111 Magalhães 2005, p. 975.
112 Pordata 2019.
113 Freire and Magalhães 2002, pp. 47–50; Magalhães 2005, p. 975.
114 Magalhães 2005, pp. 976–88.

In the 2002 survey by the Comparative Study of Electoral Systems (CSES), 47 percent of respondents answered they were 'not very' or 'not at all satisfied with the way democracy works in Portugal'. The percentage of Portuguese citizens that are satisfied and very satisfied with the way democracy works in Portugal has since decreased from 28.5 percent in 2008 to 10.6 percent in 2012.[115,116] According to Magalhães, there is no question about the diffuse support for the fundamental values of democracy, but there is an increasingly weak support for the political class and the political parties, the fundamental actors in any representative democracy.[117] Regarding the statement 'Political parties don't care about what people think', Portugal got the highest average score among surveys conducted in 31 countries, including countries which are commonly disqualified as free electoral democracies – such as Belarus, Russia or Ukraine.[118]

In their book *A qualidade da democracia em Portugal: a visão dos cidadãos* (The quality of democracy in Portugal: the vision of citizens), based on research from July 2011, right at the beginning of the crisis in Portugal, António Costa Pinto, Luís de Sousa and Pedro Magalhães painted a worrisome picture: not only do three in five Portuguese citizens think that citizens are treated unequally by the courts of justice, but, in addition to the well-known relatively low political participation compared to other European countries, distrust also affects other channels of participation: parties and unions.[119] Citizens to the right of the political centre tended to feel better represented. Citizens in the political centre felt alienated and uninterested in politics, while left-wing citizens were more likely to participate in associations and protests.[120] Citizens felt that their right to vote was insufficient and more than 70 percent of respondents felt that policymakers were not sufficiently responsible for the policies they carried out. Most citizens also felt that the system's checks and balances did not work well enough and particularly saw inadequacies in the president's control of the Government. Although people's associative and religious freedoms are guaranteed, citizens tend to be concerned about freedom of expression, guarantees of non-discrimination, and protection against police abuse.[121] Although Portuguese citizens place social rights at the centre of their conception of democracy, they perceive a lack of state capacity to implement

115 Tsatsanis and Belchior 2020, p. 80.
116 It partially recovered to 18.4 % in 2016.
117 Magalhães 2005, p. 975. See also: Freire 2003, p. 154.
118 Magalhães 2005, p. 975.
119 Magalhães 2013, pp. 21–6.
120 Lisi, Marchi and Evans 2013.
121 Gorbunova and Raimundo 2013.

social wellbeing, which has repercussions for the legitimacy of the democratic regime itself. In 2011, only one in three Portuguese people was satisfied with the functioning of democracy. According to Cabral and Magalhães, this is a consequence of the marked levels of socioeconomic inequality in the country and the comparatively low level of civic and formal education among the Portuguese, as well as the lack of communication between politicians and the masses.[122]

With the onset of the crisis, this situation only deteriorated. As Southern Europe has begun to transition from development to underdevelopment, from political processes dominated by social inclusion to processes of social exclusion, it appears that representative democracy has lost the war against capitalism, and populism is on the rise.[123]

2 The Political Economy of Austerity

2.1 Periphery and Europe

As a semi-peripheral country, Portugal today has an intermediate position in the world system. Semi-peripheral countries act as a centre in relation to the periphery – particularly in periods of expansion, they serve as chains of transmission of the centre's interests – and are peripheral in their relations with the centre. For centuries, Portugal's semi-peripheral position was based on a colonial empire that it began to conquer in the fifteenth century. Portugal played a central role in the first phase of the globalisation of capital, with the opening of international overseas trade routes and the establishment of the transatlantic slave trade in the sixteenth and seventeenth centuries. While the Portuguese empire reached a maximum size of more than 100 times the surface of mainland Portugal by 1815, its status as an economic and geopolitical power had been declining since the eighteenth century. To the benefit of the Dutch, French, and British empires, it lost influence, a trend that was reinforced by the earthquake that destroyed Lisbon in 1755. The Napoleonic wars led to the transfer of the Portuguese capital and the royal court from Lisbon to Rio de Janeiro. Tensions between the elites of Lisbon and Rio eventually led to Brazil's independence in 1822. The remaining empire, for which mainland Portugal served as the centre, also included Mozambique, Angola, Guinea, Cape Verde, São Tomé and Prín-

122 Cabral 1997, pp. 142–8, and 2000; Magalhães 2005, p. 974.
123 Santos 2016b, p. 260.

cipe, East Timor, and Macau. This empire was increasingly under pressure due to anti-colonial struggles. At the same time, Portugal maintained a position of dependence in relation to England, with which it had maintained close relations since the fourteenth century.[124]

Since the complete collapse of its colonial empire in 1974, the country has renegotiated its semi-peripheral status by becoming part of the European integration process in a peripheral position, marked by tourism and emigration, in a context of continuous reduction of national sovereignty.[125]

Semi-peripheral countries such as Portugal, Ireland, Spain, Greece, Brazil, or Mexico have social conditions similar to those of less developed countries: parallel economies, informal sectors, inefficiency of their democratic institutions, political corruption, labour market segmentation, emigration, deterioration of quality of life, urban violence, worsening inequalities, etc.[126] Portugal has a weak welfare state, compensated by a relatively strong welfare society.[127] This means that the lack of social rights must be compensated by informal community ties and solidarity, particularly in rural areas.

The basic contradictions of peripheral, dependent societies tend to be externally overdetermined. In the case of Portugal, this overdetermination has been guided by the political-economic process of European integration.[128] Portugal's peripheral and multidimensional dependent status is the antecedent of austerity policies. According to Reis et al., this is particularly the result of the Maastricht Treaty, which generated internal productive destruction and culminated in a record external debt.[129] The Maastricht model compressed the room for manoeuvre of all eurozone member states, but this compression was substantially asymmetric. It penalised peripheral countries to different degrees, condemning them to exclusion through inclusion.[130] Rather than a policy of convergence, European economic integration boosted internal uneven and combined development. In financial terms, it created a political power relationship of creditor and debtor between centre and periphery.[131]

124 The Anglo-Portuguese Treaty of friendship was signed in 1373 and is regarded as the world's oldest active diplomatic treaty. It was followed and confirmed by the Treaty of Windsor in1386.

125 Santos 2016b, pp. 42–5.

126 Santos 2016b, p. 39.

127 Santos 2016b, p. 42.

128 Reis et al. 2013, p. 24.

129 Reis et al. 2013, p. 21.

130 Pureza 2015a, p. 20.

131 Reis et al. 2013, p. 21.

Conventional analyses have placed the burden of economic problems on national economic actors, as if national states were primarily responsible for not being ready to move from a 'cohesion country' to a 'single currency country'. Peripheral countries would have been too easy-going and focused on short-term policies: structural funds would have been wasted by being allocated to sectors of the internal market instead of those involved in globalisation and European markets, in stimulating consumption instead of investment, or on cohesion rather than competitiveness. This blaming discourse will play an important role in legitimising austerity.[132] In my article 'Framing PIGS: patterns of racism and neocolonialism in the Euro crisis', I explored how this process of blaming was essential to the racist framing of the peripheral member states of the European Union, the PIGS: Portugal, Ireland (and/or Italy, Greece, and Spain).[133] This culturalisation of politics, which reduced the differences between centre and periphery to certain 'cultural characteristics and habits' – reflected in stereotypes of laziness, unproductivity, corruption, wasteful spending, and lies – legitimised a return of colonial dynamics in the eurozone through processes of economic dependence, conditional aid, and cultural hegemony. These stereotypes were used in northern Europe to legitimise harsh austerity in the south.

European integration, especially asymmetric integration in the monetary union, transferred almost all major economic policies to European institutions. These instruments included control over national currencies (and the possibility of devaluations), as well as over capital, credit creation, commerce, industry, and budgets. As a result, deliberative parliamentary politics and national sovereignty have lost control over these economic policy instruments, with EU institutions managing these policies without oversight or democratic mandate.

As previously mentioned, Reis et al. assert that the European Monetary Union was an almost inevitable outcome of the 'European Act'; a single currency was essential for the realisation of a single market and free circulation of capital.[134] This presented an opportunity to create a disciplinary mechanism to enforce the necessary neoliberal ruptures in economic policy swiftly and externally. While this functionalist perspective, based on the general interest of capital, is plausible, it is important not to overlook the national interests of the leading powers in this integration process. According to Krugman (2012b), joining or leaving the eurozone is more of a political decision than an economic

132 Reis et al. 2013, p. 22.

133 Van Vossole 2016a.

134 Reis et al. 2013.

one.[135] Germany decided to abandon its Deutsche Mark – which had been one of the most stable currencies globally – was not only because the country was assured that the policies of the new European Central Bank would adhere to German ordo-liberal, anti-inflationary, and independent principles. Germany's decision was also influenced by the fall of the Soviet Union and the reunification of Germany. The European monetary system could act as a buffer to absorb the impact of German unification.[136]

It is very difficult to calculate the precise costs of staying in or leaving the eurozone.[137] According to the dominant theory of the Optimum Currency Area (OCA), the benefits are obvious: reduced transaction costs, elimination of exchange rate risk, greater transparency and possibly greater competition because prices are easier to compare, and increased intra-European trade, which presumably 'corresponds to an increase in mutually beneficial and, therefore, productive exchanges'.[138] Critical theorists of the euro project, such as Hadjimichalis, on the other hand, argued that free trade contributed to the deindustrialisation of peripheral countries. Instead of gaining competitiveness, Southern Europe lost its productive industries because a large part of its industries, such as textiles and ceramics, were not prepared for free competition in the global market.[139] Other disadvantages of a single currency come from the loss of flexibility due to 'one-size-fits-all' monetary policies and the loss of mechanisms to respond to asymmetric shocks. According to Krugman, exchange rate devaluations – impossible within a single currency area – are the easiest method of 'adapting' the economy in periods of crisis.[140]

But more important than the general costs or benefits is the way in which they are shared.[141] It is clear, for example, that the 'winners' of the euro were mainly the competitive export industries and the major eurozone economies.[142] The perverse effect of European economic integration is that the only policy instruments left at the national level are fiscal policies, to attract capital, and labour regulations, to reduce wages. At the same time, the logic of the free market prohibited protectionism and guaranteed the free movement of capital. The consequence was that international capital became the factual arbiter

135 Krugman 2012b.
136 Reis et al. 2013, pp. 26–8.
137 Alcidi, Giovannini and Gros 2012.
138 Krugman 2012b.
139 Hadjimichalis 2011.
140 Krugman 2012b.
141 Alcidi et al. 2012.
142 Hadjimichalis 2011.

between different tax and labour regimes. This asymmetry is at the heart of the European crisis.[143]

2.2 Crisis and Austerity

Before the outbreak of the 2008 financial crisis, Portugal was already plagued by severe economic problems and macroeconomic imbalances. Olivier Blanchard wrote in 2007 that the country was marked by slow growth, low productivity, large budget deficits, large current account deficits, and no fundamental policies to change the situation.[144] Other peripheral economies of the Eurozone had seen the development of speculative bubbles and a boost in private expenditure funded by cheap credit. But during the decade before the crisis, the Portuguese economy grew just 0.55 percent per year between 2000 and 2010.[145] The increase in demand for work lead to a yearly increase in nominal wages of 6 percent, which pushed inflation to an average of 4 percent per year.[146]

When the effects of the 2008 financial crisis hit Portugal, the country had a minority government formed by the PS and led by Prime Minister José Sócrates. The government's first response to the collapse of international finance followed the strategy of most European governments and the European Commission. Trying to mitigate the internal effects of the crisis, the European Commission called for massive public investments to counteract the drop in demand and maintain stability in the financial sector. Member states were pressured to rescue private banks with public funds if necessary.[147] In Portugal, this translated into public guarantees for banks, the nationalisation of the bankrupt BPN, and countercyclical measures to combat unemployment.[148] Along with the economic recession and the collapse of tax revenues, the automatic increase in public spending due to the sharp rise in unemployment and funds allocated to the banking sector led to an increase in public deficits and public debt.[149]

Due to the worsening economic and financial situation, and particularly financial speculation against public debt, the economic crisis quickly turned into a debt crisis. This has accentuated economic and financial disparities in the eurozone, and political priorities have changed. The consolidation of public

143 Reis et al. 2013, p. 23.
144 Blanchard 2007.
145 Reis et al. 2013, p. 24.
146 Carneiro, Portugal and Varejão 2014, p. 445.
147 Costa and Caldas 2014, p. 89.
148 Costa and Caldas 2014, p. 92.
149 Carneiro et al. 2014.

accounts, the containment of debt levels, and the reduction of state spending became the guiding principles of public policies. The European Commission and national governments in Europe, many of them under pressure from the European Commission, have returned with increased force to pre-crisis neoliberal policies. Austerity became the main political concept in Europe: for liberal policymakers, the crisis would be turned into an opportunity to accelerate privatisations, break social welfare programmes, and crush workers' rights.

In Portugal, this austerity phase began in March 2010 with the consecutive introduction of four Stability and Growth Pacts (*Pactos de Estabilidade e Crescimento*, PECs). To obtain a majority vote on the PEC and state budgets, Sócrates' government, which did not have a parliamentary majority,[150] had to rely on votes, or at least abstentions, from the opposition, namely the PSD. Each of these four PECs represented a readaptation to an increasingly difficult economic environment and meant increasingly stringent fiscal measures.

On 12 March 2011, hundreds of thousands of protesters took to the streets under the slogan '*Geração à Rasca*' (Generation on the Edge). Eleven days later, and after the failure of three consecutive structural reform pacts, a parliamentary majority of the PSD, CDS, CDU, and BE rejected the new PEC4 with more austerity. The government led by Sócrates resigned. In order to meet its financial obligations to debtors, the outgoing government was forced to accept conditional international financial support, guaranteed by the International Monetary Fund and the European Central Bank. Financial support was granted under the condition of structural reforms supervised by the so-called Troika, made up of representatives from the European Commission, the ECB, and the IMF. The three main establishment parties, PS, PSD, and CDS, would negotiate with the Troika a plan for structural economic reforms, detailed in the so-called Memorandum of Understanding (MoU). The first negotiations were concluded in May 2011, but it would end up being the new right-wing PSD–CDS government led by Passos Coelho that, in consensus with the PS, would implement the MoU. This Memorandum of Understanding would be the guide for the neoliberal austerity measures that would be implemented in the following years with disastrous social, political, and economic consequences.[151]

---

150 Minority governments are relatively common in Portuguese democratic history. Examples include Guterres I (1995–1999), Sócrates II (2009–2011), Passos Coelho II (2015), Costa I (2015–2019) and Costa II (2019–2024). Moury and Fernandes (2018) even argue that, in the Portuguese context, these governments tend to be as stable and effective as majority or coalition governments.

151 Costa and Caldas 2014, p. 88, our translation.

The eurozone economy shrank by a cumulative 2.1 percent between 2009 and 2013, while it had grown by a total of 10.6 percent between 2004 and 2008. The reality was much harsher in Portugal: the GDP lost a cumulative 7.6 percent in those same years, while it had grown by a cumulative 7.9 percent in the previous five years – much less than the European average. Although the goals in terms of fiscal policy and budget cuts followed the MoU's recommendation, the effects were disastrous: between 2011 and 2012, instead of an expected contraction of 2.1 percent, the Portuguese economy lost 6.3 percent, reached 17.4 percent unemployment against 13.3 percent expected and public debt rose to 124 percent of GDP, instead of the expected 112.2 percent.[152]

Between 2010 and 2014 nominal wages fell by 8 percent in Portugal. During the same period, Greek wages fell by 27 percent and those in Cyprus by 4.2 percent. During the same period, northern European wages rose by more than 5 percent. This was not a coincidence, but rather the conscious consequence of adjustment programmes designed to restore competitiveness and 'rebalance' trade. This was done through so-called 'internal devaluation' – the only method of adjusting trade and balance of payments deficits available in monetary unions like the euro. Internal devaluation consists of the 'devaluation of labour' (cutting costs related to wages and other labour costs, such as reducing taxes, the so-called fiscal devaluation) with the expectation of boosting exports, reducing imports, and attracting investments in search of cheap labour.[153] While internal devaluation was not an openly assumed objective of the Memorandum of Understanding – some of the measures were legitimised as a solution against unemployment – the document was incredibly detailed on matters of internal devaluation, leaving no discretionary manoeuvre for the government nor social partners. At the same time, the government was incredibly zealous in its application: all attacks on labour rights were flawlessly transformed in legislation. The conditional measures included a reduction of amounts and duration of unemployment benefits, a reduced compensation for terminations of labour contracts, as well as a flexibilisation of individual

152 Costa and Caldas 2014, p. 112.

153 Caldas 2015, pp. 5–7. Monetary or external devaluation, through currency devaluation, is, according to Caldas (2015, p. 8), a better way to restore the trade balance and competitiveness, it is faster, more efficient and entails lower social costs. However, monetary devaluation is impossible as long as Portugal remains in the euro. The problem of internal devaluation in single currency areas finds its historical parallel in the gold standard between 1880 and 1914 and during the interwar period. The application of internal devaluation policies had disastrous social, economic and political impacts (Caldas 2015, p. 12).

sackings. It also included a wage-freeze, flexibilisation of labour hours, and a decentralisation of collective contracts and collective bargaining.[154]

The deficit in the balance of payments diminished by 11 percent between 2010 and 2013. According to Caldas, the decrease was the result of a reduction in imports due to the contraction of the domestic market, and not because exporting industries had become more competitive.[155] The internal devaluation did not produce the expected drop in domestic prices.[156] The new regime evidently failed to fulfil its proclaimed objective of creating jobs.[157] In addition to the direct effects of the profound economic and social crisis, the strategies adopted to respond to it had negative impacts on employment in public services and the effectiveness of labour and training policies. The result was a huge increase in the unemployment rate, due to the closure of companies, and a very large increase in minimum wage workers and low-quality jobs.[158] While in the eurozone unemployment rates rose from 7.5 to 11.6 percent, in Portugal they went from 8.7 in 2008 to 14.1 percent in 2014. These differences are even greater when we look at youth unemployment, where rates rose from 25.3 percent to 34.7 percent.

These were the adverse conditions, particularly among young people, that triggered the massive protests against austerity that began with the 12 March 2011 '*Geração à Rasca*' (Generation on the Edge) demonstration. These protests, which signalled a profound crisis of legitimacy, are the background to our inquiry into democracy.

3 Democracy as a Historical and Ideological Product

We saw how Portugal's transition to democracy was marked by various contradictions. Until 25 April 1974, Europe's longest-running dictatorship and colonial power seemed anachronistic. A few weeks later, the country was the world centre of democratic, revolutionary, and socialist experimentalism, marked by nationalisations, agrarian reform, and citizen participation.

In the aftermath of the Carnation Revolution, the European integration project was essential for Portuguese elites to guarantee the triumph of a relatively stable parliamentary liberal democracy over other alternative perspectives of

154 Caldas 2015, pp. 12–14.
155 Caldas 2015, pp. 16–17.
156 Carneiro et al. 2014, p. 444; Hespanha and Caleiras 2017, p. 47.
157 Caldas 2015, p. 14.
158 Hespanha and Caleiras 2017, p. 47.

democracy that emerged during the revolutionary period. The newly approved constitution guaranteed many of the revolution's social achievements, such as free education and healthcare. But while Portugal was trying to build a welfare state similar to European social democracies, the European Communities were already making a shift toward a neoliberal revolution that was beginning to sweep Europe. European integration would soon be accompanied by a liberal agenda of widespread privatisation and liberalisation that would reconstitute countries' economic and financial elites and quickly become an obstacle to social and economic democracy.

The integration of Portugal, a peripheral economy, into the European Union and the eurozone caused a strong process of deindustrialisation and loss of political-economic sovereignty in the country. Portugal not only transferred legal and political competences to the community level; its political economy would become increasingly dependent on matters of debt, finance, European subsidies, emigration, and tourism. With its continued integration into the eurozone, the country would further lose essential political economic instruments, especially control over its monetary policy.

Portuguese democracy, like other European democracies, had suffered for years from growing legitimacy problems. Electoral participation dwindled. Belief in parties, the judicial system, and political institutions has been eroded by depoliticisation, corruption, and inequality. As the European project, in the aftermath of the global financial crisis, entered its worst crisis yet and austerity policies dealt severe blows to social rights, public services, and living conditions, so too the legitimacy of the liberal parliamentary form of democracy seemed to enter a serious crisis. To analyse the most recent crisis, our investigation will first focus on the two interacting elements: crisis and democracy. We will begin with a theoretical and historical dissection of these two. We start with the concept of crisis, as this 'active' element at the same time will provide us with a kind of methodology that will guide us in our investigation.

CHAPTER 2

'Crisis' in the Transition to Political Science

Previous systemic crises, such as the Great Depression of the 1930s, have consistently affected the legitimacy of existing governance systems. Given that the general objective of our investigation is to disentangle the interrelationship between crisis and democracy, this chapter focuses on the first 'pole' of the relationship: the concept of 'crisis' as an analytical concept.

'The eurozone is in crisis', 'the welfare state is in crisis', 'the European economy is in crisis', 'the climate crisis', 'democracy is in crisis', 'democratic theory is in crisis', etc. 'Crisis' plays a central role in many narratives that address contemporary political, economic, and scientific situations. In the post-2008 'crisis context', a large amount of academic work in political science, economics, and sociology has focused on the effects of crisis on the economy, democracy, voting patterns, governance policies, economic behaviour, etc. A 'crisis' is an existing or developing situation – an economic recession, an explosion of geopolitical tension, a collapse of confidence, etc. – that affects other parameters to be measured or analysed. As we will see later, this very positivist approach tends to lead to the recognition that crisis is a relatively useless device, since the concept itself is questioned. However, crisis does not just refer to a moment of turbulence or imbalance, but rather to a state of affairs that requires an implicit, decisive, and immediate response. The crisis thus fluctuates between being 'real' and being 'a construction'.[1] Therefore, our approach will be somewhat different from the purely empirical or positivist perspective. First, the concept of 'crisis' will be approached as an 'subject' rather than just a concrete, objective thing. By approaching the crisis as a subject, it receives 'agency', that is, it becomes an active framework that structures the way we perceive, give meaning to and change the way we treat the things it affects – democracy in our case.

Such an approach is not only justified as a general idea that scientific knowledge on crisis improves by considering another perspective or dimension of the subject being researched. We will argue that it is essential, given the epistemological and historical nature of the concept of crisis itself. Only using this approach can one clarify how crisis functions as a crucial concept for critical and emancipatory knowledge and science.

---

1 Caldas and Almeida 2016, p. 6.

 | HTTPS://DOI.ORG/10.1163/9789004766235-004

First, I will recover a conceptual history of the concept of crisis. We will investigate the etymological and historical origins of the word crisis, from classical Greek mythology and philosophy to its modern scientific use. We will try to show how the ancient connection with the notion of judgment or final judgment, possibly through theological connotations, would translate into some idea of 'immanence' that guides us through the apparent opposition between subjectivity and objectivity in contemporary sciences. We will then briefly explore the relationship between crisis, critique, and dialectics in European political philosophy. Critique has the same etymological origins as crisis. Just like crisis, critique balances between the objective and the subjective. Both concepts are essentially contradictory. Given that a crisis situation is essentially opposed to a 'normal', 'ideal' or 'objective' state, the state of crisis and the practice of critique always involve an active form of negation. Therefore, dialectics, as the method of thinking through negation and contradiction, is crucial to understanding the concepts of crisis and critique. This part begins with a discussion of the origins of dialectics and critique in Socratic philosophy, which in turn inspired Neoplatonic theology in Europe. In modern philosophy, a similar dialectic is present in Hegel's logic. Instead of resorting to idealism, Marx will try to resolve the apparent deadlock between positive knowledge and critique, conceiving a theory in which contradictions must be 'resolved' through material and political practice.

Based on the structure of the dialectical approach, we will build an argument about how the concept of crisis is fundamentally related to the mutually interacting fields of history, science and, ultimately, politics, the latter serving as a kind of dialectical *Aufhebung* of the others.[2] We will do this by focusing on two fundamental discussions around these areas of knowledge, the first debate being the *Methodenstreit* that took place at the edge between history and science.[3] For the second debate, at the point of interaction between science and politics, we will focus on Schmitt's position on crisis – or state of exception in his own terms. We will argue that these three interacting fields of knowledge are ultimately linked to perspectives on scientific transitions between the natural, social and political sciences.

2 *Aufhebung*, mostly translated as sublation, is the German term used by Hegel to describe the process to overcome the dialectic between thesis and anti-thesis in dialectical thought.

3 *Methodenstreit* means 'methodological dispute'.

1 The Scientific Concept of Crisis

Crisis appears as a central catchword for the examination and interpretation of virtually all areas of life: social crisis, economic crisis, political crisis, ecological crisis, psychological crisis, epistemological crisis, etc.[4] However, the concept of crisis made a fundamental contribution in the development of many fields of knowledge – including politics, psychology, economy, and history – as well as in their establishment as autonomous disciplines.[5] The analysis, explanation, and possible solutions to the crisis constituted the foundations of the works of the so-called 'monuments' of European social scientific knowledge, such as Marx, Freud, Habermas, Arrighi, Gramsci, Poulantzas, etc.

However, some have questioned its usefulness as an analytical tool due to the diversity of its meanings and a subsequent devaluation effect. Its crude defining categories and variety of meanings gave traditional positivist social scientists many reasons to question its possibilities for creating systematic and scientific knowledge.[6] According to them, crisis has become an all-purpose slogan or a banal cliché. Today's terminology of crisis would be more activist and 'political' than 'scientific'.[7] This would be the reason why 'crisis' has no applicability in 'modern' behavioural social sciences and game theory.[8]

Should we then rule out a contemporary use of the concept altogether? The combination of its deeply contested character and its reach as a concept in the social sciences with its popularity in everyday speech is at least an indication of the social and political relevance of an in-depth discussion of theoretical boundaries and their practical utility. Where better to start than with the history of crisis itself?

Krisis, the ancient Greek noun, derives from *krinó/krinein* – a verb that meant to separate, choose, decide, or judge.[9] Crisis designated the existence of a situation or moment in which alternatives were restricted, and which

4 Koselleck and Richter 2006, p. 358.
5 Koselleck 2002, p. 238.
6 Starn 2005; Robinson 1968.
7 Starn 2005.
8 Robinson 1968.
9 Koselleck and Richter 2006; Starn 2005; Roitman 2011. In classical Greek, the subsequent separation into two domains of meaning – that of a 'subjective critique' and an 'objective crisis' – was still encompassed by the same term (Koselleck and Richter 2006). We can thus observe that the term anticipated 'appropriate judgment' as a crucial dimension of the concept of crisis – this means that the use of the concept of crisis presupposes an ideological perspective.

required a decision.[10] It is no coincidence that the notion of *krisis* largely entered crisis-prone medieval Europe through Jewish and Christian theology, particularly through the apocalypse in John's revelations. Apocalyptic theologies have often been the result of major social crises: Adela Collins, for example, argues that the story of revelation itself was the result of a social crisis within Judaism: the revelation deals with the perceived 'unbearable tension' between 'what was' – a complex situation involving conflicts between Christian heretics with other Jews, conflicts over wealth, and precarious and traumatic relations with Roman conquerors – and 'what should have been' – God's rule, involving the speedy, public, and communal vindication of Jesus and his followers.[11] Is it surprising then that such a story of 'crisis' – meaning a judgment before God while also containing a promise of salvation – gained resonance in a European 'Dark Age' marked by crumbling institutions, continual episodes of pestilence, Viking raids, climate change, feudal wars, and famine?[12]

But crisis didn't remain in the theological sphere. In what today would be called the 'natural scientific' form, the boundaries between physics and metaphysics were not always so clear. The current scientific use of crisis dates back to its medical significance that prevailed since the 5th century BCE.[13] Associated with the Hippocratic school,[14] crisis indicated a turning point in a disease, a phase of an illness, in which it was decided whether or not the organism's ability to heal itself was sufficient for recovery.[15] The critical process, the illness, appears objective, as empirical deviations from the normal healthy state of the organism. The patient experiences his impotence in the face of the objectivity of the disease, a subject condemned to passivity and temporarily deprived of the full possession of his powers. Crises are therefore associated with the idea of an objective force that deprives a subject of a part of his normal sovereignty.[16] However, we would not talk about a crisis if death were certain. The crisis is, therefore, never just an objective and external process. In its medical form – as in its theological form – the crisis thus designates a phase that requires an irrevocable decision, a call to action and a belief in subjective human agency.[17] This apparent contradiction between the loss of sovereignty and the need for

10 Koselleck 2002, p. 237.
11 Collins 1984; Walker Jr. 1986.
12 Koselleck 2002; Koselleck and Richter 2006, p. 359; Roitman 2011.
13 Habermas 1975a; Robinson 1968; Roitman 2011.
14 Koselleck 2002; Koselleck and Richter 2006, pp. 360–1.
15 Habermas 1975a.
16 Habermas 1975a.
17 Roitman 2011.

irrevocable choice or judgment characterises the paradoxical nature of the crisis, which transcends all aspects of the concept. Likewise, in Aristotle's introduction of crisis into the political sphere, in Rhetoric, *krisis* is the translation of judgment, corresponding to three meanings: as a faculty, as a process, and as an object.[18] In Aristotelian politics, crisis refers to a political decision that preconditions all required legal judgment, a fundamental qualitative change, a founding act between the old and the new.[19]

2 Dialectics and Critique

While in ancient Greek theological and medicinal usage the subjective and objective condition were unambiguously covered by the same term *Krisis*, in modern everyday usage we tend to separate 'crisis' and 'critique'. This separation makes it easier to understand how the interaction between the objective and subjective dimensions works. Although both terms have the same etymological origin, the separation gives rise to a 'crisis' that apparently encompasses a more 'objective condition' – a situation of economic recession, failing institutions, high unemployment – while 'critique' appears to be the 'subjective, ideological act' – an accusation or complaint against injustice, unfairness, backwardness, etc.[20]

Is it because criticising, as a verb, is a human practice, a form of resistance against dominant normativity? Michel Foucault argues that the 'art of critique' developed as a counterweight to the development of the 'arts of governmentality' in modern society. From the fifteenth century onwards, the 'art of governmentality', which was previously part of the Christian theology that constituted the backbone of the medieval apparatus of the Catholic Church, developed into the different rational sciences and disciplines that structure and reproduce all domains of social life in the modern state. In an increasingly diverse society, due to a process of division of labour, increasing inequalities, and globalisation, these forms of rational thought aim to provide systematic answers on how to govern children, the poor, the family, armies, cities, etc. The 'art of governmentality' develops in the different scientific disciplines of pedagogy, politics, and economics. At the same time, a 'critical attitude' develops, which can be defined as 'the art of not being governed like this'.[21]

---

18 Black 1978, p. 95; Sloane 2001, p. 410.

19 Koselleck 2002.

20 Ibid.

21 Foucault 1997.

Much like the art of governance gets secularised through modernity, the practice of critique, which used to be directed against religion, is becoming secularised. Karl Marx first systematised this in his introduction to *Critique of Hegel's 'Philosophy of Right'* and 'Theses on Feuerbach'. In the former, he famously wrote that while religious criticism used to be a reflection of 'the struggle against the world whose spiritual aroma is religion', in an increasingly secularised world, the task of critique becomes 'to unmask self-estrangement in its unholy forms once the holy form of human self-estrangement has been unmasked'. 'The criticism of Heaven', thus needed to turn into 'the criticism of Earth, the criticism of religion into the criticism of law, and the criticism of theology into the criticism of politics'.[22]

We will come back to this later, but the apparent separation between crisis and critique enables us to understand the contradiction between the positive and negative dimensions within the concepts of crisis and critique. As with critique, crisis is fundamentally determined by this contradiction. For Roitman it is the disjuncture between what 'ought' and what 'is' that conceives 'the formal possibility of crisis'.[23] This contradiction is what drives the methods of dialectical thinking and with it many of the dichotomies that underlie social theory. Dialectical philosophy is based on reflection on these contradictions. It is based on oppositions and negations – concepts are presented as the interaction between opposing aspects of a common whole: quantity and quality, concrete and abstract, particular and universal, process and moment. Let us think about the contradictions between the concepts of subject and object, theory and practice, validity and value, intelligible and empirical, transcendence and immanence. Crisis is an exquisite concept that allows us to explore and understand things like the interaction between oppositions.

2.1 Socrates – Questioning Discourse

As with crisis, it is common to place the historical and etymological origins of dialectical thought in ancient Greece. As a philosophical concept, critique was popularised through Plato's writings on the Socratic method of debate and questioning. In the first dialogues with Socrates, dialectics fulfils a 'critical function'.[24] Socrates was one of the first thinkers known to elaborate on the relationship between language, truth and power. The main idea behind this is the

22 TK.
23 Roitman 2011.
24 Meyer 1980, p. 284.

'problematic character' of discourse – *Logos*.[25] Socrates' perspective presupposed that words – discourses – reflected established powers.[26] This meant that the responses – positive word-based statements – reflected the power relations behind the *Logos*. Therefore Socrates was very reluctant to accept answers. According to his philosophical method, truth lies not in the answers, but in the practice of questioning itself. Truth emerged from the questioning of the authority socially invested in the leading citizens of the polis, those who were rarely contradicted due to their social position, which validated their discourse. In the end, Socrates paid a political price with his life.

Socrates, however – consistent with his position on its problematic character – never systematised the *Logos*. He practiced it on a reflexive level and therefore never had a concrete conception of dialectics.[27] While dialectics is an essential method for discovering and acquiring knowledge, as a validation procedure it struggles. Since the method negates positive discourse and knowledge, any positive truth would reflect the *Logos* and would therefore be contradictory with the method itself. This makes the transition from the dialectical to the scientific method, with its disciplinary, objective, positive character and description, particularly difficult. The concept of crisis, built around the interaction of the negative dimension (negative subjective judgment) and the positive dimension (positive objective condition), occupied a crucial place in this transition. Throughout history, philosophers have struggled to make this transition. The first was Plato himself, the one who wrote Socrates' dialogues, an act through which he intrinsically committed himself to the *Logos*.

2.2 Plato – The Idealistic Solution

In Plato we have the transition from a conception of philosophy centred on questioning to an 'ontological' conception centred on being. Dialectics lost its purely negative character. What made an answer became central to Plato's dialectic. The dialectical question–answer method became the cognitive method – a subjective characteristic, a science of judgment, to arrive at the answer – an objective statement –, rather than just the end: problematising the

25 Meyer 1980, pp. 281–83.

26 Half a century later, Aristotle considered discourse the most important condition of the political. Discourse serves to make clear what is useful and harmful and what is fair and unfair. Discourse is the precondition for his famous statement that 'man is a political animal' (Aristotle 1998, p. 1253a).

27 Meyer 1980, p. 283.

discourse.[28] Plato thus dissociates himself from Socrates: the ultimate objective of knowledge is to eliminate a problem, from which he concludes that 'questioning as such is inadequate when it comes to laying the foundations of truth'.

For Socrates the question 'What is X?' is the question presupposed in any question about X: it serves to bring forward the duality about knowledge and ignorance – or mere appearance of knowledge – about X.[29] But for Plato the Socratic question can find an objective answer because 'if we ask what X is, we presuppose that there is something that is X'. There must be a prior contact that is presupposed and required, 'since the question of the being of X bears on X itself'. 'In inquiring into what things are, we become conscious of them, and we had to be conscious of some of their properties before asking the question'.

Systematising these presuppositions about X brings us to the characteristic idealistic Platonic rationalist world of forms. Consequently, in Plato's approach, truth is no longer based on questions and answers, but on 'the objective validity of the assertion', with rationality having a monopoly of the judgment. In this approach to truth, the epistemological role of the audience is reduced to zero and the questioning itself becomes a mere rhetorical procedure, rather than playing a cognitive role. The dogmatic conception of discourse and knowledge based upon the transcendental reality will eventually form the basis of Plato's republic and have a lasting effect on neo-Platonic Christian theology.

2.3 Hegel – Dialectics in Modernity

Thinking about dialectics and the dialectical perspective on today's world inevitably leads us to Hegel. His new conception of dialectical logic is best given by the first thesis of his 1801 dissertation: '*Contradictio est regula veri, non contradictio falsi*' / 'Contradiction is the rule of truth, non-contradiction is false'.[30] Given the anti-empiricist and idealistic character of his approach, Hegel is considered by many to be a Neoplatonist. However, in contrast to medieval Christian theologians, Hegel's dialectical thought arose directly from the great social tensions that accompanied the rise of industrial capitalism. Alienation, modernisation, nation-states, social revolutions, and their reactions made him think of change over time as a dialectical process dominated by conflicts:

> The spirit of man has broken with the old order of things hitherto prevailing, and with the old ways of thinking, and is in the mind to let them all sink into the

---

28 Meyer 1980, pp. 283–84.

29 Meyer 1980, p. 288.

30 Bordignon 2012, p. 221.

> depths of the past and to set about its own transformation. It is indeed never at rest, but carried along the stream of progress ever onward … the spirit of the time, growing slowly and quietly ripe for the new form it is to assume, disintegrates one fragment after another of the structure of its previous world. That it is tottering to its fall is indicated only by symptoms here and there. Frivolity and again ennui, which are spreading in the established order of things, the undefined foreboding of something unknown – all these betoken that there is something else approaching. This gradual crumbling to pieces, which did not alter the general look and aspect of the whole, is interrupted by the sunrise, which, in a flash and at a single stroke, brings to view the form and structure of the new world.[31]

Hegel's systematic application of the method of dialectical thought to history and social processes, most famously in the *Phenomenology of the Spirit*, influenced European thought. Ibn Khaldun, had made a similar exercise in his *Muqaddimah*, in the 14th century – which, according to some, inspired Hegel – when he pointed to the importance of conflicts and economic and political crises as the driving forces behind the circular evolution of history.[32] Although repetition and conflict are also essential to Hegel's analysis, the main difference that explains the particular importance of his philosophy is that Hegel made dialectical structure the central axis of the analysis of the picture. He used it as an extraordinary method to unravel and systematise the changing world around him at the dawn of European industrial modernity. According to Wahl, the contradiction between thesis and antithesis, and the mediation that leads to synthesis, are the abstractions of the fundamental experiential basis of crisis, human alienation, despair and hope in the era of modernity.[33] History is the field where their reconciliation takes place.[34]

This holistic philosophical framework, exposed in *The Science of Logic*, allowed him to systematise reality and how knowledge about reality is constructed through contradictions in the same movement.[35] Hegel's dialectical epistemology created the possibility of critical theory – a heritage present in theoretical concepts such as the holistic approach, immanent contradiction, negation and its negation, and *Aufhebung* – opening up the possibility of devel-

---

31 Hegel 2006, p. 75.

32 Ibn Khaldun (1987) used the term *Asabiyyah*, which meant something like collective consciousness, state of mind, or ideology, in a similar way to Hegel's Spirit; and analysed its role in the change, rise and fall of civilisations.

33 Wahl 1982.

34 Roth 2019, p. 4.

35 Hegel 2010.

oping a systemic theory for social change. Hegelian thought provided a vehicle for confronting the historical and for thinking the connection between history and knowledge.[36]

Hegel himself, however, did not take up the opportunity. Hegel wanted to develop a scientific theory that could account for the 'discordant forces which were tearing modern society' in a 'united whole', comprehending the forms taken by human life and consciousness. He did not ask 'should things be', only showing the necessary place of each as a part of the whole picture.[37] Hegel's conception of science 'left no room for critical judgment', which made it politically conservative by our standards, and even by its contemporary standards, since the framework allowed for the legitimisation of the monarchy and the Prussian state bureaucracy.[38] For Marxists, Hegelian notions of mediations and dialectical change are important not because they resolve the crisis in a system, but because they point to the closure that can occur through radical historical action.[39]

2.4 Marx – Crisis and Praxis

As Plato had done with Socrates, Karl Marx attempted to resolve the dialectical approach of his inspirational source. While for Hegel 'humanity, identified as Spirit, just was, and there was nothing more to say about it', the young Marx developed the dialectical framework, placing the mismatch or contradiction between humanity and its inhuman forms as the central category of Truth.[40] Marx criticised the idealist solution to dialectics in *German Idealism*, not only in Hegel's philosophical system, but also in the work of the so-called critical Young Hegelians, such as the Bauer brothers.[41] For Marx, with Hegel, 'philosophy has sealed itself off to form a consummate, total world'.[42]

Therefore, in its confrontation with the total world, Hegel failed to understand that the activity of his philosophy only appears to be torn and contradictory, as a reflection of the torn world itself.[43] Despite Hegel's claims to immanence, according to Marx, he created a 'metaphysical subject divorced

36 Roth 2019, p. 2.
37 Smith 1996, p. 148.
38 Smith 1996, p. 148.
39 Roth 2019, p. 2.
40 Smith 1996.
41 Marx 1976.
42 Jessop and Malcolm-Brown 1990, p. 65.
43 Marx 1977.

from real historical individuals'.[44] Thus, inspired by his doctoral study on the anti-deterministic materialism of Epicurus – as the well-known cliché goes – Marx turned Hegel right side up again. Although the emphasis of Marx's analysis remains on the contradiction and not on the correspondence between concrete social formations and their ideologies,[45] he will base his dialectics on a 'materialist' core. Marx's dialectics will be based 'on real individuals, on their activity and on the material conditions under which they live',[46] in order to 'discover the rational kernel within the mystical shell' of Hegel's philosophy.[47]

Marx's solution to dialectics – answer to bridge the positive and negative perspectives of society – will be based on revolutionary practice, not the Platonic ideal. It combines both the 'comprehension and affirmative recognition of the existing state of things' and:

> the recognition of the negation of that state, of its inevitable breaking up; because it regards every historically developed social form as in fluid movement, and therefore takes into account its transient nature not less than its momentary existence; because it lets nothing impose upon it, and is in its essence critical and revolutionary.[48]

In Marx's dialectics, totality stands for the unity of these two phases – of recognition and denial. 'Crisis' represents the concrete appearance of this totality, as it functions as a moment in which the two phases – objective condition and subjective judgment – 'assert their unity, the unity of the different aspects'.[49] For Marx, these immanent principles – an 'immanent grounding'[50] given by 'critical standards … given in the historical process itself' – were necessary weapons in the struggle for progressive social change because they provided a basis for critique within historical reality. This element of practical, political and material critique is his main difference with Hegel.

---

44 Antonio 1981.
45 Antonio 1981, pp. 332–34.
46 Marx 1998, pp. 36–7.
47 Marx 2012a.
48 Marx 1873.
49 Marx 1968, p. 505.
50 In the tradition of critical social sciences – 'immanent critique' points to the 'discrepancy between the basic liberal values of freedom and equality proclaimed by the bourgeois society and the objective realities of economy irrationality' (Morrow and Brown 1994).

3 Crisis, Science, and History

The idea of giving 'crisis' a historical connotation is not limited to Hegel and Marx. Given that the dual character of crisis always implies the existence of a comparative state of judgment or differentiation, the question arises: crisis compared to what?[51] Or if we take Habermas's conceptualisation: what 'goal state [*Sollzustand*]' are we talking about when we talk about a crisis as a 'deviation'?[52] Within the paradigm of modernity, the temporal perspective, marked by increasingly rapid historical progress driven by globalising capitalism, plays an essential role in terms of comparison according to Koselleck (2002). Modernity presents itself as an era marked by 'a secular movement that sought the demystification and desacralization of knowledge and social organization'. She '*embraced the idea of progress and actively sought* to break with history and tradition'.[53] It is in this modern context that 'crisis' entails a theory of time.[54]

Such theory of time establishes a particular teleology and a moral demand of difference between past and future.[55] The idea of 'crisis' tends to conceive of change over time in terms of radical difference; as in the theological origin, crisis now predominantly marks 'a new time', with time being a category of truth. Crisis signifies a historical time 'when "the real" is made bare'.[56] World history thus becomes a judgment on the world, and history itself becomes an acting subject, enforcing a kind of immanent justice.[57] Koselleck thus argues that the concept of 'crisis' re-enters the modern social sciences through the growing importance of the discipline of history and the historicisation of the social sciences.

3.1 Historicism and Science

The debate over the integration of history into the sciences has been split into two seemingly opposing positions. One advocated the need for scientific laws over historical particularity, the other defended the primacy of history over universal scientific laws. The most famous expression of this debate is

51 Roitman 2011.
52 Habermas 1975a.
53 Harvey 1991, pp. 12–13.
54 Koselleck 2002, p. 237; Roitman 2011.
55 Roitman 2011.
56 Ibid.
57 Koselleck 2002, p. 241.

the *Methodenstreit* – an epistemological discussion about method that was at the origin of the establishment of European social sciences in the nineteenth and twentieth centuries. The opponents were the so-called German Historical School and the Austrian School. The first had German nationalist and romantic roots and emerged as a legal school in opposition to the classical and utilitarian political economy of Adam Smith, David Ricardo, and others. It used the ideas of historicity and local particularity to criticise the universalisms of 'modern' positivist scientific laws. They 'blamed economy for being "abstract"'. Instead, 'they advocated a "visualizing" (*anschaulich*) way of dealing with the problems involved. They emphasised that the issues in this field are too complicated to be described in formulas and theorems and that the "differences" cannot be comprehended by a uniform theory'.[58] According to followers of '*historicismus*', scientific laws themselves are a product of history. Thus, they themselves are continually changing and therefore are never universal.

The Austrian school, with Ludwig von Mises, Carl Menger, and Friedrich Hayek, reacted against this perspective and considered the 'ahistorical' Hume, Smith, and Ricardo as 'the most exquisite outcome of the philosophy of the Enlightenment'.[59] The Austrian theoretical school based its political and economic models on Menger's 'methodological individualism', a theoretical perspective that assumes that 'every correct theoretical abstraction of social and economic changes is the result of the actions of individuals and agents in the economy'.[60] This perspective on science is closely linked to the ahistorical neoclassical/neoliberal hypothesis of '*Homo economicus*'. According to the Austrian school, German historical particularisation ultimately leads to 'as many economic theories required as there are nations and races', and therefore denies the possibility of 'such a thing as an economic science valid for all countries, nations and ages'.[61] Wouldn't this mean that 'there could be no such a thing as a science, other than history, dealing with aspects of human action', if we took historicists seriously?[62]

The debate between positive science and history was the main inspiration for the work of Karl Popper, who came to dominate scientific epistemology in the twentieth century. Popper is often classified in the Austrian and positivist school, although he assumed himself as a critic of positivist science, which he vigorously attacked for being itself metaphysics. Popper's main criticism of his-

58 Von Mises 1984.
59 Ibid.
60 Azad 2005; Udehn 2002.
61 Von Mises 1984, pp. 7–8.
62 Von Mises 1984.

toricism is in relation to its form of historical positivism that deduces laws from history.[63] The process of falsification is central to Popper's perspective on science, and since historical laws can never be falsified, they are excluded as being scientific in advance.[64]

Popper associates this historical positivism with Marxism.[65] In doing so, however, he reduces the Marxist analysis of history to a very positivist, reductionist, and structural version of Marx's approach. The Marx that Popper criticises is a very odd analytical Marx, without dialectics. According to Popper, the problem with this historicism lies in the holistic approach to history: as 'the whole' is too complex, it can never be fully known. Therefore, all descriptions of reality must be selective, and real 'predictions', like those of the historicist approach, can never be made. As history is made up of singular events, it can only reveal trends: the best historical analysis it could give would be a 'so-far-unfalsified hypothesis'. Specifically, Popper argues that Marx's thesis of 'scientific socialism', which proposes the historical necessity of a revolution for the transition from capitalism to socialism, is unscientific, since such a hypothesis could never be falsified a priori.

Such a position on the mechanical laws of history can be found in some currents of Marxism, but it is not necessarily opposed to Marx's own perspective. The latter's approach to the 'whole' mirrors the Hegelian approach to totality, which, according to Hegel, cannot be understood analytically, but only through dialectics. If there was one person who consistently argued that man 'made' history and therefore constantly changed it, it was Marx. His development of the concept of praxis, in which objectivity and subjectivity merge in human activity, is the basis of his conception of history. We will return to this later, but for Marx history is a political project, which is scientific insofar as science is political.

Popper's initial approach to the 'principle of falsification' is, however, quite interesting from a critical perspective: it exposes some fundamental political aspects of modern scientific knowledge. Falsification is presented for the first time as an alternative to the empirical and positivist logic of the 'principle of

---

63 Historicism is the approach in social sciences which assumes that 'historical prediction is their principal aim' and that this aim is attainable by discovering the rhythms, patterns and trends of History (Suchting 1972, p. 235). Historicists see history itself as the driving force of the social construction of meanings and try to identify objective forces in order to understand and to account for the emergence of beliefs and meanings (Refudeen 1998).

64 Popper 2005.

65 Ironically, Marx's own theoretical approach develops precisely from a critique of both liberal economics and the German Historical School (Marx 2010).

induction', as a means by which science decides on the truth.[66] According to the positivist approach to science, every objective scientific theory is the product of sensory observations and must be able to be tested and reproduced in similar circumstances. Popper argued that the fundamental logical flaw in inductive reason is that one can never infer universal statements based on singular/particular statements.[67] Alternatively, he proposes a method based on deduction rather than induction. It consists of testing easily testable singular statements, deduced from a theory. If the decision of the falsification process is positive, the 'singular conclusions have been verified, then the theory has, for the time being, passed its test. But if the decision is negative, or in other words, if the conclusions have been falsified, then their falsification also falsifies the theory from which they were logically deduced'.[68]

In his *The Logic of Scientific Discovery*, he defines the criterion for falsification as 'intersubjectively tested'.[69] According to Popper, science is what has become 'justified', meaning tested and understood 'by everyone so far'. This 'intersubjectivity', 'by everyone' and 'so far', are important elements that leave room for a critical appropriation of Popper's approach. Subjectivity – in contrast to the objectivist approach of the positivists – thus plays an important role, and 'by everyone' means that science depends on the existence of social consensus, hegemony, and conflict. Furthermore, 'so far' incorporates a temporal dimension in the conceptualisation of scientific knowledge. This definition reopens the possibility of a historical dimension of science, as different 'times' can mean different judgments about what is scientifically true.

It should be noted that, in his polemic with Marxism, Popper later amends these points, giving them a liberal political content. In the corresponding footnotes, referring to *The Poverty of Historicism*, in later editions he attributes a failure of scientific evolution to the fact that knowledge is not 'free' to advance; as freedom is not guaranteed, the state of art of science can stop or even be reversed.[70] Later, in his *The Poverty of Historicism*, a critique of Marxism, he also redefines intersubjectivity in a fundamentally more liberal notion – in the Habermasian style – by adding the idea of rational deliberation to the definition: 'intersubjective rational criticism'.[71] As rational communication, rather than social struggle, for example, becomes the ultimate test of validity, he

66 Popper 2005, p. 5.
67 Popper 2005.
68 Popper 2005, p. 10.
69 Popper 2005, p. 22.
70 Popper 2005, p. 279.
71 Popper 2002.

excludes alternative and anti-hegemonic forms of scientific epistemology and sanctifies hegemonic bourgeois rationality.

Nevertheless, Popper admits that precisely in the context of 'crisis', the scientific epistemological consensus is challenged: at that point 'the conflict over the aims of science … becomes acute', and then 'the "classical" system of the day is threatened by the results of new experiments which might be interpreted as falsifications … The system will appear unshaken to the conventionalist … by blaming our inadequate mastery'. Others, including Popper, 'will hope to make new discoveries; and we shall hope to be helped in this by a newly erected scientific system'.[72] The crisis opens 'new vistas into a world of new experiences'.[73] Isn't the way Popper links 'crisis' and 'falsification' with the ideas of 'conflict', 'hope', 'a new scientific (justificatory-normative) system' to be implemented, against 'the conventionalist', to be achieved in a 'world of new experiences', a perspective very linked to Marx's 'scientific socialism' and political truth?

3.2 From a History of Scientific Dualities to the Current Crisis

In fact, 'science' has never been a uniform, well delineated body of knowledge. It is rather a gathering of continually conflicting worldviews. The recurring dualities between positive science and negative criticism, between classical economics and historicism, and between positivism and Marxism, reflect this general trend in the evolution of sciences. Kuhn conceptualised the history of science as a history of scientific revolutions that had parallels with political revolutions.[74] The paradigm shift, or scientific revolution, happens at a time of crisis, like the transition from one scientific paradigm to another. In Kuhn's work, the paradigm refers to a general approach accepted by the scientific community and 'normal science' refers to the application of paradigmatic theory to the solution and explanation of problems similar to those already solved by the paradigm.[75] In these paradigm shifts, parties to a revolutionary conflict must resort to mass persuasion and often violence.[76]

In modern social sciences, the tendency to conflict is mainly reflected in two dominant currents. Santos designates the dominant paradigm in social sciences as 'objective', characterised by the idea that it is possible and necessary to apply the canons and methodologies that have become standard in nat-

72 Popper 2005, pp. 88–9.
73 Ibid.
74 Kuhn 1996, pp. 92–94.
75 Purtill 1967.
76 Kuhn 1996, pp. 92–94.

ural sciences.[77] Originating from these same natural sciences at the end of the sixteenth century (Copernicus, Kepler, Galileo, Newton), from the nineteenth century onwards, greatly influenced by Descartes' *Discourse on the Method* (1637), this model of rationality extends to emerging social sciences. The positive technoscientific approach – which Comte conceptualised as the final historical stage of knowledge, after the theological and metaphysical, emerged as a fight against all types of feudal dogmatisms.[78] These feudal dogmatisms, such as Catholic theology and codes of honour, guided and restricted social life and legitimised despotism, irrationality, and hierarchy. The rise of this modern positive science was the intellectual sign of a rising bourgeoisie and reflected bourgeois domination and the disciplinarisation of nature and all non-civilised non-subjects, including colonials, women, the insane, animals, children, the poor, etc. It is best symbolised by the concept of social physics in the work of Comte and Quetelet, in which only objective, positivist, and empiricist methods can establish objective and universal 'natural' laws that govern society and that account for meanings independent of history.[79] Today, this ideology of technicality and rationality presents itself as the final stage of human knowledge.

The paradigm is continually opposed by a radically 'subjective' and anti-positivist tendency, inspired by phenomenology rather than empiricism.[80] These phenomenologists are sensitive to discursive constructions of reality and meaning and use values to understand history.[81] This approach tends to claim a distinct methodological status for the social sciences. Instead of copying the natural scientific method, its methodology is radically different – it is inter-subjective, descriptive and focussed on understanding knowledge; it refuses to propose universal truths and laws.[82]

Both currents have in common a reification of the human-nature divide as a basic pillar of knowledge, that is to say a naturalisation of science, excising the human, historical subject from his naturalised scientific knowledge. At the end of the twentieth century, in his analysis of the crisis of the dominant paradigm in scientific knowledge, Boaventura de Sousa Santos states that this distinction between natural sciences and social sciences, represented in the separation between positivists and anti-positivists in social sciences, became unsustain-

77 Santos 2000.
78 Comte 1868.
79 Santos 2000.
80 Santos 2000, p. 67.
81 Refudeen 1998.
82 Santos 2000.

able.[83] This unsustainability is expressed in the form of a 'crisis' of the dominant scientific paradigm. The crisis opens, in Kuhn's terms, as a 'paradigm shift period' of postmodernity, originating from changing social and theoretical conditions.[84]

In the theoretical field, one needs to point to the great advances in natural sciences in the twentieth century, such as the influence of Einstein's theory of relativity and Heisenberg's principle in quantum physics. Both had major implications for scientific epistemology, since both theories, from a natural scientific starting point, essentially point to the relativity of the distinction between subject and object, and showed how our perspective is reflected in our possible knowledge, complicating the dominant Newtonian paradigm in science.[85]

Santos does not really elaborate here on the socioeconomic conditions of this change, but a more in-depth reading of his work shows that he refers to the dynamics of global capitalism and the resistance it awakens. This capitalist dynamic implies the increasing penetration of the capital accumulation process in all spheres of human life, including knowledge and science. In doing so, capitalism profoundly restructures the socio-ecological relations of our surroundings, that is, our relations with our fellow humans and with the non-human – nature.[86] Science accompanies the capitalist colonisation of nature, playing a vital role in overcoming technical and ideological barriers to its accumulation process, through disciplinarisation, structuring and information. At the same time, this process also introduces the social contradictions and crisis tendencies of capitalism into ever larger spheres of socio-ecological life. Science, as a discourse and system of meaning, is not immune to this tendency of resistance. This helps us explain conflicting narratives about sciences.

In the context of the unsustainability of the division of natural and human sciences and against the positivist tendency to approach social sciences as natural sciences, it would be clarifying to proclaim, as Santos does, that 'all sciences are social sciences'.[87] All, including the 'exact' sciences, are products of historical social relations, in the form of narratives, historical processes, technological developments, human experiences, and dominant ideologies.

Instead of the scientific continuum between various conceptions of socially determined sciences, in which the 'natural' plays the role of only one polar-

83 Ibid.
84 Kuhn 1996.
85 Santos 2000, pp. 68–70.
86 Moore 2011.
87 Ibid.

ity and the social of another, we would propose the category of the 'political'. Rather than in the 'social', it is in the political practice of change that we can find truly conscious, subjective and collective judgment and practice. This nature–politics opposition may be surprising, but it is recurrent in contemporary critical theory, particularly when addressing issues of crisis and neoliberal hegemony. Wendy Brown, for example, uses the conceptualisation of depoliticisation to 'naturalise' racial or cultural explanations in media or academic discourses.[88] Erik Swyngedouw does the same with the climate issue, opposing naturalised and depoliticised climate discourses around carbon markets and the Anthropocene to the political movement for climate justice.[89]

4 Crisis, Science and the Political

4.1 The Context of the Political

Despite his very controversial character, Carl Schmitt has been the major inspiration for the conceptualisation of the concept of the political in contemporary critical and democratic theory. In this book, we will discuss some aspects of the work of Jurgen Habermas, Chantal Mouffe, Ernesto Laclau, Koselleck, Erik Swyngedouw, Wendy Brown, Slavoj Žižek, Giorgio Agamben, Hannah Arendt, and others who to some extent are indebted to Schmitt's work on the political and the exception. Schmitt was a German jurist and political theorist who throughout his life evolved from a Catholic conservative to a prominent member of the Nazi Party. He dedicated his work to the relationship between science and the political and is particularly interesting because he conceived of this relationship through the perspective of a critique of liberal ideology.[90] As a student of Max Weber, Schmitt developed the concept of the political as a response to the crisis of the Weimar Republic. According to Schmitt, the neo-Kantian methodologies used by Weber and his contemporary liberal colleagues were inadequate to deal with the changing conditions.[91] He accused their approach of being 'soulless', reflecting only the dominant thinking of

88 Brown 2006b.

89 Swyngedouw 2009.

90 For Schmitt the political is something that precedes morals, aesthetics or economics. As the antithesis of liberalism, the political derives its energy from every religious, moral, economic, ethical, or other antitheses (Mouffe 2005, p. 123).

91 McCormick 1999, p. 79.

apolitical modernist technicism, which reduced humans to mere machines and stripped the world and life of any real meaning.

Schmitt wasn't satisfied either with his contemporary resistance to this industrial alienation, which according to him took the form of romanticism. The simple denial of modern technical rationality by Romanticism – in the form of aesthetics – neglects the struggle of ideologies. It was, therefore, unable to transcend the dualism between soul and soullessness, characteristic of the modern age.[92] Schmitt resorts to a Hegelian dialectical approach to escape this dilemma. He writes that in contrast to 'purely natural-scientific rationalism', which 'could never grasp what is politically at stake, namely the concrete situation and the concrete moment', Hegel's:

> dialectical philosophy of history, if properly employed, provides a powerful means to free the concrete here and now, the *hic et nunc*, from the sphere of irrational intuitions or emotionally guided impressionism, and install man as the master over the irrationality of a fate ordained by God, nature, or providence.[93]

The political functions as the *Aufhebung* between modernity and its dialectical negation, romanticism, between technology and aesthetics, between science and myth.

According to Schmitt, meaning is restored by the political. In Schmitt's view, the political is defined by 'the distinction of friend and enemy'. Political contrast – based on 'decision' or judgment, of 'us' in contrast to a 'them' – locates meaning in the realm of collective identifications.[94] These shared collective identities are not aimed at escaping reality but to change it.

Schmitt's concept of the political has religious roots. Against the Protestant ethics of capitalism in Weber's work, Schmitt, as a devout Catholic, chose the political in the Roman Catholic Church, a political institution with religious fervour, giving meaning to man and society, prepared to make alliances and declare enemies.[95] As Schmitt moved away from the Church, he conceived a political theology based on nationalism and myth, which ultimately transformed him from a conservative Catholic into a reactionary supporter of Nazism. The reactionary content given by Schmitt to the political is undeniable and shows its dangers. The conception of the political as an antithesis to the liberal domestication of policies through rational argumentation and privatisa-

92 McCormick 1999; Schmitt 2017.
93 Schmitt 2014, p. 391.
94 Furner 2014; Mouffe 2005.
95 McCormick 1999, p. 73.

tion has nevertheless made it inspiring for much of our contemporary critical thinking, particularly in times of crisis of a depoliticised neoliberal hegemony.

Like Schmitt, his Italian Marxist contemporary, Antonio Gramsci, also finds inspiration for a political philosophy of praxis in the success of the Roman Catholic Church. The power of religions, particularly the Catholic Church, consists in energetically feeling the need for doctrinal union of the religious mass, preserving the ideological unity of the entire social and cultural bloc. The Jesuits are seen as the main drivers of this equilibrium, which guaranteed them an organic character in terms of philosophy and organisational solidity. The political guaranteed the relationship between intellectuals and common people in the Catholic Church.[96]

For Gramsci, the relationship between the 'superior' philosophy of praxis and 'common sense' is guaranteed by the political in the same way as within the Catholic Church.[97] But the position of the philosophy of praxis – Gramsci's term for Marxism – is nevertheless the antithesis of the Catholic position: it does not aim to keep 'common people' within their primitive 'common sense' philosophy, but rather to bring them to a superior conception of life. It should not be limited to scientific activity but form an intellectual moral bloc that enables the intellectual advancement of the masses.

4.2 Crisis, the Exception and the Political

As we have already seen, Schmitt developed the concept of the political amid the crisis of the 1930s. In the same decade, from Mussolini's prisons, Gramsci developed the concept of hegemony, to understand hegemony as a theory in an undecided political terrain.[98] The link between crisis, the political, and hegemony is not a mere historical coincidence. In this decade, the contradictions of the European capitalist system became undeniable, and the liberal consensus became unsustainable. Schmitt's concept of the political emerged at a time when the laws of the free market and cosmopolitan international law vanished in the polarisation between class, nation, and race identities. The political served as a critique of the declining liberal hegemony – this was Schmitt's aim in his critique of liberal technique – but it was at the same time the expression of its historical demise, at least temporarily, and of its rupture into conflicting ideologies.

96 Gramsci 1978, pp. 17–20.
97 Gramsci 1978, pp. 21–2.
98 Laclau and Mouffe 2001, p. XI.

Schmitt uses the concept of exception in a very similar way to how we have approached 'crisis' until now, as a moment of disruption of the normal, a need for political and even theological judgment. This state of exception contrasts with liberal, positivist science that intrinsically tries to 'banish from the human mind every exception'.[99] Schmitt claims that this relationship between norm – the normal state, consensus – and exception cannot be understood without dialectics: the exception confirms the existence of the norm, and the norm creates the exception.[100] According to Schmitt, the state of exception, particularly in his work starting with *Political Theology*, from 1922, brings with it the possibility of sovereign powers. Sovereign power concerns law-making authority beyond the law/norm, which can create a new historical political situation that irreversibly transforms its nature. Inspired by Schmitt, according to Agamben, the state of exception 'marks a threshold at which logic and praxis blur with each other and a pure violence without *logos* claims to realise an enunciation without any real reference'.[101]

The crisis thus emerges when consensus ends, when choice appears, when the political emerges. This political transgresses normal politics – the low policy dimension.[102] As such, the political also applies to scientific paradigms. There is a crisis when hegemony is challenged and therefore when scientific consensus disappears. Instead of a transition from the natural sciences to the social sciences, in a crisis we observe a necessary transition to a politicisation of the sciences.

This politicisation is not necessarily a fatal barrier to scientific knowledge. On the contrary: Schmitt had argued that in the state of exception it is the very differentiation between enemy and friend that produces meaning.[103] If we accept the premise that 'truth' is always partial, 'obscuration' – defending the friend's perspective and disregarding the legitimacy of the enemy's perspective – should be approached as a blind spot that facilitates the production of knowledge.[104] The political functions as a filter and structuring principle in the natural chaos of information.[105] It is in this context that Roitman

99 McCormick 1999, p. 223; Schmitt 1986, p. 41.
100 McCormick 1999, p. 127.
101 Agamben 2005, p. 40.
102 Mouffe 2005.
103 McCormick 1999, p. 92.
104 Roitman 2011.
105 It is worth mentioning Santos' term 'knowledge born in struggle' (Santos and Meneses 2019), which emphasises the importance of emancipatory knowledge created through political resistance against capitalism, patriarchy and colonialism. It serves as the basis for his *Epistemologies of the South*, see below.

(2011) claims that 'crisis' must be treated as an 'enabling paradox'. When from a 'critique', or a political-scientific perspective, the crisis is described as the logical outcome of historical progress, it in fact obscures the contingent political meaning of such criticism. But in doing so, the crisis functions as a lens that makes certain things visible and others not, producing particular forms of knowledge. The crisis thus effectively creates and structures a new political science.

Can we then overlook the problems with Schmitt's concept of the political? Above we referred to the reactionary content that Schmitt gave to the political. Although the crisis of liberalism was also a precondition for the social experiments of the popular fronts, the welfare state, and redistribution policies, one cannot neglect the way in which fascism could lead the crisis to political conclusions that were not progressive. As McCormick rightly points out, the concept of 'political activity' in Schmitt's work tends to fall into the trap he reproached in romantic politicians.[106] That is, like the aesthetics of romanticism, his approach is characterised by the final emptiness of the concept of the political as such, since 'the political is itself devoid of any substantive content'. The political is therefore not enough.

The consequence of this 'emptiness' is that its conceptual approach can be useful for approaches from all sorts of different political perspectives – and can therefore create 'monsters'. Isn't this described in the famous description by Gramsci (Schmitt's contemporary): 'The crisis consists precisely in the fact that the old is dying and the new cannot be born; in this interregnum a great variety of morbid symptoms appear'?[107] Although Schmitt's interpretation of the political was ultra-reactionary – in the form of a Catholic opposition to liberalism – and Schmitt's legal interpretation of the crisis, the state of exception, legitimised a fascist regime, it also allowed Schmitt's theory to become particularly relevant for thinking the political among contemporary progressive theorists.

Many contemporary 'post-Marxist' critical theorists have used Schmitt to transcend Marx and Gramsci in a postmodern era. The political seemed to be a crucial concept of critique in an age when a working-class-based socialist alternative was seen as *'passé'*, since the category of labour seemed to have become too weak, complacent, and conservative to play the role of a universal historical agent, as the driving force of emancipatory change. Ernesto Laclau and Chantal Mouffe's widely acclaimed book *Hegemony and Socialist Strategy* (2001) and Mouffe's later work are excellent examples. Schmitt's idea of the

106 McCormick 1999, p. 112.
107 Gramsci 1992, p. 33.

political would allow them to transcend the universality of capital, without the need for class. Instead, they would focus on building alliances between different identities in shifting common struggles into pluralistic democratisation. The political thus legitimised the dawn of the era of identity politics in critical theory and political practice.

But much as Schmitt accused the Romantics of becoming accommodated within liberalism as a mere form of aesthetics, a similar critique could have been directed to many forms of contemporary 'critical' identity politics that rely on the concept of the political. Instead, let us do the opposite of what Mouffe, Habermas – whose project was the removal of the 'ideological ballast' of historical materialism – and others did: let us bring Schmitt's concept of the political back into Marx's analysis. Given the conservative Catholic Carl Schmitt's ideological enmity towards Bolshevism, an honest 'Schmittean reading of Marx' might seem ridiculous, but we believe it could provide some answers to the theoretical and ideological shortcomings of Schmitt's theory and bring some considerations for a reconceptualisation of 'political' science.

4.3 Marxism as More than Political Science

Curiously, in a 1931 radio broadcast, recently republished in English in the journal *Historical Materialism*, Carl Schmitt himself proposed Marxism as the ultimate form of a political science. He considered Marx's theory and its application by Lenin particularly important in a context in which 'the political' was 'situated in a seemingly apolitical, economically determined industrial society'.[108] The political, in the form of the radical opposition between capital and labour, is the kernel of 'Marxist science'.[109]

But Marx is more than just political.[110] The most fundamental difference between Marx and Schmitt lies in the starting points for the analysis of modernity. Schmitt, influenced by Weber, considered technicity the driving force of modernity. Schmitt's focus on 'technicity', the general phenomenon of technical-economic thought and rationalisation, which incorporates both market dynamics and bureaucracy allowed him to claim that Marx and the communists ultimately shared the same cultural principles of technical development as bourgeois society.[111] Such a culturalist characterisation of technicity conceived 'the political' as the mythical antithesis of the 'scientific'. In Schmittean terms, a

108 Schmitt 2014, p. 389.
109 Furner 2014, p. 374.
110 Furner 2014.
111 McCormick 1999, p. 45.

true 'political science' would therefore be impossible, and political knowledge is doomed to mythical meanings. Not so for Marx.

A return to Marx, with a readjustment of Schmitt's conception of the political, would be, from our perspective, a more fruitful approach. Instead of technicity, Marx projected the relations of production – capital, with its processes of accumulation, commodification, and resistance – as the driving force behind modernity and the processes of alienation.[112] In fact, Marx took a much more consequential 'Schmittean' position than Carl Schmitt. The differentiation between capital and labour – the enemy and the friend according to the class perspective – brought 'the political' to the very root of the historical process behind modernity. Marxism thus assumes a true political ontology based on the category of labour. This not only makes the analysis of modernity more consistent than Schmitt's; it also allows us to differentiate between 'science' as a method and form of knowledge and the effective driving force of alienation, that is, capital.

Without question, all truth is 'practical' and 'political' for Marx in his *Theses on Feuerbach*. The second thesis says: 'The question of whether objective truth can be attributed to human thought is not a question of theory, but a practical question. It is in praxis that human beings must prove the truth, that is, the reality and power, the earthly character of their thinking'.[113] As in Carl Schmitt's 'political activity', Marx's truth is a political and historical practice. But Marx's focus on labour, capital, and the relations of production also gives more material 'substance' to the political than 'myth' ever can. Praxis brings material resources and historical agents into the process of a dialectical analysis.

Even Schmitt acknowledges this in his analysis of Marx and Hegel, when he says that socialism 'is not simply any possible type of criticism of the ills common to all times. It is not compassion for the unfortunate and poor, it is struggle against injustice, resistance and rebellion'.[114] Schmitt admits the merits of this Marxist 'scientific' dimension, meaning that the political is planted in a 'concrete rational consciousness of a historical situation as a whole, and, from this, the intention of shaping the entire situation of humanity in accordance with this consciousness'.[115] The communist doctrine on crisis completely changes the relationship between normal and exception, and thus, according

112 This is the project of political Marxism and Ellen Wood's repoliticisation of historical materialism in *Democracy Against Capitalism* (2016).

113 Held 2013, p. 190; Marx 1998, p. 569.

114 Schmitt 2014, p. 390.

115 Ibid.

to Schmitt, 'The concepts of truth and science in Marxist scientific socialism can only be understood from such a dialectical philosophy of history'.[116]

This does not foreclose the element of 'political myth'. Myth plays an important role in scientific political struggle, particularly in the conception of class opposition and class consciousness. It is present in the popular transformation from *'Klasse an sich'* to *'Klasse für sich'*, and in the universalisation of its claims as a historical agent, from a particular material interest to a universal truth. This political process and the struggle for truth that would later characterise Gramsci's conception of hegemony are already present in this long but revealing quote from Marx's *Critique of Hegel's 'Philosophy of Right'*:

> No class of civil society can play this role without arousing a moment of enthusiasm in itself and in the masses, a moment in which it fraternizes and merges with society in general, becomes confused with it and is perceived and acknowledged as its general representative, a moment in which its claims and rights are truly the claims and rights of society itself, a moment in which it is truly the social head and the social heart. Only in the name of the general rights of society can a particular class vindicate for itself general domination. For the storming of this emancipatory position, and hence for the political exploitation of all sections of society in the interests of its own section, revolutionary energy and spiritual self-feeling alone are not sufficient. For the revolution of a nation, and the emancipation of a particular class of civil society to coincide, for one estate to be acknowledged as the estate of the whole society, all the defects of society must conversely be concentrated in another class, a particular estate must be the estate of the general stumbling-block, the incorporation of the general limitation, a particular social sphere must be recognized as the notorious crime of the whole of society, so that liberation from that sphere appears as general self-liberation. For one estate to be par excellence the estate of liberation, another estate must conversely be the obvious estate of oppression.[117]

The subaltern class perspective, by definition, represents a particular point of view and defines the field of visibility. It thus rejects an 'objective-scientific' perspective as a hegemonic bourgeois 'normality' that hides its 'real interests'.[118] The alternative perspective is political, subjective, and 'hypercritical', as the overcoming step of critique/crisis. In contrast to bourgeois 'objectivity', the particular proletarian perspective gains its dimension of truth through the object-

116 Schmitt 2014, p. 390.
117 Marx 1977, p. 140.
118 Löwy 1978b.

ive possibility of being transparent.[119] For Marx, who theorises from the proletarian position – that is, from the material interests of the category of labour – the economic crisis functions as a moment in which this 'real' becomes transparent: the truth of the contradictions of the capitalist form of production, derived from the fundamental opposition between capital and labour, emerges through the crisis.

Gramsci wrote that 'a theory is revolutionary precisely to the extent that it is an element of total separation into two camps, to the extent that it is a peak inaccessible to the enemies'.[120] By 'politicizing the economy', by choosing sides, through focusing on labour – as a negative subjective human element – at the heart of capitalist reproduction in the form of value formation and commodification, Marx introduced class struggle into the very heart of the economic critique of capitalist reproduction.[121] In doing so, Marx was able to historicise capitalism. In other words, rather than presenting capitalist market mechanisms as positive natural laws to be discovered, his approach revealed it to be a contingent social formation whose present and future depended on political conflict. By placing it in relation to other historical modes of production, he opened up a possibility for change. The concept of crisis also plays a crucial role for Marx, particularly in the form of revealing the true political conflict.[122] In Marx's own words: 'In the crises of the world market, the contradictions and antagonisms of bourgeois production are strikingly revealed'.[123]

119 Löwy 1978a, p. 32.

120 Gramsci 1992, p. 156.

121 Löwy 1978a, pp. 72–3.

122 In a quote wrongly attributed to Marx by David Held (2013, p. 191), Lenin (1966) goes further in this logic and proclaims: 'Revolutionaries sometimes try to prove that there is absolutely no way out of the crisis. This is a mistake. There is no such thing as an absolutely desperate situation ... Trying to "prove" in advance that there is "absolutely" no way out of the situation would be sheer pedantry or playing with concepts and catchwords. Practice alone can serve as true "proof" in this and similar issues'.

123 Marx 1968, p. 500. The character of 'revelation' derived from Marx's immanent critique is, through Marx's intellectual influence on economics and the social sciences, reflected in many contemporary mainstream uses of the concept of crisis. In contemporary economic discourse, crises – for example, when a financial bubble bursts – divulge the alleged false value based on speculation and reveal the true value, the fundamentals of the economy (Roitman 2011). 'Crises surface when the balance between supply and demand, between production and consumption, between the circulation of money and the circulation of goods is disturbed to such an extent that recessions and deterioration become visible everywhere' (Koselleck 2002, pp. 242–43).

4.4 Frankfurt School and Crisis

In the post-crisis era, in a context of betrayal of the social democracy and frustration of the German revolution and Stalinisation of the Soviet revolution, the best-known exponent of critical theory, the Frankfurt School, struggled to cope with the relationship between crisis and dialectics. Political events and revolutionary practice did not coincide with the expectations derived from the Marxist theory of the day.[124] The fact that dialectical materialism was confronted with a complete loss of scientific and critical credibility due to its incorporation into the ideological legitimation of a particular autocratic regime has led to several adaptations of the critical approach in which the logic of Marx and Hegel remains present.[125] Critical theory attempts to overcome the subjectivist/objectivist polarisation. It overcomes positivist and humanist knowledge through a theory of political action,[126] meaning that 'the critical theory of society is, in its totality, the unfolding of a single existential judgement'[127] in which the unifying elements are that a part of the critique is introduced at the metatheoretical level, as a practical commitment to social criticism and advocacy.[128]

Some of them were inspired by George Lukács' critique in *History and Class Consciousness* of the 'determinist' and 'positivist' interpretation of historical materialism by 'orthodox Marxism', which neglected the central importance of human subjectivity.[129] According to Lukács, who, like Schmitt was a student of Max Weber, there is no objective reality on which social theorists can reflect passively. Instead, the theorist is a participant in an ongoing class conflict. Historical materialism therefore does not have for Lukács any meaning outside the struggle of the proletariat – in contrast to both 'orthodox Marxists', who considered historical materialism a predefined historical theology, and Habermas, who later tried to depoliticise historical materialism. The Marxist claim to objectivity and truth can never be separated from the practices of a specific social class. But Lukács argued that 'the standpoint of the proletariat' and, consequently, of Marxism, transcends the 'one-sidedness' and distortions of other social theories and class ideologies, due to its role as a universal social class.[130]

---

124 Held 2013, pp. 17–23.
125 Morrow and Brown 1994, p. 89.
126 Morrow and Brown 1994, pp. 53–60.
127 Horkheimer 1976, p. 227; Morrow and Brown 1994, p. 97.
128 Morrow and Brown 1994, p. 110.
129 Lukács 1971.
130 Held 2013, p. 21.

The early Horkheimer, in contrast to other members of the Frankfurt school and his own older pessimistic perspective, still defended a theological-political class perspective close to that of Lukács's 'standpoint of the proletariat'.[131] He argued that the practical role of the theorist was to articulate and help develop class consciousness:

> To all those who are primarily concerned with the unhampered development of human potential and of justice, these classes must appear as the decisive structural principle of our time, for the realization of such goals depends on their elimination. There are other differences, other structural principles which, given the same interest in the free development of men and justice, may appear as fundamental as social classes ... Nevertheless, the distinction according to social classes is superior to the other points of view, for it can be shown that while the elimination of classes would entail a change in the other antitheses, the reverse is not true ... The elimination of classes is therefore the decisive principle ...[132]

However, from the 1930s onwards, the Frankfurt Institute for Social Research and the most influential currents of critical thought moved away from Marx's political perspective and retreated to Hegelian idealism to overcome differences in social theories through an interdisciplinary approach inspired by holism and dialectics.[133] After the Second World War, the destructive political experiments of fascism and the loss of faith in the degenerate Stalinist Soviet Union led to a definitive departure from traditional Marxist doctrines. Held exemplifies this with Horkheimer's focus on 'remembering', 'recollecting', or capturing a past in danger of being forgotten, and Marcuse's defence of personal gratification and individual self-emancipation (against those who would simply argue that liberation arises from changes in the relations and forces of production).[134]

The most significant example is Horkheimer and Adorno's *Dialectic of Enlightenment*. In this work, they developed a purely negative perspective on knowledge in general. The first chapter of *Dialectic* uses Hegel's claim that there is an internal relationship between the Enlightenment and an ethics of utility

131 Held 2013, p. 23, our translation.
132 Horkheimer 1978.
133 Horkheimer (1993, p. 11) saw this as '[...] a reformulation on the basis of the new problem constellation ... of the old question concerning the connection of particular existence and universal Reason, of reality and Idea, of life and Spirit'.
134 Held 2013.

and terror.[135] According to their new perspective, knowledge and rationality were only possible through alienation and control. Therefore, rationality and enlightenment always led to totalitarianism. Fascism and Stalinism were thus seen as the ultimate result of the Enlightenment. Hegel's dialectical perspective would thus transform into a purely negative dialectic, with no room for an *Aufhebung* to resolve or escape historical contradictions, as Marx had proposed. Given the importance of *Aufhebung* for the notion of crisis and for critical social theory in general, this meant an intellectual closure of the possibility of emancipation. The work of Horkheimer and Adorno thus signifies a fundamental pessimistic break with the Marxist and critical tradition so far. By focusing on criticising all forms of domination and at the same time refusing to specify 'what is to be done', they 'antagonize all those who seem to require a hard and fast doctrine to guide their action'.[136]

The restructuring of the political economy in post-war Europe and state intervention separating crisis tendencies from class tensions reinforced the rather cynical perspective of the Frankfurt School and paved the way for the 'cultural' – and therefore apolitical – impulse in critical studies. Another path was taken by Habermas, who was not as pessimistic as Horkheimer or Adorno were in the latter part of their lives and accused them of undervaluing democratic traditions.[137] In his book *Legitimation Crisis* (*Legitimationsprobleme im Spätkapitalismus*), Habermas explores how the apparent overcoming of the underlying class contradictions in capitalism through state intervention and the growing importance of technology made 'advanced' capitalism vulnerable to other types of crisis tendencies.[138]

Habermas was inspired by *The Fiscal Crisis of the State* by James O'Connor, from 1973. O'Connor argued that to ensure the loyalty of the masses and maintain legitimacy, as a consequence of the contradictions of capitalist production, the state must pay the cost of those who suffer the 'costs' of economic growth.[139] Over time, the development of capitalism led to the decline of the family, communities, and other non-capitalist spheres of production that played a vital role in the reproduction of life and value. This has led to a huge increase in the aggregate of social needs and a tendency for an increasing majority of the population to become dependent on the state. This results

135 Held 2013, p. 151.
136 Held 2013, p. 353.
137 Held 2013, p. 252; Morrow and Brown 1994, p. 144.
138 Habermas 1975a; Morrow and Brown 1994, p. 186.
139 O'Connor 2002, p. 8.

in a budgetary or fiscal crisis, with the State crisis being the expression of the crisis tendencies of capitalism itself.[140]

Also, for Habermas, crisis tendencies manifest themselves at the point of their political eruption, that is, at the point at which the existing political system is delegitimised. Habermas distinguishes four possible crisis tendencies: economic crisis, rationality crisis, legitimation crisis, and motivation crisis.[141] Economic crises obey the logic expressed in the law of the tendency of the rate of profit to fall, in which the state either mediates or acts as a collective capitalist [*Gesamtkapitalist*] that makes capital accumulation the substance of political planning. These crises will assert themselves as a social crisis and will lead to political struggles in which the class opposition between the owners of capital and the wage-dependent masses will again become manifest. The very logic of the crisis is altered by the displacement of the contradictory steering imperatives of market to the administrative system. Political crises exist in the form of the so-called rationality crisis, in which the administrative system is unable to reconcile and fulfil the imperatives received from the economic system, leading to a disorganisation of the state apparatus and the way it manages the spheres of life; or in the form of a legitimation crisis, in which the legitimating system cannot maintain the required level of loyalty from the masses. The latter calls into question the structure of the depoliticised public realm and therefore the formally democratic guarantee of the autonomous private disposition of the means of production.[142] Sociocultural crisis tendencies manifest themselves in the sociocultural system responsible for the social integration of a society and translate into a departure from the existing order and a lack of motivational commitment.[143] Haberman writes:

> Legitimation crises result from a need for legitimation that arises from changes in the political system (even when normative structures remain unchanged) and that cannot be met by the existing supply of legitimation. Motivational crises, on the other hand, are a result of changes in the socio-cultural system itself, becoming apparent at the level of cultural tradition (moral systems, worldviews) as well as at the level of structural change in the system of childrearing (school and family, mass media). In this way, the residue of tradition off which the state and the system of social labour lived in liberal capitalism is eaten away (stripping away traditionalistic padding), and core components of the bourgeois ideology

140 O'Connor 2002, p. 40.
141 Habermas 1975a, p. 145; Morrow and Brown 1994, p. 187.
142 Habermas 1975a, pp. 45–7, 60.
143 Habermas 1975a, p. 48; Held 2013, p. 258.

> become questionable (endangering civil and familial-professional privatism). On the other hand, the remains of bourgeois ideologies (belief in science, post-auratic art, and universalistic value systems) form a normative framework that is dysfunctional. Advanced capitalism creates 'new' needs it cannot satisfy.[144]

The increasingly strong focus on legitimacy, legitimacy claims, and communication will set Habermas on the path to a programme of critical research centred on a rationalist, communication-based approach to politics. He wanted a theory of knowledge that was able to escape accusations of being the ideology of the working class or the dogmatic claims of elitist speculative philosophers – referring to analytical philosophy. According to Habermas, one of Marx's main shortcomings was that he merged both interaction and labour into the category of social praxis, thus reducing communicative action to instrumental action. Habermas will give primacy to the former, which he considered to be the basis of the communicative and symbolic activities through which life was constituted.[145] He will rescue the communicative aspect in what would be his linguistic turn. Consequently, a focus on consciousness and knowledge based on material conditions would be misplaced; language itself is the basis, or the means through which we represent reality.[146]

Habermas never developed an explicit ontological position, although his fundamental distinction between work and social interaction assumes one.[147] It will serve as the basis for his 'reconstruction of historical materialism', which preserves the structure of the Hegelian Marxist critique of reason but rejects the primacy of work. It considers epochal changes based on changes in normative structures and not in relations of production.[148] This new 'credible' historical evolutionism is guided by a practical interest in emancipation upon which rational bases for knowledge can be formulated. Due to its reflexive status, he considers this theory of social evolution also informative for the purposes of political action.[149] Such an approach, going beyond objectivism and relativism, avoids the extremes of anti-foundational postmodernism, as its critical realism presupposes a reality outside discourse, even if it can only be known through it.[150]

---

144 Habermas 1975a, pp. 48–9.
145 Morrow and Brown 1994, pp. 144, 155.
146 Morrow and Brown 1994, p. 154.
147 Morrow and Brown 1994, p. 155.
148 Morrow and Brown 1994, p. 171.
149 Habermas 1975b; Held 2013, p. 270.
150 Morrow and Brown 1994, p. 165.

According to Habermas, we cannot know Being itself, because our knowledge is always mediated by interpretation. Habermas's critical theory recognises that science is ultimately based on a social consensus mediated by language.[151] Habermas bases the possibility of rational argumentation on the creation of a public sphere dominated by rational deliberation.[152] This created the democratic potential to complete the Enlightenment project of human emancipation and will serve Habermas's approach to deliberative democracy. Although Habermas's analysis of the legitimation problems of late capitalism serves as inspiration for our analysis of the democratic crisis, his assumption of rational bases separate from the category of labour as an ontological foundation moves Habermas's model of democracy away from Marxism and a 'political' scientific approach to democracy, which is our main approach. Although Habermas's analysis of the legitimation issues of late capitalism inspires our analysis of the democratic crisis, his model of democracy diverges from Marxism by separating the rational foundations of the category of labour as an ontological foundation. This departure is less aligned with our primary approach, which uses a 'political' scientific perspective on democracy.

5 Crisis, Critique and Political Science Now

We have seen that the concept of crisis is full of contradictions. These originate from the ancient meaning of the Greek concept of crisis, or *kritein*, which involves both an objective and a subjective dimension, a moment of choice. Rather than viewing the contradiction as ambiguity, confusion, or a limitation to its scientific usefulness – as many scientists do – we explored the clarifying potential inherent in the contradiction itself. To do so, we first explored how crisis is closely linked to critique and contradiction based on a historical analysis of these concepts and a brief exploration of their use in the history of European thought, particularly in dialectical thinkers from Socrates to Marx. We argued that understanding and using the contradictory concept of crisis allows us to address two fields of knowledge that are often seen as being in epistemological opposition to science, namely the field of history and the field of politics. We saw how the crisis offered a way out for the *Methodenstreit* between the arguments of the particularities of knowledge on the part of the historicists and the search for universal laws on the part of the positivists. The crisis marks

151 Morrow and Brown 1994, pp. 155–65.
152 Haberman 1991.

the temporal coincidence of the political need for universal truths, as well as the knowledge of their own historical particularity and, with it, the possibility of political change.

The potential of the crisis to reintroduce the political and the historical into scientific knowledge is even more important in our contemporary context of neoliberal hegemony in decline, which portrays our reality as being post-historical and post-political – post-historical, as in Fukuyama's 1989 assertion of the end of history, post-political in the form of technocratic policies, accepted by almost all sectors of the political spectrum. The crisis crushes hegemony in the sense that it reveals that post-political consensus is no longer possible and political conflict arises. More than in any other context, the crisis paves the way for a historical and political form of science. In a context of crisis, we see true antagonistic politics emerge, in contrast to the agonistic version that Chantal Mouffe and others developed during a period of liberal-democratic consensus. Although these contradictions can be channelled into different forms of identities (of class, race, nationality, ideology), they become, at least temporarily, irreconcilable during crises.

However, crises are not emancipatory as such. Despite important theoretical contributions to the critique of liberalism and the conceptualisation of the political, Schmitt's own political position also showed that crisis, the state of exception and the political can be profoundly reactionary. The political opening of hegemony is not necessarily full of emancipatory content – it is not only the possibility of a 'new world to be born', it is also 'a time of monsters'.[153] Crises can legitimise deeply exclusionary and fascist reactions, as in the European refugee crisis or the rise of nationalism and populism in the aftermath of the global financial crisis. In our contemporary context, the crisis has also been used to legitimise future neoliberal policies – rather than a death of the old society in the Gramscian sense, the time of monsters is a temporal strengthening of the old society. Naomi Klein's *The Shock Doctrine* was a first example of how neoliberal globalisation used exceptionalism and crisis situations to promote the interests of global financial capital.[154] António Casimiro Ferreira and José Manuel Pureza also made this case in their analyses of Portuguese austerity.[155] In his book *Linhas Vermelhas* [Red lines], Pureza, for example, defends the hypothesis that austerity and the euro crisis represent a new configuration between crisis and exception that he calls 'crisis-as-politics': instead of the crisis

153 Gramsci 1992, pp. 32–3.
154 Klein 2008.
155 Ferreira 2011; Pureza 2015b.

being just a 'moment of disruption of the normal', the crisis has become a political strategy of elites to destroy an existing normativity – under the guise of an important exception, exceptionalism is normalised and becomes permanent.[156]

The crisis therefore requires the question of choosing a side in science. Reiterating the introduction: instead of removing the 'ideological ballast' of historical materialism, when analysing concrete crises, such as the 'crisis of democracy' or the 'legitimation crisis' of the state, it must be argued that the 'ideological ballast', and with it a political practice, is the most valuable critical and crucial element in the whole approach, without which the whole theoretical approach does not make 'sense'.

We have focussed on various interactions between language and politics and discussed the problematisation of the *logos* by Socrates, according to whom the structure of argumentation, words, and discourses reflected established power relations. We focussed on the linguistic turn in critical theory that recognises that science is ultimately based on a social consensus mediated by language.[157] Habermas's critical theory – probably still the most influential theory on language and democracy – assumes the existence of an external reality, but argues that we cannot know this real Being, because our knowledge is always mediated by interpretation and language. The only thing we can know is communication itself. We assumed that this conundrum is a consequence of his ontological rejection of labour as the main political category of knowledge.

Our approach, by contrast, is based on this original Marxist political ontological assumption: that is, we assume a 'reality' of political conflict, or rather, of political economy. Within this perspective, language (and therefore ideology), discourses, and science have a dialectical interaction with political economy. Discourse is both socially constitutive and socially conditioned: linguistic-discursive textual structures are assigned a crucial function in the social production and reproduction of inequalities, power, ideology, and authority. And at the same time, power and control manifest themselves in language.[158] Ultimately, this interaction is determined by political economy or class struggles, but language also reflects and influences these struggles. Today's discourse is socially characteristic of the economic, social, and cultural changes of late modernity.[159] Therefore it is extremely important to analyse the different dis-

156 Pureza 2015b.
157 Morrow and Brown 1994, pp. 155–65.
158 Blommaert 2005, p. 25; Wodak 2011, p. 51.
159 Blommaert 2005, p. 25; Chouliaraki and Fairclough 1999, p. 4.

courses on the issue of democracy and its relationship with class interests and political economy.

The biggest difference between the approach that will guide our analysis – critical discourse analysis – and Laclau and Mouffe's theory of discourse (the most influential in critical democratic theory) is that the objects of analysis in our method are oral and written discourses within their social context as reflections of social conflict, instead of the entire social being considered as a discursive construction.[160]

The literature of democratic theory has produced a wide range of studies that address the relationship between liberalism and democracy, as we will see. The search for solutions to the crisis involves affirming new interpretations and new diagnoses of the crisis. We will return to this later, but the first step towards these statements is the study and scrutiny of the crisis discourse that still predominates in the public space.[161] We will analyse the discourses of the political and economic elites regarding their meanings of democracy. We will focus on the articulation between contested neoliberal austerity policies and the democratic discourse to legitimise them.

We will not reiterate the entire political-economic context. However, based on our approach to the concept of crisis, it is essential to begin with a recap of the economic crisis in Portugal and the various ways in which it has been addressed. Perspectives on this crisis are closely linked to corresponding views on democracy. We focus on the main concepts and pillars of neoliberal ideology in general. We define and historicise neoliberalism and analyse how depoliticisation and culturalisation play an important role in its legitimation and reproduction.

In a third part we focus on how democracy is used to legitimise the government and its neoliberal policies. We distinguish the formal approach, the substantive approach and the exceptional approach. In the fourth part we illustrate these conclusions based on a critical discourse analysis of interviews with two of the main neoliberal policymakers responsible for neoliberal austerity measures in Portugal. We will analyse how the strategies of depoliticisation, formal legitimation and exceptionalism play a role in their legitimating discourses. In the end, we seek to summarise the main characteristics of what can be called the democratic discourse of austerity.

160 Brito 2016, p. 49.
161 Caldas and Almeida 2016, p. 10.

CHAPTER 3

Democratic Theory: History and Crisis

The Portuguese Revolution of 1974, which overthrew the Salazar dictatorship, is often referred to, most notably in Huntington's work, as the starting point for what was perceived as the historic triumph of liberal democracy.[1] This period was celebrated as the 'end of history' and the culmination of human and social evolution. For nearly three decades after the end of the Cold War, liberal democracy remained largely unquestioned – an extraordinary status for a concept that exemplifies what Gallie described as 'essentially contested concepts,' meaning that 'different persons or parties adhere to different views of the correct use of some concept [recognising] that one's own use of it has to be maintained against these other uses'.[2]

For the first time in a long period, the uncontested status of liberal democracy began to wane during the 2008–12 crisis period, and its inherently contested nature resurfaced. Questions emerged. Can one really talk about 'democracy' when policies are controlled by foreign institutions and dictated by financial markets? Is an electoral system alone sufficient to guarantee genuine democratic governance? What about the *'Democracia real yá!'* movement?[3] Should democratic policies be guided by those who were elected three years ago or by the 'mob' that takes to the streets today? What about 'democratic' governments that implement policies that break their election promises? What if policymakers deny the legitimacy of ex-post electoral accountability?

These questions force us to abandon 'democracy' as an abstract concept. A more productive approach focuses on the interactions between historical political events and conceptualisations of democracy itself. Democracy will therefore be approached as a contested concept – contested not only in democratic theory, but also as a product of historical, material, social and political struggles, and as an ideological construct through which we make sense of the world and attempt to change it.

1 Huntington 1991.
2 Gallie 1955/1956, p. 172.
3 'Real Democracy Now!' was one of the iconic slogans of the *indignados* movement against austerity and the 'political cast' in the Spanish State and inspired the Portuguese movements (Baumgarten and Díez García 2017).

 | HTTPS://DOI.ORG/10.1163/9789004766235-005

1 Schools and Waves of Democracy

Many libraries are filled with a wide variety of literature on democracy, presenting countless contradictory theories and approaches to the concept. Leonardo Avritzer summarises some of them: democratic elitism,[4] liberal utilitarianism,[5] republicanism,[6] pluralism,[7] critical social theory,[8] among others.[9] In his classic *Models of Democracy*, David Held elaborates on eight different models of democracy: republican conception of self-governing community, liberal democracy, Marxist conception of democracy, elitist democracy, pluralism, legal democracy, participatory democracy, and deliberative democracy.[10]

Traditionally, many overviews and categorisations of these theories are presented in chronological order, as if they were part of a theoretical evolution, with democratic theory evolving through contradictions between existing democratic theories, rational arguments, and empirical democratic realities over the centuries. Although a purely rational evolutionary model of the history of democracy is untenable, we will use a historical perspective, in particular Samuel Huntington's 'waves of democratization', to provide a reference.[11] It is no coincidence that Huntington's book begins with a symbolic reference to the Portuguese revolution. According to Huntington's *The Third Wave*, the history of democracy in the 20th century follows a pattern of ups, in which countries tend to democratise, and downs, in which countries tend to fall into de-democratisation or return to dictatorships. Huntington distinguishes three waves, which coincide with three major debates in democratic theory distinguished by Boaventura de Sousa Santos.[12]

1.1 From the Classic Approaches to World War

With roots in the American and French revolutions and ending with the rise of fascism, the first wave of democratisation spans Hobsbawm's long nineteenth century and was primarily a European and North American phenomenon.[13]

4 Schumpeter 1976.
5 Downs 1957.
6 Arendt 1972; Rousseau 2001.
7 Dahl 1971.
8 Habermas 1998.
9 Avritzer 2002.
10 Held 2006.
11 Huntington 1991.
12 Huntington 1991; Santos 2005.
13 Hobsbawm 1994.

Still indebted to Enlightenment authors such as Rousseau and Montesquieu and to the republican ideas of the Renaissance that originated in eleventh-century Italian city-states and the rediscovery of ancient Greek literature, early modern democratic theory was primarily opposed to authoritarian rule, based on theology and lineage, that dominated Europe for centuries. Held distinguishes between developmental republicans who, inspired by the Greek *polis*, saw political participation as an integral part of a good life and influenced Rousseau, and protective republicans, who were inspired by the balance of powers of the Roman republic and influenced Machiavelli and Montesquieu's separation of powers.[14]

Rousseau argues that the State develops when human beings leave their 'state of nature' – a time when humans were fundamentally equal and free – to civil governments as a response to 'individual weaknesses and egoistic desires, common miseries and natural disasters'.[15] This government should develop through a 'social contract': a universally recognised agreement that presupposes free citizenship, implying direct participation in the creation of laws that regulate each person's life and, therefore, excluding representation. Citizenship is a collective practice based on collective rationality: decision-making must follow the 'general will' – a common public good – and not the 'will of all' – the private aggregation of individual wills.[16]

Reason and the separation between public and private play a vital role in distinguishing between the common good and the interests of any citizens in future republican and liberal democratic theory. Held defines liberalism broadly as 'the attempt to uphold the values of freedom of choice, reason and toleration in the face of tyranny, the absolutist system and religious intolerance'.[17] As ideology of the new bourgeoisie, liberalism presupposes that citizens should be free to pursue their own preferences in religious, economic, and political matters and therefore defends a constitutional state, private property, and a competitive market economy, trying to find a 'balance between might and right, power and law, duties and rights'.[18] The state must have a monopoly on coercive power to guarantee 'free trade', business, and family life and simultaneously it must be restrained to protect the political and social freedoms of citizens. For some early modern theorists, such as Hobbes, individuals must entrust their rights of self-government to a single, powerful authority, the

14 Held 2006, pp. 29–36.
15 Held 2006, p. 45.
16 Held 2006; Rousseau 2001.
17 Held 2006, p. 59.
18 Held 2006, p. 59.

Leviathan; for others, such as John Locke, law making and enforcement are transferred to the government, solely to ensure the conditions for individual freedom in civil society. For classical liberals, property exists before society and government. As a theory of proprietors, the liberal theory of the time was elitist: legitimate government did not take into account the political freedoms of the working class, women, and people of colour, nor was it based on regular elections or universal suffrage.[19] Citizenship, with its responsibilities and rights, only existed to preserve 'life, liberty, and estate': the democracy necessary to meet the requirements of future market logics.[20]

During the traumatic political and economic events that began with the First World War, marking the beginning of the initial 'reverse wave', this approach to democracy became progressively unsustainable. Despite this 'reversion', the era ushered in a fruitful period for democratic theory, which continues to exert a significant influence on contemporary democratic thought.[21] It opened the first big debate on democratic theory of the twentieth century: is democracy desirable? The debate involved the works of intellectuals such as Weber, Kelsen, Schmitt, Schumpeter and Michels.[22]

Weber saw democracy as a necessary counterweight for society, while Michels's 'Iron Law of Oligarchy' theorised how elite rule is inevitable.[23] In the same period, scholars from the Frankfurt School criticised the new mass society, in which elites controlled populations through mass parties and the mass media, and which made individual rationality unsustainable. The early liberal-democratic theory, based on this rationality, entered into a serious crisis.[24]

Carl Schmitt was one of the first to warn about the consequences of the introduction of mass parties, extended democracy, and collective authority that would obstruct rational political discussion and democratic consensus.[25] 'Parties ... do not face each other today discussing opinions, but as social or economic power groups calculating their mutual interests and opportunities for power'.[26] During the crisis, different Enlightenment values became incompatible: projects of social equality seemed to endanger liberal ideas of individual freedom. This created a distrust in the 'demos' itself.[27]

19 Held 2006, p. 64.
20 Held 2006; Macpherson 1977.
21 Santos and Avritzer 2005.
22 Santos 2005.
23 Maley 2011; Santos 2005, pp. X–XI.
24 Avritzer 2002, p. 14.
25 Avritzer 2002, p. 13.
26 Schmitt 1988, p. 6.
27 Santos 2005.

Worried about the growth of mass totalitarian movements of Nazism and Stalinism, Hannah Arendt defended a strict separation between the social question and the political question. According to Arendt, social needs create irrationality and a potential for totalitarian violence, since Robespierre's prioritisation of social equality over the rights and freedoms of citizens led the French Revolution to terror and doom, and should therefore be kept out of the political sphere.[28]

Joseph Schumpeter's democratic elitism, which asserted that classical substantive democracy is impractical due to the inability to know the general will, has emerged as the most influential response to these challenges.[29] According to Schumpeter, democracy must be reduced to a formal method of elite selection, in which citizens choose representatives from among freely competing political parties. Also referred to as minimalist or procedural democracy, liberal representative democracy became the most influential theory after the traumas of World War II, Nazism, Stalinism, and the Holocaust. Winston Churchill called it 'the worst form of government except all those others that have been tried'.[30]

The advent of the Cold War and the new balance of power between East and West gave rise to a diversity of other liberal democratic theories. Some, like that of Downs, are extensions of Schumpeter's theory to a full-fledged utilitarian economic theory of democracy, with the valorisation of political apathy.[31] Others, such as Arendt's liberal constitutionalism, gave special importance to constitutions, international law and the universal rights of citizens that should protect the democracy of majorities. A combination of both laid the foundation for Robert Dahl's work on the pluralistic nature of elites.[32]

1.2 Learning with the 'South'

During the Cold War period of relative stability between Western liberal democracy and the Soviet popular democracy model, social struggles in the West were contained through the liberal-democratic consensus and the welfare state. Through this balance, some alternative models emerged, such as participatory and developmental democracy.[33] Most of the challenges and innovations

---

28 Arendt 2016, pp. 54–7.
29 Schumpeter 1976.
30 Raymond 1992, p. 124.
31 Downs 1957; Avritzer 2002; Mouffe 2000, p. 82.
32 Dahl 1971; Santos and Avritzer 2005.
33 Santos and Avritzer 2005, pp. X, XXXV.

to democratic theory have originated in the peripheries of the capitalist world. The colonial wars and decolonisation processes in the 'Global South', as well as the civil rights movement in the United States, gave rise to different articulations of racial and anti-colonial theories with democracy in the works of Aimé Césaire, Malcolm X, and Franz Fanon.[34] The dependency school and those who, in the tradition of Immanuel Wallerstein, studied the (semi)peripheral countries of the world system brought important contributions, even though many did not reach mainstream political theory.

Malcolm X rejected American democracy as the ideology of the ruling race and class, pointing to the inconsistency between universal principles and their actual practice.[35] Behind democracy 'is a system of exploitation, of outright humiliation, degradation, discrimination'.[36] For the black population, democracy is nothing more than a police state.[37] Frantz Fanon adopts the Marxist critique of democracy as a bourgeois class project but problematises the differences between the metropolitan and colonial contexts. While the strong bourgeoisies maintain the claim to 'universal democratic ideas', even if fundamentally racist, the new economically powerless bourgeoisies of developing countries are incapable of establishing coherent class domination; they imitate European democratic phraseology but reveal themselves to be incapable of minimal forms of humanism.[38]

Malcolm X rejected American democracy as the ideology of the ruling race and class – pointing to the inconsistency between the universal principles and its actual practice.[39] Behind democracy – 'is a system of exploitation, of outright humiliation, degradation, discrimination':[40] for the black population, democracy is nothing more than a police state.[41] Frantz Fanon adopts the Marxist critique of democracy as a bourgeois class-project but problematises the differences between the metropolitan and the colonial context. While strong bourgeoisies maintain the pretence of 'universal democratic ideas' – even if fundamentally racist – the new economically powerless bourgeoisies in the

34 In his own approach to the concept of non-imperial 'Global South', Santos (2007, p. 22) tries to unify both kinds of peripheral struggles, as he conceives 'Global South' not just as a pure geographic construct, but rather as a metaphor of unjust and systemic human suffering provoked by global capitalism and colonialism.

35 Rabaka 2002.

36 Malcolm X 1992, p. 47.

37 Malcolm X 1966, p. 66.

38 Fanon 2005.

39 Rabaka 2002.

40 Malcolm X 1992, p. 47.

41 Malcolm X 1966, p. 66.

developing countries are unable to establish a coherent class domination: they mimic the European democratic phrases but prove incapable of minimum forms of humanism. The easiest solution is the single-party system with flawed parliamentary rules.[42] Like Huntington, Fanon concluded that democracy is difficult in the neocolonial world, but while Huntington defended the temporary sacrifice of democracy for the need for stability, Fanon argued that this stability is impossible because the neo-bourgeoisie is nothing more than the indirect rule of the metropolis.[43] It is well known that according to Fanon, such an anti-colonial project 'can only triumph if we use all means to turn the scale, including, of course, that of violence'.[44] It is therefore no surprise that, according to Fanon, armed citizens are the best guarantors of democratic rights. He envisions militia training and participation as an informal school for civic and patriotic consciousness, literacy, and technical and organisational knowledge.[45]

During the 'second reverse wave', which saw several progressive South American governments brought down by right-wing military coups, democratic elitism was strongly challenged, by losing the crucial role of collective action in defending democracy and by being unable to distinguish between democratic and authoritarian elites. It confused anti-institutionalisms that destroy the political process with 'forms of collective action of voluntary associations, social movements and other forms of participation' that form a key element of democracy.[46]

This leads to the second major debate, about the structural conditions of democracy and its relationship with capitalism. The so-called 'democratic transitions' school attempted to adapt elitist democratic theory to the realities of the Global South, recognising the role of authoritarian elites in Latin America, whose anti-democratic attitudes during economic conflicts and crises – in which they saw their interests challenged by the popular classes – undermine the possibility of democracy in the periphery.[47]

They advocated for 'democratic transitions', defined as periods 'in which an institutional arrangement aiming at the establishment of political competit-

42 Fanon 2005, p. 110.

43 Adam 1993, pp. 502–4.

44 Fanon 2005, p. 3. In the French edition: '[...] *ne peut triompher que si on jette dans la balance tous les moyens, y compris, bien sûr, la violence*' (Fanon 2011, pp. 452–53).

45 Adam 1993, p. 507.

46 Avritzer 2002, p. 24.

47 O'Donnell, Schmitter and Whitehead 1986; Schmitter and O'Donnell 1986; Avritzer 2002, p. 27. For the case of Southern Europe and Portugal, see also: Giner 1986; Maxwell 1986, 1997.

iveness between democratic and authoritarian political actors is reached'.[48] These periods are necessary to build mutual trust between classes, so that anti-democratic elements disappear.[49] Democratisation cannot be defined by a set of empirically identifiable variables – such as Lipset's prerequisites of democracy – but only through a long process of persuasion and forcing non-democratic elites to adopt democratic attitudes within democratic institutions.[50] Remaining too institutionalist and elitist – the popular masses are assigned only a secondary role[51] – it is no surprise that an exponent of this like Przeworski continues to be an apologist for a minimalist conception of democracy.[52]

1.3 The End of History

The empirical, positivist school, with a prominence of comparative political science, is today probably the most influential approach to the study of democracy. 'Empirical political theory' is an adaptation of the elitist, aggregate democratic model, integrating the 'empirical' criticism made by the transitions school.[53] It had its predecessor in Lipset's international comparative study on the social requirements for democracy, which stated that conflicts generated by inequality put the survival of democracy at risk. The approach of Avritzer and Lijphart studied the influence of various electoral designs on the working of democracy, but the most influential example is probably that of Huntington, the *Third Wave* itself.[54] It makes a historical comparison of the number of democratic nations – defined by open, free and fair elections – and concludes that economic growth not only creates the possibility of 'affording' for democratic governance, but also that rapid growth alters power relations and gives rise to political tensions that disrupt the prevailing order, often toppling authoritarian regimes. Economic growth therefore tends to lead to democratisation.[55]

Huntington's third wave began with the Portuguese revolution of 1974. When the fascist regime of the *Estado Novo* was replaced by a provisional government of socialists, communists, and liberals, and soviet-like forms of popular-democratic participation emerged everywhere, few would have imagined a

48 Avritzer 2002.
49 Avritzer 2002; Schmitter and O'Donnell 1986.
50 Lipset 1959; Avritzer 2002, p. 27; Rustow 1970, pp. 344–45.
51 Avritzer 2002.
52 Przeworski 1999.
53 Mouffe 2000, pp. 81–2.
54 Avritzer 2002, p. 25; Huntington 1991; Lijphart 1984, 2012, and 1994.
55 Fraser 2001; Huntington 1991.

future marked by the hegemony of liberal democracy and its articulation with neoliberalism.

Based on the liberal ideas of individualism and free trade developed by the Austrian and Chicago Schools, neoliberalism emerged as a response to the global collapse of profits, the crisis of the welfare state, the oil crisis, and the debt crisis of the seventies and early eighties.[56] It argues that a society is more efficient when public policies are efficient in market terms and the state is minimal.[57] With its focus on the problems of debt, inflation and money – hence it is called monetarism – it gained traction under Reagan and Thatcher. The scope over which democratic policies would be applied would be radically reduced with constant attacks on the social democratic welfare state and through privatisation and liberalisation policies. The collapse of the Soviet Union and the emergence of a unipolar world without a balance of power between West and East – and between social classes – reduced the room for manoeuvre of reformist parties and trade unions. At the very moment that Giddens popularised a 'third way', former social democrats, such as New Labour, accepted neoliberal premises.[58]

Economic globalisation and trade liberalisation, actively promoted by the IMF, WB, and WTO within the framework of the Washington consensus, have made governments increasingly dependent on the goodwill of markets and financial institutions. Neo-Keynesian Thomas Friedman labelled it a 'golden straitjacket', focusing on private sector growth and exports, a low public deficit, debt and inflation policies, the reduction of state bureaucracy, the abolition of trade tariffs, and the deregulation and privatisation of industries, banks, pensions, capital markets, and telecommunications. As we have seen, in Europe this was accelerated by the implementation of the Common Market and monetary integration since Maastricht.

Politically, the result was a sharp reduction in the political spectrum and a compression of the public sphere. Neoliberal reforms transformed the political citizen into an individual *homo economicus*, a depoliticised subject whose 'freedom of choice' obeyed the rational laws of supply and demand as consumer and producer in a global market economy. The result has been designated as a 'post-political' or 'post-democratic' world,[59] in which management has taken the place of politics.[60]

---

56 Palley 2005; Roberts 2012.
57 Palley 2005.
58 Giddens 2012.
59 Mouffe 2005; Swyngedouw, 2007; 2011.
60 Rancière 2005.

2 The Crisis of Democracy and Its Alternatives

'Third wave' liberal democracy was thus marked by two paradoxes: between the global spread of democracy and its dramatically reduced scope – the so-called 'low-intensity democracy'[61] – and the 'double pathology' between the phenomenon of people not wanting to participate – dramatic abstention and the fact that citizens feel less and less represented.[62] In this context, academic debates flourished around the 'gap between citizens and politicians', 'good governance', 'populism', 'electoral fragmentation', and 'democratic legitimacy', particularly around European governance structures.[63] Fuelled by abstention in European elections, criticism of the 'undemocratic' structure and growing Euroscepticism, the debates revolved around the apparent inadequacy of national democracy in the context of supranational integration, Europeanisation, and globalisation.

Empirical political theory and comparative political science have remained faithful to formal, elitist definitions of democracy.[64] Huntington's approach, for example, neglects international and local dynamics, scope, participation, and redistributive aspects. They tend to have a teleological character. In an attempt to 'compromise' and 'complexify', authors such as Schmidt and Rosanvallon framed the problems through the scale and different 'dimensions' of democracy – distinguishing inputs, outputs and other aspects of legitimacy, but the most influential currents in political theory are constructed without profoundly discussing the concept of democracy itself.[65] This is a crucial flaw – not just theoretically, but particularly because the meanings of democracy tend to undergo drastic changes during crises.

Authors critical of the dominant liberal approach have pointed out other shortcomings. This resulted in four main critical models: the 'aggregative model', the 'deliberative model', the 'agonistic model', and 'demodiversity'.

2.1 Participatory Democracy

Rousseau's participatory conception of democracy did not survive the emergence of a complex administration and specialised bureaucracies in the mod-

61 Gills and Rocamora 1992; Santos and Avritzer 2005.
62 Santos and Avritzer 2005.
63 Magnette 2003; Santos 1995b, p. 286.
64 Cheibub, Gandhi and Vreeland 2010.
65 Rosanvallon 2013; Schmidt 2013.

ern state and was further problematised due to 'excessive' participation in the context of the Bolshevik revolution and Nazi Germany.[66] This changed in the late 1960s with the growing 'crisis of democracy': built on the traditions of revolutionary and popular participation, 'participatory democracy' would become the 'New Left' model for moving beyond the opposition between orthodox Marxism and liberalism.[67]

With the social objective of combating apathy and estrangement of the poor masses, participatory democracy involves the direct participation of citizens in key institutions, including workplaces and local communities, ensuring accountability and openness, and minimising bureaucracy, while conditions must be guaranteed through redistribution and public services such as childcare.[68] Participation is a pedagogical experience of active and conscious citizenship: in addition to bringing political efficiency and sovereignty in relation to centres of power, it fosters human development and a sense of community.[69] Direct democracy or self-management could not simply replace the state – and without representation, bureaucracy fills the gap. Therefore, participatory democracy is seen as complementary to representative democracy.

Participation models have been particularly successful in democratic transitions in the Global South, mainly in the form of participatory budgeting, due to their ability to transfer practices and information from social movements to administrative levels.[70] The involvement of citizens counterbalanced the state bureaucracies left behind by dictatorships. Participatory democracy also allowed the recognition of alternative citizen identities for those who had always been excluded in a historically violent context.[71] It enabled articulations between 'new' identities based on gender, informal classes, and ethnicity, with 'old' identities linked to unions, liberation movements, and left-wing political parties.[72]

Participatory budgets were often initiated by progressive parties such as the Workers' Party (*Partido dos Trabalhadores*) in Porto Alegre, Brazil, or the Communist Party of India in Kerala. They combine elements of representation and participation at the local level and a broad public debate about rules of par-

---

66 Santos and Avritzer 2005, p. XXIX.
67 Held 2006.
68 Ibid.
69 Held 2006; Pateman 1970.
70 Santos 2005, p. XLVI.
71 Santos 2005, p. XLVII.
72 Santos 2005, p. xlviii.

ticipation, deliberation and distribution. Between 1997 and 2000, around 140 Brazilian municipalities[73] and 1500 cities around the world[74] adopted them.

However, several vulnerabilities remained: exclusionary elites who do not accept people from the lower classes in the same spaces strongly contested participatory experiences.[75] Furthermore, participatory democracy has also shown potential for co-optation, adulteration, and integration, to the extent that it has lost its democratic and emancipatory potential. Santos and Davidson, for example, show how the participatory budget of Vallejo, California, emerged from a nationwide fiscal and austerity crisis.[76]

2.2 Deliberative Democracy

Deliberative democrats are equally critical of the limits imposed by democratic elitists, but in contrast to participationists, they are concerned about the potentially harmful influence of irrational masses guided by unbridled desires, individual interests, ignorance, and myopia.[77] Democratic decision-making should be based on 'reasonable political judgment' and 'reflective preferences', rather than on the will of those involved. Decisions should be based on a space for critical and rational argumentation and not on direct participation; not on the predetermined will of individuals, but on the process of its formation.[78] By decoupling the common good from the means to achieve it, deliberativism is an expanded form of proceduralism, but it approaches proceduralism as a social practice and not as a method of establishing government.[79]

Habermas and Rawls provided much of the intellectual apparatus of deliberative democracy.[80] In his reconstruction of a 'historical materialist' analysis of democracy, while rejecting 'its philosophical ballast' – the intellectual and political perspective of the working class – Habermas attempted to recover the link between democracy and liberalism.[81] In his theory on the public sphere and communicative action, Habermas defends the historical co-originality – and possible reconciliation – of fundamental individual rights and popular sovereignty.[82]

---

73 Santos 2005.
74 Davidson 2018.
75 Santos 2005, p. lii.
76 Santos 2005, p. lv; Davidson 2018, p. 556.
77 Held 2006, pp. 231–34.
78 Held 2006, p. 233; Manin 1987, p. 351.
79 Santos 2005, p. XLIV.
80 Medearis 2005.
81 Gunaratne 2006, p. 1; Habermas 1985, p. 383; Morrow and Brown 1994, p. 187.
82 Haberman 1991, 1998.

As bourgeois domination is not based on direct control, but on economic domination in the private sphere, its relationship with political power is different from that of other classes in history: the capitalist renounces the direct personal exercise of government. Instead, since the advent of commercial capitalism in the seventeenth century, the bourgeoisie has demanded the right to know what the state does with its taxes, giving a public character to the relationship between the state and society. Between the private sphere and the state, a space developed for a free and rational discourse on power, separating individual reflection from material interests and the domestic economy from personal subjectivity. The origin of this 'public sphere' and deliberative democratic practices is located in bourgeois salons, cafes, and a set of voluntary associations that constituted a civil society, disconnected from the market and the state.[83] In the public sphere, political decisions are reached through deliberative discussion among free, equal, and reasonable citizens.[84] Face-to-face interaction allows for new forms of civic participation and republicanism in democratic theory, through 'communicative action' – a politicisation through language and rational understanding that makes it possible to achieve a generalisable interest.[85] Ideally, the rational balance of arguments and interests requires an 'ideal speech situation'.

Habermas and other deliberationists, such as John Rawls, are not naive enough to deny the obstacles to the ideal situation.[86] Rawls's original position and Jürgen Habermas's ideal speech situation were developed precisely to integrate the 'social point of view'.[87] Obstacles are conceived as 'empirical' – given the practical and empirical limitations of social life – and thus the ideal speech situation is maintained as a 'regulative idea'.[88] The deliberative model has therefore been extensively criticised as elitist: by insisting on public reason, it solidifies the structural disadvantages that marginalised groups face. As an exponent of the Frankfurt School, Habermas should know how structural power relations shape ideologies and discourses, but he is silent about such structural disadvantages.[89] The 'Eurocentric',[90] 'national', 'bourgeois', and 'patriarchal' public sphere tends to reproduce a capitalist, sexist,

83 Avritzer and Costa 2004, p. 707; Habermas 1991.
84 Habermas 1998; Mouffe 2000, pp. 81–87.
85 Avritzer 2002, pp. 40–42.
86 Rawls 2009.
87 Held 2006, p. 239.
88 Mouffe 2000, p. 88.
89 Medearis 2005, pp. 62–4.
90 Habermas himself said that his work is of importance only to Western societies because

racist, Eurocentric, and colonial rationality.[91] Through different degrees of linguistic and rationalist exclusion of women, non-Western cultures and epistemologies, lower social classes, etc., around four-fifths of the world's population is preventively barred from fully participating in democratic discourse.[92]

Critics such as Slavoj Žižek assert that Habermas's theory can be seen as 'postmodern' because it tracks the left's transition from Marxist historical materialism to the acceptance of the liberal capitalist economy as the prevailing paradigm. By separating the issue of deliberative democracy from the structural inequalities inherent to capitalism, Habermas intended to free historical materialism from ideological 'ballast', but limited its radical emancipatory potential.[93] This detachment allowed the theory to become mainstream and central within the liberal canon of democracy, despite its critical origins.

2.3 Agonistic Democracy

Since the linguistic turn in the 1970s and 1980s, 'discourse' has become central to democratic theory.[94] *Hegemony and Socialist Strategy* by Laclau and Mouffe would be an innovative work in this field. Like Habermas's approach, it is also the fruit of a transition to a post-Marxist analysis, and the social is also conceived as a discursive space. Based on a creative reinterpretation of Gramsci, Laclau and Mouffe privilege the idea of 'political articulation' and 'hegemony' to the detriment of the 'Hegelian/naturalist' categories of traditional Marxism.[95]

Laclau and Mouffe's reconceptualisation of hegemony centres on the concept of 'structural undecidability' in the construction of a hegemonic subject. They argue that their emphasis on 'contingent articulation' reveals the fundamental dimension of politics, suggesting that hegemonic transitions rely entirely on political articulation and not on pre-existing entities such as class interests. Thus, the hegemonic subject is not inherently tied to the Hegelian concept of a universal class or to the Marxist notion of the proletariat as a universal class. Rather, it is constitutively 'political' and does not lead to the dissolution of the state and the end of politics.[96]

---

of its limited Eurocentric vision; and that 'modernisation' is not synonymous with 'westernisation' (Tong 2000, pp. 10–11).

91 Avritzer 2002; Gunaratne 2006.

92 Santos 1995c.

93 Gunaratne 2006, p. 135; Habermas 1985, p. 383.

94 Medearis 2005.

95 Laclau and Mouffe 2001.

96 Laclau and Mouffe 2001, pp. x–xii.

According to Laclau, Marxism, since its inception, faced a fundamental asymmetry between the effective consciousness of actors and their historical interests. He criticises the Marxist tradition for not subjecting the notion of interests to rational critique, instead reinforcing its existence through the dichotomy between '*Klasse an sich*' and '*Klasse für sich*' ('class in itself' and 'class for itself'). In today's context, this complexity is intensified by the erosion of fixed identities such as 'worker' or 'petty bourgeoisie'. Furthermore, Laclau argues that the classical category of working class is deeply Eurocentric and inadequate for analysing peripheral areas of the world.[97]

Different positions of the subject – depending on residence, institutional apparatuses, and forms of cultural, racial, and sexual oppression – became issues of political mobilisation. This inverted the notion of classical subjectivity, focusing instead on the subject's shifting positions within a framework defined as 'discourse'.[98] Articulation occurs through the constitution of chains of equivalences, reflecting the plurality of demands and existing in an unstable tension between subordination and autonomous empowerment. Laclau and Mouffe's hegemonic articulation works through a dialectic between difference, determined by particularity, and equivalence, through the articulation of particularities in a situation of antagonism. The hegemonic relationship is the possibility of a body transcending antagonism, by representing universality.[99] In classical Marxism, the worker represents universality to transcend the particular forms of capitalist exploitation. The post-Marxism of Laclau and Mouffe denies the ontological centrality of the working class and presupposes a subject that is always open and ambiguous.[100] Laclau's classic example is populism, whose social differentiation and logic of equivalences are based on the oppositions 'people/oligarchy' and 'nation/imperialism'.[101]

From this discursive approach, Mouffe developed the 'agonistic model of democracy'.[102] Like deliberativism, it does not assume pre-constituted political identities, but regards the separations between a rational public sphere and a plural private sphere, and between 'procedural' and 'substantial' elements, to be unsustainable.[103] Mouffe criticises deliberative theory for disregarding the inherent and inevitable tension between democratic and lib-

97 Laclau 1986.
98 Laclau 1986.
99 Laclau and Mouffe 2001, p. XIII.
100 Laclau and Mouffe 2001, p. 2.
101 Laclau 2005, p. 4.
102 Mouffe 2000, p. 83.
103 Mouffe 2000, p. 97.

eral logics – a tension that cannot be eradicated, but only managed through negotiation, with compromises that offer a temporary respite in an enduring confrontation.[104] The antagonistic approach excludes the possibility of final reconciliation, rational consensus or the fully inclusive 'we' of the Habermasian model.[105] Instead of ideal speech and consensus, power and antagonism are at the heart of democratic politics. The challenge is to make power more compatible with 'democratic values'.[106]

Mouffe (2000) argues that to truly embrace pluralism, democratic theory must relinquish the pursuit of rational consensus and undergo a process of 'repoliticization'.[107] Drawing inspiration from Carl Schmitt's concept of 'political' – differentiated from 'politics' – Mouffe maintains that the political conflict, inherent to the friend-enemy categorisation, was neutralised by liberal hegemony. She proposes transforming the Schmittean notion of 'enemy' into a democratic 'adversary' within an 'agonistic' model of politics, opposing the liberal pluralist 'aggregative' approach. This shift emphasises the role of antagonistic confrontation as a fundamental aspect of democratic existence, challenging the notion of rational conciliation and promoting acceptance of diverse interpretations of liberal democratic principles.

Mouffe interprets the events that followed the crisis of neoliberal hegemony as a 'populist moment', in which right-wing and left-wing populism take centre stage.[108] She argues that the political frontier must be built on a 'transversal populist mode' that transcends social sectors defined in sociological terms, focusing instead on new forms of subordination that have emerged outside the production process, with demands around the environment, sexism, and racism. This strategy implies an antagonistic relationship between the 'people' and the 'oligarchy' to counter right-wing populism. While right-wing populism emphasises national sovereignty and restricts democratic rights to 'nationals', left-wing populism has to deepen democracy through different trajectories, with the aim of uniting people with other previous political affiliations.[109]

When austerity policies began to affect broad sectors, occupation movements such as Syntagma Square in Greece and 15M in Spain challenged neoliberal hegemony. Mouffe (2000) rejects the dichotomy between these movements and political parties, viewing the aim of some social movements to go

104 Mouffe 2000, p. 93.
105 Laclau and Mouffe 2001, p. XVII.
106 Mouffe 2000, pp. 99–100.
107 Mouffe 2000.
108 Mouffe 2018.
109 Mouffe 2018, p. 83.

'beyond politics' as a form of political withdrawal, which is itself a reflection of neoliberal hegemony.[110] She envisions a left-wing populist strategy centred on the emergence of a new type of radical populist party that articulates with social movements – such as *Syriza, Podemos, La France Insoumise, Die Linke*, the transformation of the Labour Party under the leadership of Corbyn, the success of Bernie Sanders in the USA, and the Left Bloc in Portugal.

2.4 Demodiversidade

Boaventura de Sousa Santos's concept of demodiversity was developed to describe 'the peaceful or conflictual coexistence of different democratic models and practices'.[111] Santos is inspired by the metaphor of ecology, proposing forms of heterogeneous plurality and sustainable interactions against the monoculture of modern science and its predatory character.[112] Similarly, demodiversity is a critique of and an alternative to hegemonic, liberal, and representative Western democracy. Based on a global comparison between the 1960s, when liberal democracy seemed confined to a small corner of the West while in the rest of the world other political practices claimed to be democratic in light of autonomous criteria, and the 1990s, when diversity gave way to the imposition of a single, universal liberal democracy, demodiversity is conceptualised negatively – as a 'loss'.[113] The main factors that contributed to this decline included the collapse of the Soviet Union and the incorporation of liberal democracy into the political conditionality of structural adjustment programmes.

The existence of demodiversity created possibilities for intercultural dialogue, cultural hybridisation, and convergence. The decline of demodiversity is problematic as liberal democracy, rooted in a specific modern Western cultural framework, is coercively imposed, perpetuating colonial and imperialist dynamics. The disparity between the ideal practice and the real practice of democracy, as highlighted by Santos, also reaches extreme levels: the existing form of democracy diverges so much from its ideal that it seems more like a caricature, thus undermining the legitimacy of democracy itself.[114]

While Laclau and Mouffe propose an approach where democracy functions as an empty signifier, requiring the removal of concrete practices to build

110 Mouffe 2000.

111 Santos and Mendes 2017, p. 70. Our translation. In the original: '*A coexistência pacífica ou conflitual de diferentes modelos e práticas democráticas*' (Santos and Mendes 2017, p. 70).

112 Santos 2007, pp. 22–3.

113 Santos 2005, pp. LXI–LXIV; Santos and Mendes 2017, p. 70.

114 Santos 2005, pp. LXIV–LXV.

identity through a Schmittean polarisation, Santos's hypothesis is based not on the emptying of concrete experiences, but on helping to translate them in the search for political harmony based on shared causes.[115] Boaventura de Sousa Santos disagrees with Laclau that democracy, emancipation, freedom, and equality are empty signifiers. Their empty condition exists rather because its substantive contents were intentionally emptied by capitalism, colonialism, and patriarchy.[116]

For Santos, the political struggle must focus on preventing the emptying of these concepts. However, the nature of Santos's demodiversity raises questions about whether it is a political objective or just an empirical phenomenon, and how it correlates with the crisis. As all sides of the conflict call for democracy, social and political conflict is reflected in various interpretations of the concept of democracy itself. Liberal democratic hegemony dissolves into the emergence of a series of conflicting practices and narratives. Consequently, demodiversity emerges as an empirical reality born of the crisis. Rather than being seen as a political or moral objective, it appears as a temporary phase in the search for a new hegemonic order. Demodiversity not only reflects the crisis of the liberal-democratic model but, following the logic of Ellen Wood, it also highlights the inability of the left to present a viable working-class democratic alternative capable of transcending liberal democracy and capitalism.[117]

3 Crisis of the Alternatives and a Restart of History

Until the global economic crisis of 2008, the intersection of democracy and political economy had been, for several decades, practically ignored. Times of crisis serve as crucial moments for understanding historical processes, including the interactions between economic crisis and democracy. Crises are moments when contradictions are exposed and truths are revealed. During the initial phase of the crisis and the European austerity measures that followed, the apparent success story of European integration fell apart and brought questions of democracy and legitimacy back to the forefront of public and academic debate and political struggles.[118] Authors such as Bosco and Verney or McGiffin warned of a 'democracy without choices' or 'a bloodless *coup d'état*'.[119] The fol-

115 Monedero 2017.
116 Monedero 2017, pp. 90–92; Santos 2016b, p. 259; Santos and Mendes 2017, p. 32.
117 Wood 1998, 2016.
118 Scharpf 2012; Schmidt 2013.
119 Bosco and Verney 2012; McGiffen 2011.

lowing decade was marked by increasing polarisation, giving rise to new protest movements around the world, from Occupy Wall Street to the Arab Spring and the *Indignados*, including the Yellow Vests in France and popular uprisings in Chile, Ecuador, and elsewhere. The decade also saw the electoral triumph of authoritarian and populist leaders such as Trump, Bolsonaro, Boris Johnson, and Orban.

Similar to comparable crises such as the Great Depression of the 1930s, the current crisis has not only affected democratic legitimacy but also scrutinised established democratic theories and explored the potential for new ones. In our subsequent investigation, we assume that the historical evolution of democratic models arises from the very social struggles they seek to address. Emerging social movements and growing protests, many of them calling for 'real democracy', have led to new ideas and fostered public debate around alternative perspectives and critiques of liberal democracy. The background of the crisis and its conceptualisation will play a crucial role in our analysis.

I argue that the hitherto existing 'state of democratic theory' reflects liberal hegemony. Not only in the democratic elitism of Schumpeter and Przeworski and in the positivist empiricism of Huntington do we find a liberal core, but also among critical theories such as the deliberativism of Benhabib and Habermas and even in radical and agonistic schools. Apparent critics of the liberal approach generally refrain from abandoning liberal ethics or, alternatively, fail to present a comprehensive strategy and political economy capable of sustaining alternative democratic models. Even Santos admits that 'democratizing democracy' represents only a temporary response to the lack of alternatives to capitalist globalisation, as long as there is no socialist alternative on the agenda.[120]

By separating democracy from the organisation of political economy, democratic theorists restrict themselves to idealism and pragmatism: Mouffe's agonistic horizon, for example, fails to take confrontation as the very condition of democracy to its ultimate consequences and brings democracy back to the existing liberal consensus on what the 'democratic game' is. These limitations imposed by predefined rules obscure the historical reality that democratic politics and the process of democratisation have consistently involved ideological confrontations – often characterised by violence – that challenge the established rules of the 'democratic game'. The achievement of universal male suffrage is inseparable from the Bolshevik revolution and the First World War, and French 'freedom and equality' are inseparable from the Jacobin terror.

120 Santos 2005.

Mouffe's acceptance of the 'rules of the game', based on 'freedom and equality', merely reflects the ideological hegemony of an era. Rather than forming the basis of democracy, the rules governing the democratic process have historically functioned as a compromise, serving to obstruct or delay further democratisation. These rules represent a conservative response to social emancipation, a form of Gramscian passive revolution.[121]

While representatives of deliberative, radical, and agonistic democracy celebrate internal conflicts as 'true' democracy, our approach anticipates that the fundamental tensions of capitalism ultimately lead to crises of legitimation, characterised by the hegemonic disruption of existing democratic rules.[122] Understanding democracy in a crisis context requires conceiving it beyond established democratic rules. This study highlights the importance of 'anti-currents' – those that reject established democratic rules – as fundamental in understanding the historical trajectory of democracy. Rejection of established democratic norms, continuous contestation of democratic rules, and resistance to adhering to or challenging them are an integral and fundamental part of democratising practices and democratic change.

This takes us back to the approach rooted in dialectics, negativity, and the Schmittean concept of the political. The reluctance of democratic theorists like Arendt and Mouffe to cross liberal boundaries limits their scope. To rescue democratic theory from the neoliberal paradox and salvage its emancipatory potential, a more fruitful approach should therefore begin with a historical analysis of the impossible relationship between capitalism and democracy and refocus on the social struggles that shaped and contested democracy.

3.1 Capitalism and Democracy

Capitalist and democratic relations are structured antagonistically. Capitalist relations are structured around the private ownership of the means of production, the exploitation of wage labour, and the exchange of commodities, which ultimately constitute two predominant and opposing social classes and determine the power of the citizen.[123] Those outside the capitalist class find

121 Gramsci's concept of passive revolution 'refers to the capacity of dominant classes in periods of crisis and societal transformation to pre-empt, deflect or absorb revolutionary struggles "from below" and reconfigure the state and the economic structure "from above" to their advantage'. It serves to understand the different capacities of elites in exploiting changes in global capitalism and adapting to popular pressures (De Smet and Bogaert 2017, p. 212).

122 Habermas 1975a.

123 Mandel 1982.

their desires curtailed by limited purchasing power and their freedoms restricted by the discipline of the employment contract and the need to survive. Democratic relations, based on the principles of popular sovereignty and equal decision-making capacity among citizens, have a naturally opposite logic. This is why Marx argued that true democracy was impossible under capitalism.[124] But democracy also developed along with and because of the dynamics of the capitalist political economy, as an 'antagonistic symbiosis'.[125]

In the core capitalist nations, the historical connection between the emerging bourgeoisie and liberal democracy, which would reach its full development in the nineteenth century, originated from the revolutionary class character of the bourgeoisie in feudal societies. These were predominantly based on inheritance, family, personal allegiance, and serfdom. Its aristocratic ruling class ruled based on theology, lineage, and military strength.[126] When, as an exponent of increasing trade, manufacturing industry, and urbanisation, a powerful new bourgeoisie developed, its interests soon became incompatible with feudalism. Feudal decentralisation limited free trade and investment, and serfdom limited the availability of free labour.

Several reasons explain the push for democracy in the transition from feudalism to capitalism. Through the creation of a working class and its tendency towards inequalities and crisis, capitalism triggered popular uprisings that led to democratisation. Due to the much-needed national alliance with the popular classes against the remnants of feudalism, the bourgeoisie had to articulate a counter-hegemony based on democratic sovereignty, freedom, and rationality. The growth of the capitalist economy also generated a margin for concessions. Capital's tendencies toward internal competition created a peacefully disunited ruling class without a single centre and therefore it needed an independent elected and deliberative representation. Furthermore, the bourgeois government is impersonal; it thrives regardless of who is in power. While feudalism could never be governed by a peasant party, capitalism is perfectly compatible with a Labour Party government.[127]

Old Athenian democracy inspired modern liberal democracy. However, there are important differences. While in liberal democracy civic equality coexisted with social inequality, in Athenian democracy political equality coexisted with socioeconomic inequality and transformed it, albeit at the expense of slaves, who were excluded from democratic participation. This is why 'the

124 Held 2006.
125 Dahl 1999, p. 187.
126 Therborn 1999, pp. 55–61.
127 Therborn 1977, pp. 29–31.

common good' in modern democratic theory has an 'abstract character', while in Athenian democracy the common good was a social practice. The abstract character is a consequence of the difficulty of uniting extremes of social inequalities and conflicting interests.[128]

Another major difference is the absence of liberalism in Greek antiquity. According to Wood, liberalism has aristocratic origins, as it emerged through aristocratic opposition to the advent of centralised states and absolute monarchy.[129] It can be traced back to *Magna Carta* and Cromwell's revolt. The idea of freedom – safeguarding feudal liberties and powers – is rooted in pre-capitalist privilege versus sovereignty and is therefore certainly not democratic by intent. This liberty is later reflected in the demand to make government taxation dependent on representation and control by the propertied classes: 'No taxation without representation' would form the basis of census (property-based) suffrage. While liberalism was reappropriated for more democratic purposes by progressive forces since the seventeenth century, notably in the notions of civil liberties and human rights, identifying or even replacing democracy with liberalism was a counter-revolutionary project. By shifting the locus of power from landlordism to property, capitalism separates property from privilege: the benefits of privilege give way to pure 'economic' advantage.[130]

Capitalism is unique in its ability to sustain private property and surplus extraction without the need for direct political authority. The state guarantees the public enforcement of property law and class relations are reproduced in the privately owned factory. This leads to conceptualising relations of production as an economic matter between private individuals in civil society and the separation of the economy as a separate private sphere.[131] This separation, which originated in the feudal lord's concern to keep the absolutist sovereign out of local affairs, would later restrict the political influence of the working class in the new emerging class struggle. Following Marx, others such as Karl Polanyi, Jürgen Habermas, and Ellen Meiksins Wood have theorised the division between public and private spheres, which reflects the ideological distinction between politics and the economy, the distinguishing feature of modern capitalist society.[132]

128 Wood 2016, pp. 202–12.
129 Wood 2016, pp. 229–33.
130 Wood 2016, pp. 203, 208.
131 Santos 1995c, p. 414. Wood 2016.
132 Habermas 1991; Polanyi 2001; Wood 2016.

According to Karl Marx, civil or bourgeois society – *bürgerliche Gesellshaft* – is the sphere of action of socioeconomic transactions, the sphere of the bourgeois historical subject, a 'natural state' of the selfish individual.[133] Commodity fetishism plays a crucial role in the naturalisation of capitalist exploitation in the private sphere.[134] The private rule of the capitalist class is based on the ownership of the means of production, whose intrinsic character is governed by market exchanges. Its universal goal – to make profits as efficiently as possible – structures social relations with individuals from different social classes, as well as within their own class. This leads to a focus on 'juridical equality, unequal rewards for unequal competitive performances ... and a consciousness of the prices of objects and men ... and awareness of the prices of objects and men' and requires subjection to and qualification for rational calculation, orderliness, thrift and continuous effort.[135] This 'despotism of the workshop'[136] and the dictates of the market driven by competition and profitability constitute a coercive force 'capable of subjecting all human values, activities and relations to its imperatives to a totalitarian extent that no ancient despot could have ever dreamed of'.[137]

The state, which accompanied the institutionalisation of national markets, the establishment of a power structure with a centralised bureaucracy, the unification of territories and languages, the development of a national ideology, and the institutionalisation of bourgeois democracy, becomes 'a separate entity, beside and outside civil society ... the form of organization that the bourgeois necessarily adopt for both internal and external purposes, for the mutual guarantee of their properties and interests'.[138] Given the subjacent class struggle, the institutionalisation of the political sphere tends to represent a balance between class relations. The subordinate classes in bourgeois society, in particular the working class, play only 'a small part in determining the existence of law and the State'.[139] Marx exemplifies this in his analysis of the Bonapartist government:

> not directly involved in the struggle of capital and labour; it professed to save the working class by breaking down parliamentarism, and, with it, the undis-

133 Bobbio 1997, pp. 27–31.
134 Santos 1995c, p. 414.
135 Therborn 1999, pp. 57–8.
136 Mandel 1982, p. 243; Santos 1995c, p. 415.
137 Wood 2016, p. 254.
138 Marx 1998, p. 99.
139 Marx 1998, p. 349.

> guised subservience of government to the propertied classes. It professed to save the propertied classes by upholding their economic supremacy over the working class; and, finally, it professed to unite all classes by reviving for all the chimera of national glory .... In reality, it was the only form of government possible at a time when the bourgeoisie had already lost, and the working class had not yet acquired .... Under its sway, bourgeois society, freed from political cares, attained a development unexpected even by itself.[140]

The bourgeois state, at least at its core, and in contrast to the feudal state, tends to be governed by an impersonal rule of a constitutional and public nature, instead of the private legal possession of any specific group.[141] But this 'democratic rule' in the public sphere only exists at the expense of coercive rule and exploitation in the private sphere. At the same time, the state can ostensibly belong to everyone, namely through universal suffrage.[142]

The public sphere is the privileged space of the new democratic ideology and political activity; a sphere that, according to Habermas, had its origins in the development of new means of communication – books, newspapers and political pamphlets – and in the emergence of bourgeois salons, meetings of upper class people who opened their homes for public debates on public affairs, science, culture, etc. They played a crucial role in the ideological struggle between the developing bourgeoisie and the established aristocracy, as they made it possible to win the battle within civil society.[143] Articulating the rising bourgeois classes with other layers, such as peasants and workers, it allowed the former to channel the misery of the poor into a social force capable of ending the fading feudal governance and push towards a bourgeois revolution. This space for debate – which excluded the illiterate masses – became the cornerstone of the deliberative dimension of liberal democracy, from early parliamentary traditions and discussions to diverse liberal democratic theories.

Once the early exclusionary principles of liberal democracy were established, the democratisation of democracy would be the result of emancipatory struggles by other social classes and groups in society. The rise of the organised working class, whose relative exploitation through the production of surplus value has been the driving force behind the process of capitalist accumulation,

140 Marx 2012b, p. 36.
141 Santos 1995c, p. 415.
142 Wood 2016, p. 40.
143 Butler et al. 2000, p. 47.

has probably had the greatest impact on the history, institutionalisation, and functioning of democracy.[144]

To begin capital accumulation, initial capital and free labour were needed and neither was widely available at the dawn of capitalism. In feudalism, work was generally not free: it was subject to serfdom or community service. And if it was 'free', it was generally scarce, as people only worked as much as was necessary to live. Many preferred to use their labour on common land and with their own tools. A massive process of proletarianisation was necessary, which would eliminate obstacles to the constitution of labour as a universal commodity, a consequence of a development that occurs before the 'normal' accumulation process, the so-called primitive accumulation. Marx wrote this famous passage:

> The free workers are therefore free from, unencumbered by, any means of production of their own. With the polarization of the commodity-market into these two classes, the fundamental conditions of capitalist production are present. The capital relation presupposes a complete separation between the workers and the ownership of the conditions for the realization of their labour. As soon as capitalist production stands on its own feet, it not only maintains this separation, but reproduces it on a constantly extending scale. The process, therefore, which creates the capital-relation can be nothing other than the process which divorces the worker from the ownership of the conditions of his own labour; it is a process which operates two transformations, whereby the social means of subsistence and production are turned into capital, and the immediate producers are turned into wage-labourers. So-called primitive accumulation, therefore, is nothing else than the historical process of divorcing the producer from the means of production. ... To become a free seller of labour-power, who carries his commodity wherever he can find a market for it, he must further have escaped from the regime of the guilds, their rules for apprentices and journeymen, and their restrictive labour regulations. Hence the historical movement which changes the producers into wage-labourers appears, on the one hand, as their emancipation from serfdom and from the fetters of the guilds, and it is this aspect of the movement which alone exists for our bourgeois historians. But, on the other hand, these newly freed men became sellers of themselves only after they had been robbed of all their own means of production, and all the guarantees of existence afforded by the old feudal arrangements. And this history, the history of their expropriation, is written in the annals of mankind in letters of blood and fire.[145]

---

144 Mandel 1982; Marx 1982.

145 Marx 1982, pp. 874–75.

With the increase in 'the accumulation of capital, the class struggle develops, and hence the class-consciousness of the workers as well'.[146] The emergence of the working class and its antagonism with capital forced democracy to move from a counter-aristocratic hegemony to the institutional space of a new class struggle.

The individual citizen emerges from the same process that produced free, abstract labour in the economic sphere: through the alienation of the peasantry from their means of subsistence and their social, juridical, and political ties to the village community.[147] While the dissolution of traditional prescriptive identities represented a move towards individual 'freedom', the new powers and rights of citizenship were accompanied by the separation between the economic and the political. The 'devaluation of the political sphere' and the consequent subjugation of working citizens within the depoliticised market are fundamental characteristics of the devaluation of citizenship in contemporary democracy.[148]

The only relationship that working citizens maintain is that of representation. In the Athenian context, representation, restricting government to a small group, was considered an oligarchic tendency in public affairs. 'Representative democracy' is an American novelty: in their goal of sustaining a propertied oligarchy with the electoral support of the masses, American federalists wanted a large republic to make representation inevitable. Representation was thus conceived as a gatekeeper of the public will – the very antithesis of ancient Greek *isegoria*, which implied equal rights for citizens to participate in assemblies.[149]

For a long time, even this restricted representation was denied to the working class. Even if we leave aside the suppression of women's suffrage – which affects the majority of the working class – universal male suffrage was only guaranteed after the First World War in most European countries. Previously, suffrage was restricted to property-owning elites who paid poll taxes. People who lived in poverty or were economically dependent on employers were considered incapable of making rational, independent political decisions and were therefore denied the right to vote. Early bourgeois 'democracy' would today be considered profoundly undemocratic, not only due to its profound inequality and its deeply racist, sexist, anti-Semitic, and highly exclusionary practices, but also due to the harsh repression against unions and political organisations. Only rich, white, male citizens participated democratically: the expan-

146 Marx 1982, p. 808.
147 Wood 2016, pp. 209–11.
148 Wood 2016, p. 211.
149 Wood 2016, pp. 214–17.

sion of citizenship and democratisation was essentially the result of later social struggles, in particular against capitalism.

3.2 Socialism and Democracy

Overcoming the separation between the political and economic spheres has been crucial to any attempt at political democratisation under capitalism. This separation tends to be reflected in a separation between political struggles, which concern formal rights of deliberation, representation, citizenship, legal equality, and economic struggles, which concern issues of inequality, food, wages, living conditions, etc. Within the class struggle this separation is expressed in the phenomenon of 'economism', the 'natural' focus of working-class struggles, particularly in the trade union movement, on purely economic demands such as wage increases and job security.

As demonstrated earlier, the segregation of spheres was only possible through primitive accumulation, where the state intervenes coercively on behalf of the expropriating classes. This leads us to Marx's conclusion that the secret of capitalist production is 'political': the continued national and international integration of capitalism requires greater state intervention in the planning and containment of class conflict.[150] Subordinate social classes tend to discover the political dimension of economic struggles in periods of crisis. Therefore, it is the state, and not private interests, that becomes the main target of resistance and political revolution during crises. The distinction between the economic and the political in capitalism is precisely what makes the unity of political and economic struggles for emancipation necessary, it is what makes socialism and democracy historically synonymous in capitalism.[151] The forthcoming sections will highlight some key concepts and debates in the history of socialism and democracy. Although the scope of this book does not allow for the historical and political detail that many of these debates deserve, a brief overview is essential for a contemporary, historically informed Marxist approach to democratic socialist strategy.

Due to historical circumstances, particularly Stalinism, 'dictatorship of the proletariat' is probably the most controversial expression associated with Marxism. However, its significance should not be overlooked. It was used by Marx to address the question of socialism and democracy, transforming it into a critical starting point. Furthermore, the philosophical relationship with the

150 Wood 2016, pp. 19–21.

151 Wood 2016, pp. 47–8. Santos (2003, p. 67) in this context defines socialism as 'limitless democracy'.

concepts of crisis, state of exception, and sovereignty makes the discussion of the term even more important. For Marx, the dictatorship of the proletariat was equal to socialism: a period of transition in which the working class becomes the ruling class until class distinctions disappear and the state 'withers away'. Democracy thus goes through a transition from capitalism to communism.[152] Neither Marx and Engels, nor even Lenin, wrote a concrete plan for what such a 'dictatorship' would look like: it was a political abstraction, whose practical dimension depended on their own contemporary experiences, the Paris Commune for Marx and the Russian Revolution for Lenin.[153]

The Paris Commune demonstrated the dialectic between democratic form and revolutionary content.[154] Our contemporary everyday language, which conceptualises dictatorship and democracy as two irreconcilable opposites, would not characterise the Paris Commune as a dictatorial regime. Instead, we would speak of some form of radical democracy that extends popular representation and participation to the bureaucracy and judiciary, through universal suffrage, rigorous accountability and revocability of delegates, the abolition of internal hierarchies, and the replacement of the army by the 'armed people'.[155] It served as historical confirmation of the predictions, two decades earlier, in *The Communist Manifesto*: 'The proletariat can only come to power through the violent overthrow of the bourgeoisie … to raise the proletariat to the position of ruling class, to win the battle of democracy'.[156]

In *State and Revolution*, Lenin (2015) famously quotes Marx:

> The Commune … appears to have replaced the smashed state machine 'only' by fuller democracy: abolition of the standing army; all officials to be elected and subject to recall. But as a matter of fact, this 'only' signifies a gigantic replacement of certain institutions by other institutions of a fundamentally different type. This is exactly a case of 'quantity being transformed into quality': democracy, introduced as fully and consistently as is at all conceivable, is transformed from bourgeois into proletarian democracy; from the state (a special force for the suppression of a particular class) into something which is no longer a state proper …. The dictatorship of the proletariat represents simultaneously with an immense expansion of democracy, which for the first time becomes democracy for the poor, democracy for the people, and not democracy for the money-bags,

152 Lenin 2015, p. 127.
153 Balibar 2017.
154 Kivotidis 2019.
155 Kivotidis 2019.
156 Marx 2013, pp. 77, 93.

> the dictatorship of the proletariat imposes a series of restrictions on the freedom of the oppressors, the exploiters, the capitalists.[157]

According to Marxist theory, state power represents the political dominance of a single class. In capitalist societies, state power is exercised unilaterally by the bourgeoisie. Given that state power faces constant threats due to the evolution of class struggle, it must adapt to maintain its authority. Thus the only possible 'alternative' to bourgeois state power is for the proletariat to maintain equally absolute control over state power, even if it is impossible to predict the moment and the particular form in which this will occur.[158]

Rosa Luxemburg, who is often cited as an early critic of the authoritarian turn in the Soviet Union, warned against conceptualising dictatorship and democracy as opposites. She denounced the reformist social democrats who favoured 'democracy' – liberal democracy – against revolutionary dictatorship, at the same time as she denounced the concentration of power in a few men, a bourgeois model of dictatorship. She summarised the relationship between dictatorship, democracy and socialism as follows:

> Socialist democracy is not something which begins only in the promised land after the foundations of socialist economy are created … [and] in the interim, have loyally supported a handful of socialist dictators. Socialist democracy begins simultaneously with the beginnings of the destruction of class rule and of the construction of socialism. It begins at the very moment of the seizure of power by the socialist party. It is the same thing as the dictatorship of the proletariat …. This dictatorship consists in the *manner of applying democracy*, not in its *elimination*, but in energetic, resolute attacks upon the well-entrenched rights and economic relationships of bourgeois society, without which a socialist transformation cannot be accomplished. But this dictatorship must be the work of the *class* and not of a little leading minority in the name of the class – that is, it must proceed step by step out of the active participation of the masses; it must be under their direct influence, subjected to the control of complete public activity; it must arise out of the growing political training of the mass of the people.[159]

The dictatorship of the proletariat is, therefore, not some kind of finished programme conceptualised by enlightened leaders. It is not a policy or a strategy

157 Lenin 2015, p. 126.
158 Balibar 2017.
159 Luxemburg 2004b, p. 308.

that involves a specific form of government or institutions, but rather a historical reality that covers the entire period of transition to communism, developing within the framework of capitalism through the active struggle against it. It is not, therefore, a path or a political 'option' in the transition to socialism that can or should be 'chosen' in certain historical conditions, as in the 'backward' Russia of 1917, and that can, under equal conditions, be exchanged for another, opposite 'democratic' transition path in politically and industrially 'advanced' Western Europe. As it is not a question of choice, it cannot be 'abandoned', just as the class struggle cannot be 'abandoned', except in words and at the cost of enormous confusion.[160]

The use of the concept of dictatorship by Marx, Engels, Rosa Luxemburg, and Lenin addresses the sovereignty of the proletariat, but does not fully coincide with Schmitt's use of the term in legal theory. Carl Schmitt used the term in the Roman sense: dictatorship is a temporary situation in which full sovereignty is given to someone in the context of a state of exception for the purpose of defending the Constitution and restoring order and normality.[161] In the Marxist interpretation, the dictatorship is not a conservative institution to restore 'normality'. Quite the opposite, it serves to fundamentally change it, to create history.

Among the socialists who rejected the concept of dictatorship of the proletariat is Eduard Bernstein, whose book *The Prerequisites of Socialism and the Tasks of Social Democracy* represented an absolute revision of Marxist theory in 1899. *In The Prerequisites of Socialism* – also translated as *Evolutionary Socialism* – Bernstein rejects the revolutionary character of the proletariat and promotes universal voting rights and social reforms as an alternative peaceful path.[162] Bernstein's refutation of some basic premises of revolutionary socialism is the result of a disagreement with Marx's theory of the crisis of capitalism: he sees no tendency towards ever deeper crises and therefore no moment of truth of capitalism that would lead to a dictatorship of the proletariat.[163] Bernstein also questions the proletariat as a class.[164] He emphasises their internal diversity and contradictory interests, as opposed to the homogeneous and universal class that capitalism should have created. According to Bernstein, socialism is therefore much wider than the class struggle in modern society: it takes

160 Balibar 1977, pp. 8–10.
161 McCormick 1999.
162 Bernstein 1909, p. 145.
163 Bernstein 1909, pp. 73–94.
164 Bernstein 1909, p. 103.

the form of several explanations; it can be a state power, but also a movement, a perception, or an objective (equality, justice, cooperative economy).[165] The reformist social democrats only spoke of the dictatorship of the proletariat to dissociate themselves from it, thus abandoning the distinctive element between proletarian revolution and bourgeois reforms.[166]

Ironically, the first successful socialist revolution in Russia of 1917, and the subsequent revolutionary threat in Western Europe, changed the power relationship between classes in such a way that social democratic reformism seemed viable: considerable concessions could be achieved within the sphere of liberal democracy. Against these reformists, Marx had already warned that social rights, their 'formulation, official recognition and proclamation by the State', were just the result of long class struggles disguised by 'parliamentary fantasy'.[167] Under pressure from the strengthened and confident working classes, economic and political elites quickly implemented universal male suffrage to co-opt their leadership. This would eventually lead to welfare societies; formal democracy gained some substance by reducing inequalities and promoting the integration of the working class in the co-management of the capitalist political economy. The politicisation of economic struggles led to an expansion of democracy from political formality to civil society.[168]

The aforementioned expansion through the co-optation of social democracy in Europe at the end of the First World War entangled the question of democracy with imperialism and colonialism. As postulated by several Marxist theorists, the process of partial substantial democratisation, which conferred benefits on the working class without needing a revolution, was facilitated at the expense of peripheral regions.[169] The theories of imperialism by Hilferding, Lenin, and Luxemburg attempted to explain how the dynamics of accumulation would give rise to imperial conflicts: Hilferding argued that the emergence of finance capital in the early twentieth century intensified competition between nation-states and imperial practices.[170] For Lenin, imperialism is a new phase of capital development in which financial capital takes control of the state and its international relations.

For Rosa Luxemburg, the dynamics of imperialism and violent appropriation are a permanent repetition of what Marx identified as the initial phase of

165 Bernstein 1909, p. 95.
166 Balibar 1977, p. 17.
167 Marx 1982, p. 184.
168 Bobbio 1997, p. 156.
169 Bukharin 1977.
170 Willoughby 1995.

capitalist development: the phase of primitive accumulation, in which capital was constituted and workers and materials are attracted to the accumulation process by brutal violence. Rosa Luxemburg argues that capitalism did not cease this process of accumulation through dispossession, involving the plundering of colonies, war, resource extraction, and exploitation of nature. She identifies it as an ongoing phenomenon, parallel and interconnected with the normal, or expanded, accumulation of capital, which depends on the extraction of surplus value from the working class.[171] Similarly, David Harvey suggests that capitalism needs something 'external' to itself to stabilise internal contradictions and conflicts.[172] Regardless of the primary driver, be it underconsumption or overaccumulation Lenin and Rosa Luxemburg[173] state that imperialism, in contrast to the thesis of classical liberal political economy, which suggests that state intervention in imperialism contradicts free market capitalist principles, is an intrinsic component of capitalism.

Both attribute the 'betrayal' of social democracy and its collaboration with nationalism during the First World War – the German SPD in particular – to the incorporation of the reformist leadership of the labour movement and the labour aristocracy into the capitalist state. This 'betrayal' implies the abandonment of internationalist and revolutionary goals, opting instead for chauvinist nationalism, as demonstrated by the support for imperialist war by German workers to prove their patriotism. From the perspective of the working classes of imperialist countries, imperialism brought certain advantages, such as higher wages, which led to the integration of working-class organisations into the bourgeois state structure. Almost all workers and mass organisations have become integral parts of the capitalist system.[174] As domestic opportunities for capital accumulation were constrained by a strengthened working class, rising wages, social concessions, and labour rights, national capital found stronger incentives to seek profits beyond its national borders. Whether for the pursuit of new markets, for the export of capital and investments, or for the exploitation of cheap resources and natural assets, the national state placed its coercive power behind the interests of national capital. Within the framework of imperialism, the specific interaction between democracy and peripheral regions emerges. In a world divided by the spheres of influence of the great imperialist powers, democratisation faces specific challenges in peripheral,

171 Luxemburg 2016.
172 Harvey 2005, pp. 140–41.
173 Lenin 1999, pp. 108–9; Luxemburg 2004a, p. 327.
174 Bukharin 1977, p. 24.

colonised, and dependent nations. It is in this context that the discussion about the relationship between 'democratic demands' and 'socialist demands' within Marxist theory arises.

The concept of 'democratic demands' originates from the Marxist notion of bourgeois-democratic revolution. Historically, 'democratic demands' have been associated with the emancipation of the progressive bourgeoisie from feudalism and absolutism, while 'socialist demands' aim at the overthrow of capitalism. Given that socialism can only emerge from capitalism – since capitalist development creates the working class and the material conditions for socialism – many Marxists have argued that there is a teleological evolution of the stages of development that should guide the policies of socialists. In regions still characterised by feudal or absolutist conditions, socialists should advocate the establishment of democratic capitalism. Only after the establishment of such a system, when the contradictions inherent to capitalism were mature, would socialist demands come to the fore.[175]

The theories of uneven and combined development and permanent revolution proposed by Leon Trotsky significantly challenged this perspective and have since served as a primary Marxist framework for analysing the relationship between democracy and the periphery. Trotsky's approach was inspired by the critique of colonialism developed by Parvus in 1907 and shaped by the experiences of the Russian revolutions of 1905 and 1917. It postulates that in countries marked by underdevelopment and dependence in a global context of imperialist development, national bourgeoisies lack the strength, autonomy and progressive role necessary to lead a traditional liberal bourgeois revolution. Furthermore, as Fanon observed, in the (neo)colonial context, local elites function only as agents dependent on the coloniser, whose economic interests are not invested in promoting independent national economic development, but rather in facilitating the plundering of the country by imperialist interests.

In this context, Trotsky argues that the only progressive and revolutionary class is the working class. It is the only class that, in alliance with the peasantry, is capable of carrying out the historical tasks of the bourgeois revolution. As imperialism does not provide the conditions for independent liberal bourgeois development, the pursuit of 'democratic' demands automatically assumes an anti-capitalist, anti-imperialist and therefore socialist character. This constitutes the essence of Trotsky's theory of permanent revolution, according to which, due to the dynamics of uneven and combined development, 'demo-

---

175 Laclau 2005, pp. 125–27.

cratic and socialist revolutions would fuse into a single process whose outcome would be workers' power'[176] Trotsky writes:

> With regard to countries with a belated bourgeois development, especially the colonial and semi-colonial countries, the theory of permanent revolution signifies that the complete and genuine solution of their tasks of achieving *democracy and national emancipation* is conceivable only through the dictatorship of the proletariat as the leader of the subjugated nation, above all of its peasant masses.[177]

More than a century has passed since the emergence of the theory. But according to Löwy, the idea of permanent revolution is still indispensable today for a radical political strategy.[178] The world system is still characterised by inequality between the centre and the periphery, between highly industrialised countries and the 'underdeveloped world' of the Global South, and these dynamics still influence the forms and practices of democracy today.

The defeat of the revolutions in Western Europe after the First World War and the triumph of reformism sparked a renewed debate among Marxists about strategic positions regarding democracy and parliamentarism. Discussions on the question of parliamentarism dominated the Second Congress of the Communist International in 1920. Nikolai Bukharin distinguished four different positions.[179]

Reformists, dominant in most European parties and workers' organisations, upheld the belief in achieving socialism through legal reforms and participation in parliamentary democracy. Over time, a substantial part of the representatives of the working class and party factions were assimilated into the bourgeois parliamentary apparatus, abandoning their anti-systemic position. In radical opposition to the reformists, the anti-parliamentarians emerged as legitimate children of the opportunism and parliamentarism practiced by the social democrats.[180] Within this anti-parliamentary faction, there were two main groups, each with different reasons for rejecting parliamentary tactics. The first group, the principled anti-parliamentarians, included anarchists and

---

176 Callinicos 1982.

177 Trotsky 2010, p. 310.

178 Löwy 2010, p. 145.

179 Bukharin 1977, pp. 20–1. Nikolai Bukharin was a Russian Bolchevic who wrote extensively on imperialism, editor of *Pravda* after the October revolution; he was executed by the Stalinist regime in 1938.

180 Bukharin 1977, pp. 30–1.

trade unionists opposed to the political action of workers' parties, such as the North American Industrial Workers of the World (IWW), who voted against the *Theses on Communist Parties and Parliamentarism* at the end of the congress. These anarchists and syndicalists were vehemently opposed to any form of centralised authority.

In contrast, the Italian socialist representative Amadeo Bordiga defended an anti-parliamentary position based on a Marxist critique of bourgeois democracy.[181] Bordiga asserted that bourgeois democracy and parliamentary systems inherently served as defence mechanisms for capitalism. He defended the priority of dismantling these bourgeois institutions before any efforts towards building a workers' state or transitioning to communism. The belief that all confrontations between hostile parties and all struggles for power should be carried out through election campaigns and parliamentary debates should be dismantled. Bordiga also emphasised the dangers associated with electoral activity, including the diversion of resources and attention from other vital party functions. He advocated boycotting elections and bourgeois democratic institutions, particularly in Western Europe, where parliamentary democracy held a strong ideological position. According to Bordiga, communist parties could only achieve significant progress if they became directly involved with the dictatorship of the proletariat and the workers' councils, abandoning any contact with bourgeois democracy.[182]

Against the position of Bordiga and the German left communists who emphatically rejected 'any reversion to parliamentary forms of struggle, which have become historically and politically obsolete', Lenin wrote a well-known pamphlet entitled *'Left-wing' Communism: An Infantile Disorder*.[183] He considers this a manifestation of weakness: how could the working class trust a revolutionary leadership if it considers itself too weak to confront capitalism in its own parliament? Furthermore, calling for the advancement of the councils' alternative to parliament makes no sense when these workers' councils do not yet exist: 'Parliament is a product of historical development which one cannot abolish from the world until one is strong enough to scatter the bourgeois parliament'.[184] Just as historical experiences do not arise artificially, neither can councils or soviets be created artificially.

While rejecting the reformist, parliamentary path to socialism, Lenin criticises the anti-parliamentarians for confusing two distinct meanings of 'parlia-

181 Bordiga 1977.
182 Bukharin 1977, p. 33.
183 Lenin 1966, p. 56.
184 Lenin 1977, pp. 51–52.

mentarism being obsolete'.[185] Though parliamentarism may be theoretically obsolete as an element of decadent bourgeois capitalism, it is not practically obsolete because large segments of the working class still adhere to bourgeois democracy. A considerable portion of the proletarian petty bourgeoisie, less progressive workers, and small peasants believe that their interests are represented in parliament: 'one must combat that through work in parliament and teach the masses the truth through facts. The backward masses cannot be taught by theory, they need experiences'.[186]

Only through pedagogical experience will the organised working class be prepared to adopt a regime based on councils and dissolve the parliamentary system.[187] For the time being, Marxists should engage in electoral battles and campaigns to prepare for the dissolution of parliamentarism from within. In certain cases, only by being a member of parliament – even within the most reactionary parliaments – can one combat bourgeois society and parliamentarism. Revolutionary crises often manifest themselves as parliamentary crises and need a 'combination' of mass action outside parliament with an internal opposition sympathetic to the revolution. Simultaneously, rigorous and uncompromising criticism must be directed, not against parliamentarism or parliamentary activities, but against leaders who are unable and 'unwilling' to use elections to parliament and parliamentary activity in a revolutionary and communist way.[188]

Another significant debate within the left during the 1920s and 1930s centred on political articulation, more specifically on the choice between united front and popular front strategies. The concept of a united front first emerged in 1922, during the Fourth Congress of the Communist International.[189] After the setback of the German revolution, it was proposed as the most effective method to guide communists towards gaining the support of the majority of workers. It was presented as a political tactic to unite all factions of the working class, encompassing trade unions and working-class parties, including social democratic, anarchist, and Catholic workers' associations against capital. This tactic of political articulation should not be confused with 'electoral combinations' of leaders in pursuit of one or another parliamentary objective, but rather be approached as a process that happens from below, rejecting at the same time an

185 Lenin 1966, pp. 56–65.
186 Lenin 1977, p. 52.
187 Lenin 1966, p. 59.
188 Lenin 1966.
189 Riddell 2011.

'organisational fusion of all the 'workers' parties'.[190] Trotsky called it 'the tactic of fusing the masses on the basis of transitional demands'.[191] The underlying idea was that through practical involvement in the struggle, socialist conclusions would naturally emerge, since a workers' government cannot be achieved or sustained without a revolutionary confrontation with the bourgeoisie. He simply said:

> The united front tactic is an initiative whereby the Communists propose to join with all workers belonging to other parties and groups and all unaligned workers in a common struggle to defend the immediate, basic interests of the working class against the bourgeoisie ... it is the experience of struggle that will convince workers of the inevitability of revolution and the historic importance of Communism ... The real success of the united front tactic depends on a movement 'from below', from the rank-and-file of the working masses. Nevertheless, there are circumstances in which Communists must not refuse to have talks with the leaders of the hostile workers' parties.[192]

The united front is often contrasted, but sometimes also confused, with the tactic of the popular front, which originated in France. In 1935, Communist and socialist leaders began talks about joint political action to combat the growing French fascist movement, which would eventually lead to popular front governments under the leadership of Léon Blum. The tactic was replicated in republican Spain, where Communists joined forces in government with anarchists, social democrats, and liberal republicans to combat Franco's fascists. In 1935, the Communist International formally recognised this approach as its official doctrine, supplanting the ultra-sectarian stance of the 'third period', which had identified social democracy and other socialist movements as its main political adversaries, labelling them social fascism. Driven by rank-and-file agitation 'from below' within various national sections, internal debates and factionalism within the Comintern leadership, and the USSR's need for security in the face of Nazi aggression, the communists followed Giorgi Dimitrov's call for a 'popular front' that did not distinguish allies on the basis of class – like the united front – but included all progressive forces willing to join the fight to defend democracy against fascism. It included liberal, republican and progressive sectors of the bourgeoisie and was widely applied, from labour disputes and participation in international brigades to involvement in electoral processes.

190 Riddell 2011, p. 1158.
191 Trotsky 2007, p. 10.
192 Riddell 2011, pp. 1157–159.

Notably, in the United States, this tactical approach even prompted communists to extend critical support to Franklin Roosevelt.[193]

Other Marxists, particularly the Left Opposition that gathered around Leon Trotsky, who was banished from the Soviet Union after Lenin's death, remained faithful to the old united front tactic. They criticised the tactics of the popular front as much as they did the sectarian line of the 'third period', and argued that it represented a tendency toward class collaboration and opportunism. They posited that these tactics not only diverged from the Marxist conception of socialism and the dictatorship of the proletariat as 'real democracy', but also asserted that the popular front tactic would ultimately prove ineffective in the struggle against the rise of fascism.

While Comintern loyalists defended parliamentary democracy against fascism at all costs, the Left Opposition argued that fascism was itself the consequence of the insoluble contradictions of capitalism and liberal democracy. An interclass front weakened and confused the working class. Fascism had to be faced by the working class and the left based on a programme of social emancipation and eventually revolution. While Comintern loyalists crushed their united front adversaries, in many cases through physical elimination and show trials, they were unable to prevent the rise of fascism across Europe. The popular front experiments in Spain and France ended up defeated. In many countries, the old 'democratic' capitalist elites became supporters of fascism rather than defenders of liberal democracy, while communists and the rest of the left became the main targets of repression.

The popular front doctrine ended abruptly in 1939, with the Molotov-Ribbentrop non-aggression pact between Nazi Germany and the Soviet Union, removing Communists loyal to Moscow from anti-fascist struggles. After failed negotiations on a collective security treaty, Stalin saw the pact with Hitler as the best guarantee for the USSR's geopolitical survival. The pact would be short-lived, and Operation Barbarossa would reestablish the Allied alliance.

From that moment on, geopolitical interests, determined by well-agreed spheres of influence, would regulate communist strategies towards liberal democracy. In the liberal West, communists led by Moscow advocated a stage approach that followed a logic similar to that of the popular front: liberal parliamentary modernisation and capitalist modernisation were defended as a temporary objective that would prepare a socialist transformation in an indefinite future. In its own sphere of influence, the Soviet Union would impose, often through military force, one-party Stalinist regimes, so-called 'people's demo-

---

193 Barrett 2009, pp. 531–33.

cracies', which redistributed wealth but denounced as 'bourgeois' the notions of individual and formal liberties.

The ideological divide between the Western and Eastern blocs has shaped contrasting perspectives on democracy and human rights, reflecting their own geopolitical and economic interests. This balance of powers between West and East and between capital and labour allowed for the development of the European social model, characterised by various forms of welfare capitalism and the institutionalisation of social citizenship.[194] This model promoted a trans-class institutionalisation of democracy with formal and substantive dimensions, accommodating social conflict and facilitating the emergence of trans- or extra-class conflicts and post-materialist movements: conflicts over race, gender, sexuality, and ecology emerged through their own interactions with the capitalist political economy, apparently independent of class. Popular front doctrine remained a spectre that guided many Marxist and post-Marxist organisations and intellectuals long after more precise formulations had been forgotten. Barrett argues that it has profoundly influenced the civil rights movement, the feminist movement, the New Left, and Eurocommunism, up until the recent left-wing populist approach to democracy.[195]

The incorporation of subaltern identities in the democratisation process cannot be understood in isolation from the extensive integration of and into the working class, through the substantial proletarianisation of women and colonised subjects and mass migration from peripheral regions.[196] As social conflicts take root in a capitalist framework, they express the same inherent contradictions in new forms and fields, such as through the escalating conflict over gender, racism, Islamophobia, and the electoral rise of far-right movements.

4 Democracy in Today's Crisis

Democracy has been an essentially contested concept throughout modern history. For at least two centuries, theorists have developed dozens of theories and approaches, including classical republicanism, utilitarianism, elitism, constitutionalism, anticolonialism, empiricism, liberalism, deliberative approaches, participatory approaches, agnonism, and socialism. As every form of scientific knowledge is not only historical, but also political, and crises have the property

194 Esping-Andersen 2013.
195 Barrett 2009, pp. 543–46.
196 Santos 1998.

of exposing the contradictions of processes, we conclude that Marxist theory – with its ontology based on the opposition between labour and capital – is the best approach to understanding democracy throughout the history of capitalism, particularly during a serious crisis at the end of 30 years of neoliberal hegemony.

If we start from the premise that the 'struggle for democracy ... is in what it will mean'[197] or that democratisation consists of a 'dispute over the meaning of democracy',[198] Ellen Wood reminds us not to overlook that the conflict between capitalism and socialism can be conceptualised as a clash between different forms of democracy.[199] We have observed how the struggle between capital and labour has shaped democratic processes, in which capitalism safeguards its interests by separating the political and economic spheres, representative democracy serves capital's oligarchic agenda, and the construction of individual liberal citizenship mirrors the alienated worker.

In her critique of Laclau and Mouffe, Wood states that the challenge of analysing democracy and formulating political strategies is not a mere linguistic issue.[200] Wood argues that the theorist's responsibility does not lie in depleting democracy of its particular ideological content, but rather in elucidating its distinctive character and essence.[201] Only by adopting this approach is it exposed that what appears to be universal, capitalist democracy, is, in reality, particular. In other words, one should not separate the ideological concept from its specific historical conditions, in which it represents the vested interests of a particular class, in order to repackage it as a universal principle. Instead, it is necessary to delve deeper into the historical factors that facilitated the generalisation of a specific interest of a particular class and gave it an appearance of universality.[202] The very diversity of meanings of the democratic concept arises at the point where fundamental class interests diverge, while the capitalist claim to exclusive ownership over democracy is based on the fusion of the various meanings.[203]

In the contemporary crisis of democracy, critical theorists need to trace it back to an opposition between capital and labour and between capitalism and socialism. The historical experiences of the working classes and debates about

197 Žižek 2006, p. 37.
198 Santos and Avritzer 2005, p. XLV.
199 Wood 1998, p. 134.
200 Wood 1998, p. 135.
201 Wood 1998, p. 153.
202 Wood 1998, p. 153.
203 Wood 1998, p. 134.

socialist strategies and tactics need to be condensed into political knowledge that can be used to build alternatives for fundamental change. The crisis of democracy is a crisis of capitalist hegemony. Democratic legitimacy relies on a hegemonic consensus regarding the interpretation of 'democracy'. However, the crisis reflects underlying social contradictions, resulting in the dissolution of the previously established consensus. As divergent yet potentially legitimate interests emerge, social dissent focuses on the conceptualisation of democracy itself, giving rise to disparate narratives and perspectives.

From a Marxist perspective, the objective of our inquiry is inherently dual: not only to expose the mechanisms by which this crisis unfolds, but also to propose strategies for achieving an alternative and universally applicable notion of democracy. Simultaneously, it is imperative to remain cautious against the dangers of co-optation and ideological obfuscation, which can dilute or distort the emancipatory potential of such an endeavour.

CHAPTER 4

Democratic Austerity

Since the linguistic turn – a consequence of the ontological rejection of labour as a primary political category of knowledge – most critical theory has assumed that science is ultimately based on a social consensus mediated by language.[1] Habermas's critical theory recognises an external reality, but we cannot know it except through interpretation and language. In our approach, we assume a 'reality' of political conflict, or rather, of political economy. Language – and therefore ideology, discourse, and science – has a dialectical interaction with political economy. Discourse is both socially constitutive and socially conditioned: linguistic-discursive textual structures have a crucial function in the social production and reproduction of inequalities, power, ideology, and authority, while power and control are manifested in language.[2] Ultimately, this interaction is determined by political economy and class struggles; today's discourse is socially characteristic of the economic, social and cultural changes of late modernity.[3] Examining democratic discourses in relation to class interests and political economy is therefore vital. Oral and written democratic discourses will therefore be examined in the conflictual relationship within their social context. The search for solutions to the contemporary crisis involves affirming new interpretations and new diagnoses of the crisis that are closely linked to their respective perspectives on democracy. We will analyse the discourses of political and economic elites about democracy, focusing on the articulation between the contested neoliberal austerity and the democratic discourse used to legitimise it.

1 The Context: Three Ways to Read the Crisis

The 2008 global financial crisis led to a deep recession in European economies, with a sharp increase in unemployment, public deficits, and disparities between the centre and the periphery. In Portugal, unemployment rates increased from 8.7 percent in 2008 to 14.1 percent in 2014; youth unemployment increased from 25.3 percent to 34.7 percent. GDP lost an accumulated 7.6

1 Morrow and Brown 1994, pp. 155–65.
2 Blommaert 2005, p. 25; Wodak 2011, p. 51.
3 Blommaert 2005, p. 25; Chouliaraki and Fairclough 1999, p. 4.

HTTPS://DOI.ORG/10.1163/9789004766235-006

percent, while it had been growing an accumulated 7.9 percent in the previous five years.[4] To contextualise the different democratic perspectives on the crisis, it is important to briefly distinguish the three main perspectives of political-economic analysis: neoclassical, (neo-)Keynesian, and Marxist.

Neoclassical economic models constitute the dominant framework in traditional business schools and inspire most European policymakers. Neoclassicist models are a reinterpretation of classical liberal theories such as those of Adam Smith and David Ricardo, successors of the monetarist models, and are based on three methodological premises: methodological individualism (assuming a hypothesis of *homo economicus*), methodological balance, and methodological instrumentalism. Monetarist economists regarded government intervention in the economy as undesirable. They stated that problems such as lack of information, bureaucratic delays, inflation, and unreliability of politicians, as postulated by public choice theory, made any form of state intervention harmful.[5] According to neoclassical economists, led by prominent theorist Robert Lucas, governments' efforts to stabilise the economy were deemed futile. Instead, they argued that such interventions would exacerbate price uncertainty.[6]

According to this perspective, crises are a consequence of the failure of the state and of mistaken public policies, thrifty governments, a privileged public sector, an unsustainable social security, and corrupt and irrational public agents. The result is a lack of competitiveness and high public debt. These systemic failures of the state are revealed during the crisis through the judgment of the market; when investors understand the risks, states lose access to markets and enter into financial and economic collapse. The crisis therefore represents a moment of reckoning with the irresponsible behaviour of the state, with the financial markets as final judges. The discursive success of neoclassical economics gave it an effective – politically oriented – dominance over alternative economic models.[7] This neoclassical perspective hegemonised the idea of so-called 'trickle-down economics', which assumes that the accumulation of profits by private companies and financial markets drives the production of wealth and economic efficiency that, in the end, benefits everyone. The neoclassical model is translated into neoliberal policy that assumes that economic crises are resolved by 'obeying the judgment of the markets' and reducing government interventionism. Political guidelines include cutting public spending, reducing primary deficits, privatizing public services, and internal

4 Eurostat 2020.
5 Heylen 2014, pp. 57–8.
6 Heylen 2004, pp. 563–65.
7 Arnsperger and Varoufakis 2006, p. 6.

devaluations – which means reducing labour costs through the reduction of wages and taxes and making work more flexible. During the crisis, Reinhart and Rogoff's book *This Time Is Different*, which establishes a correlation between high levels of (public) debt and low levels of economic growth, would be mobilised as the most popular scientific legitimisation of austerity policies.

The dominant opposition against the neoliberal approach is inspired by John M. Keynes' *The General Theory of Employment, Interest and Money*. The Great Depression convinced scholars that markets were rife with flaws and required public guidance. Traditional Keynesians believe that the government should adjust levels of economic output through fiscal and monetary interventions. Neo-Keynesians accept some neoclassical criticisms and are somewhat restrained. They prefer 'coarse tuning' to fine tuning, only cancelling out huge production imbalances. Since the Maastricht Treaty, many Keynesians have been critical of European economic policies, particularly the European Central Bank's inflation control directives, as well as stability and growth pacts.[8]

The Keynesian and neo-Keynesian approach is not so much critical of capitalism as it reproaches the neoliberal approach as self-defeating. Politically, it originates from the class compromise between the industrial bourgeoisie and the working class during the great depression of the 1930s. As a transclassist perspective, it has become the hegemonic economic perspective since the Bretton Woods conference in 1944. Bretton Woods created an international financial architecture tied to the dollar, with capital controls. Institutionally, it was based on the International Monetary Fund, the World Bank and GATT – General Agreement on Tariffs and Trade, currently the World Trade Organisation.

Keynesianism legitimised the big post-war economic reconstruction programmes, the developing countries on the periphery, and the welfare state in the core countries of the world system. Financial crises – as opposed to overproduction crises – were relatively rare in this system.[9] This perspective has been losing strength with the advent of neoliberalism and the crisis of the welfare state in the 1980s, the collapse of the Soviet Union, and the acceleration of neoliberal globalisation. It only returned to the centre of academic and popular debates during the apparent practical failure of neoclassical models and austerity measures. Leading figures in the Keynesian approach today include Paul Krugman, Joseph Stiglitz, and Paul De Grauwe, as well as Piketty and Wolf.[10]

---

8 Heylen 2004, pp. 39–40.

9 Harvey 2011, p. 32.

10 Paul Krugman 2012a, 2012b, and 2015; Joseph Stiglitz 2002, and 2013; Paul De Grauwe 2010; De Grauwe and Ji 2013; Piketty 2014.

In the short period following the 2008 financial crisis, Stiglitz described what he called the 'new Keynesian consensus': everyone saw the crash as the sign of a bloated and dysfunctional financial system that had misallocated capital. Instead of managing risk, deregulated financial markets created systemic risk.[11] Financial deregulation, along with easy money, contributed to excessive risk-taking. Monetary policy would be relatively ineffective in recovering the economy, even if easier access to money could have prevented the total collapse of the financial system. Therefore greater confidence in fiscal policy would be necessary, with an increase in public spending.

From this perspective, the financial crisis was caused by a credit bubble, defaulted loans in the housing market, and trade imbalances between geopolitical rivals. At the eurozone level, the euro crisis that unfolded in the aftermath of the global financial crisis was caused by structural imbalances in financial trade between member states of the European monetary union. This was caused by different economic situations and the lack of fiscal transfers to serve as a buffer. Keynesian economists have blamed the lack of a European economic government and financial integration, the lack of a coordinated response to the banking crisis, and irrational austerity policies for the worsening of the Union's structural problems.[12]

Thus, according to the Keynesian perspective, when the bubbles of financial speculation burst, the crisis revealed the disastrous effects of different neoliberal policies, particularly the unsoundness of financial liberalisation. At the same time, the euro debt crisis showed the failure of liberal plans for a monetary union. As a solution to the crisis, neo-Keynesians proposed fiscal stimulus, public investment or even nationalisations, higher wages to increase purchasing power, stricter financial regulation, and international integration.

Marxist economic theory is often reduced to distorted and oversimplified formulas, such as the 'progressive immiseration of the working class' and the 'ever-worsening economic crisis'.[13] However, Marx never predicted any sudden and automatic collapse of the capitalist system in a 'final' crisis, due to a single economic 'cause'.[14] Marx describes capitalism based on the immanent contradictions of the commodity form: 'These forms therefore imply the possibility of crises, though no more than the possibility'.[15]

---

11 Stiglitz 2013.

12 De Grauwe 2010; De Grauwe and Ji 2013; Krugman 2012a.

13 Mandel 1982, p. 23.

14 Mandel 1982, p. 83.

15 Marx 1982, p. 209.

Based on an extensive study of Marx's *Capital,* a critique of the works of Smith,[16] Ricardo and Sismondi,[17] and an extensive study of the history of the crises of capitalism between 1815 and 1908,[18] Rosa Luxemburg concludes that the problem of capitalism must be considered part of the periodic cycle and crises – that crises do not constitute the problem of capitalist reproduction in itself,[19] but that they are a method to 'get to the bottom' of the problems of capitalism.[20] The life purpose of capital is capital accumulation – profit is its universal driving force. Capitalist production only begins in a historical sense when exploitation goes beyond the simple distribution between the values of workers' production and the cost of productive capital. This means that in the production process there is a need to reserve a certain part of the value for accumulation. But one of the problems of capitalism, according to Luxemburg, is that, on the consumption side of capitalism, there is a need to be able to find consumers for this surplus production of value, which in a capitalist society can be neither capital nor labour. Who will be the consumer of societies' production of goods that must be sold to make accumulation possible?[21] From the beginning, capitalism has depended on an exchange relationship with other forms of external societies – a metabolic (*Stoffwechsel*) mechanism. As these processes of exchange faced 'difficulties' from the natural economy and frozen social relations, capitalism relied on 'heroic measures' of political force and violence. The export of accumulated capital and the demand for customers in non-capitalist lands led to the ruin of indigenous production, stripping them bare and subjecting them to oppression. But as the non-capitalist world becomes smaller and smaller, the competitive battle between groups of capital leads to 'world economic crises, wars and revolutions'. Through this process, capitalism paves the way for its own downfall, whether through the fact that it cannot continue its imperialist drive beyond the point where the world consists only of capitalists and wage workers and thus accumulation will no longer be possible. At the same time, it sharpens class contradictions to the point of rebellion by the international proletariat against the continued existence of capitalism.[22]

16 Luxemburg 2016, pp. 21–41.
17 Luxemburg 2016, pp. 119–52.
18 Luxemburg 2014, pp. 461–84.
19 Luxemburg 2016, p. 11.
20 Luxemburg 2016, p. 355.
21 Luxemburg 2016, p. 357.
22 Luxemburg 2016, p. 361.

David Harvey further develops this argument. An examination of capital flows reveals to him six potential barriers to accumulation that produce a prolonged crisis:

> i.) insufficient initial capital ii.) scarcity or political difficulties with the labour supply, iii.) inadequate means of production – the so-called natural limits. iv.) inappropriate technologies and organizational forms versus resistance or inefficiencies in the labour process and vi.) a lack of demand backed by money to pay the market.[23]

So far, capitalism has survived many predictions of its imminent demise.[24] According to Harvey, financial crises serve to rationalise the irrationalities of capitalism – reconfigurations and new models of development. There is no evidence that this crisis political project of free market neoliberalism will fall on its own. How to get out of the crisis depends on the balance of class forces.[25]

Inspired by Rosa Luxemburg, David Harvey argues that since the crisis of 1973–1982, capitalism has been confronted with a serious underlying demand problem: how to absorb ever-increasing amounts of surplus capital in the production of goods and services.[26] We have 'a world awash in surplus liquidity', with less and less surplus capital being absorbed into production and global profit margins falling. Growth faces severe environmental, market, profitability, and spatial constraints.[27] Over the last 30 years, capital has only managed to escape the crisis through wage stagnation, 'going global' (neoliberal globalisation, particularly through the integration of Southern women into the world economy[28]), and through privatisation and financial deregulation.[29] Since then, neoliberal policies have been designed to recover profit margins; these have included wage containment (illustrated in the growing wealth

---

23 Harvey 2011, p. 47. This development is questioned by Marxist economist Michael Roberts (2018) in a recent debate with David Harvey. While Harvey argues that Marx did not strictly have a 'labour theory of value', but goes far beyond Ricardo's, since according to Marx value is only realised in the market, Roberts argues that Marx had a labour theory of value, but that, unlike Ricardo, this was based on abstract work, and not on concrete work – for which Roberts claims to have empirical evidence. Based on this perspective, Roberts (2012) grounded his crisis theory exclusively on Marx's law of the tendency of the rate of profit to fall, while Harvey brings in other factors.

24 Harvey 2011, p. 47.

25 Harvey 2011, pp. 10–12.

26 Harvey 2011, pp. 15–30.

27 Harvey 2011, pp. 28–30.

28 Harvey 2011, pp. 15–16.

29 Harvey 2011, pp. 24–8.

inequalities since that time) through attacks on trade unions and labour flexibilisation, as well as the influx of cheap labour through the immigration of second-class workers/citizens and the globalisation of trade, on the one hand, and attacks on indirect wages through the dismantling of the welfare state and the collapse of state investment, on the other hand. The lower purchasing power and lack of public investment were compensated through financial deregulation and a huge inflation of private investments based on high-risk credit. These policies gained pace with the collapse of the Soviet Bloc, the main geopolitical and ideological enemy of the capitalist West, leading to neoliberal hegemony and the weakening of the labour movement. In doing so, it also eliminated the power relationship that supported the social compromise and Keynesian policies of the welfare state.

Neoliberal financialisation was thus born from capitalist needs. It was this financialisation and the increase in leverage of financial institutions that ended up causing problems for banks in the 2008 crisis.[30] Financialisation reached its limits in the crisis. It revealed the unsustainability of these policies, since the ever-growing system of financial credit – fictitious capital that has fewer and fewer connections with the 'real' material economy – could not expand infinitely.

Although Marxists recognise some of the Keynesian critiques of neoliberalism, they also understand the neoliberal critiques of Keynes in the capitalist context. This duality is overcome by historically grounding validity and criticism in their particular position through a class analysis of the capitalist system. Although the Marxist perspective takes into account the neoliberal and Keynesian perspectives, it rejects the depoliticised character of both; it historicises them and instead sees the economic crisis with a political alternative, basing the legitimacy of the anti-capitalist perspective on the interests of the working class. The solution to the crisis, and in particular its material social effects on workers, is thus present in the anti-capitalist struggle and in overcoming the capitalist production process, in order to create an economic system in which the drivers of the economy are the interests of workers.

1.1 Democracy in Times of Austerity

The first government response to the crisis was expansionist, based on the Keynesian perspective of the crisis. The Portuguese government of José

30 Harvey 2011.

Sócrates translated the EC's call for massive public investments into public guarantees for banks, the nationalisation of the bankrupt BPN bank, and countercyclical measures to combat unemployment.[31] However, the countercyclical response was short-lived, and the neoliberal or neoclassical perspective returned as the dominant framework for policymakers and technocrats to frame the crisis. When the economic crisis turned into a debt crisis, Europe's national governments, under pressure from the European Commission, returned to pre-crisis neoliberal policies with redoubled force. Austerity has become the main political concept in Europe.

In Portugal, the austerity phase began in March 2010 with the introduction of the subsequent PEC (Stability and Growth Pacts). Given its minority position in parliament and the explosion of social protests in the streets, the PS minority government was unable to implement increasingly stringent budgetary measures. The government fell in March. Eventually it would be the new right-wing PSD-CDS government led by Passos Coelho, in consensus with the PS, that would implement structural economic reforms in exchange for loans to guarantee financial stability.[32]

During the global financial crisis and the subsequent eurozone crisis, many proclaimed the bankruptcy of neoliberalism itself as an economic theory and ideology. The global financial crisis showed that financial deregulation brought capitalism to the brink of collapse, that low wages caused a lack of demand, and that private banks and companies could only avoid bankruptcy through state interventionism and public investment. The proclamations applied to the European Monetary Union, which was based on the neoliberal principles of fiscal balance, debt control, and wage depression.[33]

But instead of the collapse of neoliberalism, we had austerity. After the collapse of the financial system, the shadow banking system regrouped: it resisted criticism and eluded all attempts to impose new regulations. It proved capable of imposing its power and hegemony through the implementation of austerity in Europe.[34] What is austerity? For the right, the argument is simple: austerity means you can't spend more than you earn; a principle of sound finance. We must tighten our belts and settle, or at least control, public debts as quickly as possible.[35] Austerity represents a principle of good finan-

31 Costa and Caldas 2014, pp. 89, 92.
32 Costa and Caldas 2014.
33 Seymour 2014.
34 Louçã and Ash 2017, p. 28.
35 Seymour 2014.

cial practice and public policy that follows the basic argument of the infamous paper by Reinhart and Rogoff that would guide EU policies in the following years.[36]

While austerity policies are legitimised as a form of spending cuts that would help the economy, in economic and political reality they have the opposite effect. There is widespread consensus among economists that austerity measures are pro-cyclical policies and actually deepen the economic recession.[37] Austerity creates a negative spiral in periods of economic recession: lower public investment and lower wages create lower consumer demand, which creates lower private investment. Why, then, did policymakers choose austerity over expansionist policies, and what is the relationship between neoliberalism and austerity? Richard Seymour argues that austerity is not just a continuation of neoliberal policies of permanent austerity: it is a new phase of neoliberalism in the form of its own exception.[38] The neoliberal content of austerity measures is far from new, but through austerity it returns radically in the crisis.[39]

From the onset, austerity measures and structural reforms met with great social resistance. There are different arguments to explain why austerity is considered incompatible with democracy: austerity excludes political alternatives, policies are imposed from outside, austerity is criticised as unconstitutional, it attacks social rights that are the basis of social democracy and the democratic consensus of the post-war welfare state, and huge crowds protest austerity in the streets, claiming that they are the people and want 'Real Democracy Now!'.

The implementation of austerity measures was not, however, accompanied by a discursive abandonment of the idea of democracy by political decision makers. Perhaps the only exception was the former leader of the PSD in the opposition, Manuela Ferreira Leite, who at the beginning of the global financial crisis, in November 2008, wondered if 'it wouldn't be a good idea to have six months of suspension of democracy in Portugal'.[40] Throughout the crisis period, policymakers generally claimed democratic legitimacy for these measures and defended them against criticism. Political decision-makers thus articulated discourses on democracy and austerity.

---

36 Reinhart and Rogoff 2010.

37 Krugman 2015; Stiglitz 2014.

38 Seymour 2014.

39 Ferreira 2012, p. 69.

40 Lusa 2008. Our translation. In the original: '*não sei se a certa altura não seria bom haver seis meses sem democracia*'.

2 Elements of Austerity–Hegemony

In social theory, it is common to address problems of legitimation, dominant ideas, consensus, discourses, and ideology in terms of hegemony. Hegemony occurs when one social class exercises power over another social class beyond coercion or law, through cultural consent and recognition of leadership. The term was first used by Plekhanov in 1905 but became particularly well-known in political theory due to the works of Italian communist leader Antonio Gramsci.[41] According to Peter Thomas, hegemony was originally a theory 'forged to theorise and guide the proletariat's alliance with other subaltern classes',[42] a class alliance of the proletariat with other exploited groups, especially the peasantry, in a common struggle against the oppression of capital.[43] Only from 1922 onwards did hegemony appear as 'the domination of the bourgeoisie over the proletariat', in which the bourgeoisie confined 'the latter to a corporate role, by inducing it to accept a division between political and economic struggles in its class practice'.[44]

Gramsci valued civil society, and his first model of hegemony even excluded the state when considering the foundations of bourgeois power; his second model corrected this unilaterality, by proposing the simple preponderance of the state. Bourgeois hegemony was now seen as being 'co-present in civil society and the state alike'.[45] Ideology is thus shared between civil society and the state, while violence belongs only to the state.[46]

One of the basic elements of hegemony, according to Gramsci, is common sense – common sense in contrast to the 'good sense' of philosophy.[47] Philosophy is the critique and overcoming of religion and common sense. Common sense is a historical product and consists of the ideas of everyday life. Common sense ideas – their language, associations, and arguments – offer an entire inter-

---

41 Laclau and Mouffe 2001, p. XII; McLean and McMillan 2003.

42 Thomas 2009, p. 60.

43 Anderson 1976, p. 19.

44 Thomas 2009, p. 57.

45 Thomas 2009, p. 66.

46 Anderson 1976, p. 32.

47 Gramsci 2011, p. 173. According to Trotsky (1986, pp. 24–5), common sense is the 'lowest form of the intellect is not only necessary under all conditions but under certain conditions is also adequate. Common sense's basic capital consists of the elementary conclusions of universal experience: not to put one's fingers in fire, whenever possible to proceed along a straight line, not to tease vicious dogs … and so forth and so on. Under a stable social milieu common sense is adequate for bargaining, healing, writing articles, leading Trade Unions, voting in parliament, marrying and reproducing the race'.

pretative repertoire that builds, regulates, and controls the available knowledge about what surrounds us, delimiting the terms of public debate and preventing us from thinking beyond these same ideas.[48]

Gramcsi writes:

> Every social stratum has its own 'common sense' which is ultimately the most widespread conception of life and morals. Every philosophical current leaves a sedimentation of 'common sense': this is the document of its historical reality. Common sense is not something rigid and static; rather, it changes continuously, enriched by scientific notions and philosophical opinions which have entered common usage. 'Common sense' is the folklore of 'philosophy' and stands midway between real 'folklore' (that is, as it is understood) and the philosophy, the science, the economics of the scholars. 'Common sense' creates the folklore of the future, that is a more or less rigidified phase of a certain time and place.[49]

According to Boaventura de Sousa Santos, modern science seems built against common sense, which it considers superficial and illusory.[50] Since common sense means the obvious and obviously useful knowledge versus the incomprehensible and prodigious knowledge of science, and science thrives 'on the prejudice of pretending to be unprejudiced', they appear in opposition to one another. However, they imply each other and are part of the same cultural constellation of capitalist modernity:

> Common sense is practical and pragmatic. It reproduces knowledge drawn from the life trajectories and experiences of a given social group and asserts that this link to group experience renders it reliable and reassuring. Common sense is self-evident and transparent. It mistrusts the opacity of technological objectives and the esoteric nature of knowledge, arguing the principle of equal access to discourse, to cognitive and linguistic competence. Common sense is superficial, because it disdains structures that cannot be consciously apprehended, but for the same reason it is expert at capturing the horizontal complexity of conscious relations both among people and between people and things. Common sense knowledge is non-disciplinary and non-methodical. It is not the product of a practice expressly devised to create it; it reproduces itself spontaneously in the daily happenings of life. Common sense accepts what exists as is. It favours

48 Soeiro et al. 2013, pp. 5–10.
49 Gramsci 2011, p. 173.
50 Santos 1995c, p. 46.

> actions that do not provoke significant ruptures in reality. Finally, common sense is rhetorical and metaphorical; it does not teach, it persuades.[51]

'Common sense' ideas have been widely used to legitimise austerity measures: 'the country/we live beyond our means', 'debts must be paid', 'the welfare state is unsustainable', 'we all have to contribute' – all or a combination of some of these 'common sense' examples. Although common sense may be an expression of the bad faith of some individuals or groups, it is not when the contrast between common sense and good sense manifests itself in large parts of the population. It is the expression of deeper contrasts in the historical-social order.[52]

As a consequence of the 2008 crisis, for some time it appeared that there would be an imminent intellectual defeat of neoliberalism due to the exposure of its irrationality. But instead, the crisis brought austerity and an unlimited 'state of exception' that hollowed out democracy and created a new transfer of wealth from labour to capital, in the name of the 'common good'.[53] Impoverishment and austerity were presented as inevitable, this was repeated in political discourse, reproduced in everyday life, and reinforced by the media. 'Common sense' is the most powerful engine for manufacturing consent. Its effectiveness is based on the simplicity and moral weight of its formulations. Even if citizens do not explicitly support it, it generates resignation.[54] The contradictions of common sense can be exposed by confronting it with reality and trusting in the 'good sense' of citizens. This good sense explains the outbreaks of social mobilisation and resistance against domination. According to Soeiro et al., the rupture with common sense is the first step towards the construction of another emancipatory common sense.[55] Santos defines this emancipatory common sense as 'a discriminating common sense constructed to be appropriated in a privileged way by oppressed, marginalized or excluded social groups, and effectively strengthened by their emancipatory practice'.[56]

To analyse democratic austerity discourses, we will define and develop some of the basic aspects that support this contemporary common sense. In the first part we return to neoliberalism as an ideology and develop it further. We also focus on two aspects that are linked to the functioning of neoliberal hege-

51 Santos 1995c, p. 47.
52 Gramsci 1978, pp. 13–14.
53 Soeiro et al. 2013, pp. 5–10.
54 Ibid.
55 Soeiro et al. 2013, p. 11.
56 Santos 1995c, p. 48.

mony: depoliticisation and culturalisation. The second part of this section will analyse what we consider to be the three dimensions on which this austerity democracy is based: substantive legitimacy, formal legitimacy, and the idea of exception. These elements sometimes appear synchronised, sometimes in apparent opposition to each other, but they all play a crucial role in maintaining hegemony.

2.1 Neoliberalism

Common sense has been synonymous with neoliberalism for some time. Developed by political and economic elites to overcome the crisis of the 1970s, the neoliberal discourse has been the hegemonic legitimising discourse in recent decades.[57] As we saw in the introduction, neoliberalism is a reaction against the Keynesian economics of the welfare state and finds its theoretical basis in the Chicago School of political economy, with authors such as Von Hayek, Friedman and others.[58]

A large amount of literature has been written to analyse, describe and criticise neoliberalism. Important authors include David Harvey, Slavoj Žižek, Chantal Mouffe, Eric Swyngedouw, and Wendy Brown. In his *A Brief History of Neoliberalism*, David Harvey describes:

> neoliberalism [is] in first instance a theory of political economic practices that proposes that human wellbeing can best be advanced by liberating individual entrepreneurial freedoms and skills within an institutional framework characterized by strong private property rights, free markets and free trade.[59]

In common usage, neoliberalism is equated with a radically free market. But more than that, it is a successful class political project that coalesced in the crisis of the 1970s to restore the conditions for capital accumulation and the power of economic elites. Almost all states have adopted – sometimes voluntarily, sometimes through external coercion – some version of neoliberalism and have implemented practices of deregulation, privatisation, and withdrawal of the state from many areas of its social functions.[60]

Neoliberalism includes maximising competition and free trade achieved through economic deregulation, the elimination of tariffs, and a series of

57 Mylonas 2012, p. 648.
58 Brown 2003.
59 Harvey 2007, pp. 2–3.
60 Harvey 2007, pp. 13–19; 2011, p. 10.

business-friendly monetary and social policies linked to the vicissitudes of globalisation or the policies of the International Monetary Fund and the World Bank.[61] This:

> is a discourse which is backed by the strength of all the economic and social forces (the banks, the multinational companies, politicians, and so on) who are trying to make flexibility – the new global capitalism – even more of a reality than it already is. Neoliberal discourse contributes its own particular, symbolic, form of strength to the strength of these social forces.[62]

According to Brown, neoliberalism is more than a set of free-market economic policies that dismantle welfare states and privatise public services in the North, destroying efforts towards democratic sovereignty or economic self-determination in the South. It is not just an ideology that arises from or masks an economic reality, but is a specific form of expressly amoral normative political reason that organises the political sphere, governance practices, and citizenship, a political rationality that governs the criteria of the sayable, the intelligible, and the truth:

> Neoliberalism casts the political and social spheres both as appropriately dominated by market concerns and as themselves organized by market rationality. That is, more than simply facilitating the economy, the state itself must construct and construe itself in market terms, as well as develop policies and promulgate a political culture that figures citizens exhaustively as rational economic actors in every sphere of life.[63]

According to Marion Fourcade-Gourinchas and Sarah Babb (2002), critics of neoliberalism have understood the neoliberal transformation as a manifestation of capital's increasing control over labour or the imposition, by international agencies and financial institutions, of disciplinary policies (e.g. conditional loans, retaliatory measures) that ultimately serve the interests of the world's hegemonic power, the United States.[64] One of the main drivers of this has been the process of globalisation and trade liberalisation steered by the World Bank and the IMF. The drive for trade liberalisation should improve a

61 Brown 2003.
62 Fairclough 1999, p. 72.
63 Brown 2006a, p. 694.
64 Fourcade-Gourinchas and Babb, 2002.

country's income, according to the Ricardian scheme of comparative advantages: 'by forcing resources to move from less productive uses to more productive uses'.[65]

Its advocates have argued that neoliberal measures simply 'work' better than statist ones; neoliberalism moved the analytical focus away from economic debates towards the normalisation in the teaching of business schools and in the training and practices of the business community of 'experts' with 'technical knowledge': executives, managers, analysts, traders, market experts, etc.[66] The neoliberal discourse legitimises phenomena through 'macroeconomic and neoliberal language, giving rise to a dehumanizing narrative that reduced human history to its economic constituents at the expense of any social or political traits'. It affects the way citizens see themselves, as well as the opportunities available for social and political change: 'the belief in the absence of political alternatives would lead citizens to shy away from an angry response to the current crisis'.[67]

2.2 Depolitisation

In the context of the rise of neoliberalism, different theorists have focused on the concept of the political and depoliticisation, as central to a critique of capitalist discourse and specifically neoliberal discourse. We have already discussed the Schmittean model of the political, of which Chantal Mouffe's approach is probably the best-known contemporary example. Another model is undoubtedly that of Rancière. This author criticises the agonistic schema of the political, particularly the notion of antagonism where the 'content' is irrelevant. He argues that politics has its own universal measure, namely: equality.[68] Rancière starts from a very Aristotelian political approach, starting from a human as a political animal who had an interest in co-governing his polis:[69] According to Rancière, politics begins with:

> the emergence of an active agent without a place in the social edifice, demanding to be included in the public sphere, to be heard on equal footing by the ruling oligarchy: being recognized as a partner in political dialogue. But against Habermas, political struggle is not a rational debate between multiple interests but …

65 Stiglitz 2002, p. 59.
66 Louçã and As, 2017, pp. 187–8; Springer, Birch and MacLeavy 2016, p. 324.
67 Temple, Grasso, Buraczynska, Karampampas and English 2016, p. 570.
68 Rancière 2011, p. 4.
69 Aristotle 1998, p. 1253.

> the struggle for one's voice to be heard and recognized as the voice of an equal partner.[70]

Swyngedouw elaborates: 'This is not just a question of mutual incomprehension that can be managed through a Habermasian communicative act, but rather an expression of a "*mésentente*" (the original title of Rancière's book on politics, problematically translated as 'Disagreement'), a misunderstanding that is "constitutive"'.[71] This event-based approach to the political is also found in Badiou, according to whom the political emerges through the process of political subjectivation: through the appearance of those who disturb the state of the situation in the name of 'equality', 'the people', the 'common' and 'the democratic'.[72]

The concept of the political is contrasted with the conceptualisation of politics – or police. Politics, or policymaking (*la politique* in French) refers to public management: the power games between political actors, the everyday choreography of negotiation, formulation and implementation of rules, tactics, institutions, and technologies of government that give society some form of temporal coherence. Police, or policying, refers in Rancière's work to the hard and soft technologies of administration, all activities that create order.[73] The political, on the other hand, refers to the agonistic struggle over fundamental questions surrounding the environments we inhabit, how to produce them. There is a tendency for the former to suture and, ultimately, foreclose the latter.[74]

Swyngedouw defines the concept of depoliticisation based on Chantal Mouffe's and Slavoj Žižek's approach to the political.[75] Depoliticisation or the post-political is used here as a container concept, which according to Swyngedouw means 'a reduction of the political, it evacuates, if not forecloses, the properly political and becomes part and parcel of the consolidation of a post-political and post-democratic polity'.[76]

Depoliticisation takes the form of the increasing dominance of a series of interrelated forms of management and governance techniques designed to maintain and nurture the uninterrupted accumulation of economic wealth.

---

70 Žižek 2004, pp. 69–70.
71 Swyngedouw 2014, p. 126.
72 Swyngedouw 2014, p. 124.
73 Swyngedouw 2009, p. 128.
74 Swyngedouw 2014.
75 Mouffe 2005; Swyngedouw 2009, 2014; Žižek's 2000.
76 Swyngedouw 2009, p. 602.

Politics is 'reduced to the administration and management of processes whose parameters are defined by consensual socio-scientific knowledge'.[77] Depoliticisation is characterised by Swyngedouw as the externalisation of problems that are integral/inherent to the relations of global neoliberal capitalism. Or as Žižek says: 'In post-politics, the conflict of global ideological visions embodied in different parties competing for power is replaced by the collaboration of enlightened technocrats, economists, public opinion experts'.[78] According to Norman Fairclough:

> It is part of a widely observed narrowing down of the political spectrum – parties are becoming increasingly similar in their policies, and the differences between them are increasingly differences of style … the predominance of a single economic-political discourse across the political spectrum.[79]

This depoliticisation is consistent with the ideas of New Public Management that the majority of right-wing and social democratic policymakers have adhered to in recent decades. Managers are seen as the ideal political decision-makers, while 'politicians' – and above all, the demands of democracy – are disposable as 'fat … that has to be cut from an overweight State'.[80] Swyngedouw summarises the elements that characterise a post-political conception of post-democracy: 1) The externalisation of problems that are integral/inherent to the relations of global neoliberal capitalism, while the side effects are portrayed as a total threat; 2) Populist policies that elevate the interest of an imaginary 'people' to a universal level and, therefore, close the 'opening of spaces that allow the universalization of the demands of particular groups or classes'; 3) the 'enemy' or target of concern is continually externalised and disembodied, always vague, ambiguous, unnameable and uncountable, and ultimately empty; 4) the target of concern can be managed through a consensual dialogic policy and, consequently, demands become depoliticised and politics naturalised.[81]

While this rhetoric might have been expected to come under pressure in the aftermath of the financial crisis, the market-oriented neoliberal discourse

77 Ibid.
78 Žižek 2000, p. 198.
79 Fairclough 1999, p. 78.
80 Pureza 2015b, p. 91. Our translation. In the original: '[…] *"os políticos" – e sobretudo, as exigências da democracia – são descartáveis como "gorduras"'*.
81 Swyngedouw 2009, p. 613.

has not weakened.[82] One of the first elements of this depoliticising discourse on the nature of the crisis was the characterisation of the eurozone crisis as a debt crisis.[83] As such, the crisis appeared as the consequence of poor public governance, while the capitalist crisis, the role of financial markets, the role of monetary choices, and inequalities were fundamentally ignored.[84] It transferred capitalism's structural responsibility for socioeconomic failures to the State, to the 'excessive consumption' of citizens and the government.

2.3 Culturalisation

One of the aspects of this depoliticising discourse is the culturalisation of politics.[85] Brown and Mamdani define 'culturalization of politics' as a discursive process that reduces all culture to 'a tangible essence that defines it and explains politics as a consequence of that essence'.[86] This process 'analytically vanquishes political economy, states, history, and international and transnational relations. It eliminates colonialism, capital, caste or class stratification, and external political domination from reports of political conflict or instability'.[87] At the same time, it strips liberal democratic institutions of any association with culture, ignoring that liberalism is culture: the culture of the dominant classes at the centre of the world system.[88] The solution presented for the wrong political-economic 'culture' that led to the state of exception is to literally liberalise it, through privatisation, individualisation, transparency and political reform. It is in this context that we must think about concepts such as 'a new political culture', a new work ethic, flexibilisation of labour, anti-corruption, making the state more efficient, etc.

For centuries, northern Europeans described the Mediterranean people as a lazy culture. Some place it in the second modernity, the moment when the core of the world system and its ideological centre moved from the Iberian Peninsula to Northwest Europe,[89] others point to the importance of the Napoleonic wars as a crucial moment in the constitution of the Mediterranean image.[90] In

---

82 O'Rourke and Hogan 2012, p. 4.
83 Mylonas, 2012.
84 O'Rourke & Hogan, 2012.
85 These paragraphs are based on an article I published in *Patterns of Prejudice*. Cf. Van Vossole (2016a).
86 Brown 2006b; Mamdani 2004, p. 17.
87 Brown 2006b, p. 20.
88 Brown 2006b.
89 Santos 2012.
90 Herzfeld 1984.

line with the racist ideology of the nineteenth century, western Europeans were ranked on the hierarchical scale as ascending from the dark-skinned and passionate southern Europeans towards the light-skinned and reasonable northern Europeans.[91] This racist ideology sought to present European culture as of 'pure' origin and, above all, free from oriental influences.[92]

The identity of the 'Mediterranean' was constructed in contrast to the 'European'. The culturalisation of the Mediterranean, or Mediterraneanisation, has been characterised by a typical exoticism. For centuries, millions of northern Europeans have associated the word Mediterranean with the eternal dream of a perfect vacation, poetry, visual arts, and music. Its people are what northerners are not: talkative, emotional, civilised, passionate, tanned. Today, 'Mediterranean' has become more of a folk concept based on tourism and a general interest in roots and tradition. Mass tourism, a consumer activity practiced mainly by citizens of the global North, has commodified this interest in 'exotic' cultural diversity, being reified into a known consumable object, as if the Mediterranean world were a theme park.[93]

This racist imaginary has historically been strengthened by mutual migratory relations between the periphery and the centre. The enormous wave of emigration of the 1960s – due to repressive political regimes, poverty, and lack of prospects for economic development – has been repeated recently. In 'highly developed' receiving countries, these people have often been confronted with racism and treated as second-class citizens – to the point that 'blacks' from the former colonies of the Netherlands, for example, even tend to consider them as black, basing this designation on common experiences of colonial and Mediterranean immigrants.[94]

This Mediterraneanisation was not restricted to popular discourses, it also colonised the social sciences, especially anthropology. Before the popularisation of the PIGS concept by the *Financial Times* during the recent crisis, the 'exotic' concept of 'Club Med' and the concept of PIGS already existed in economic discourses during the 1980s and 1990s.[95] At the same time, the tradition of comparative political science, the mainstream of political science, tended to categorise southern Europe as a non-democratic part of Europe – with Spain, Portugal, and Greece experiencing military and fascist dictatorships until the 1970s – a categorisation based on cultural values and economic underdevelopment.

91 Goldberg 1993.
92 Van Vossole 2016a.
93 Frykman 1999.
94 Essed 1991.
95 Lopreite 2011.

During the economic boom years of the 1990s and early millennium, the racist imagery remained hidden beneath the surface. The flood of structural funds, the fall in interest rates after the implementation of the euro, and the higher growth rates in the European Union have deflated the existing xenophobic picture on the European periphery. For a decade, Ireland and Spain were symbols of neoliberal success.

After the great recession, the peripheral countries of the eurozone were placed in the position of scapegoats for the economic crisis and the near collapse of the eurozone. A cultural narrative resurfaced that placed the origin of the crisis in Athens and the rest of the periphery.[96] This was intended to explain the current situation as the result of corrupt local politicians, irresponsible behaviour of citizens and consumers, state inefficiency, low productivity combined with high and uncompetitive wages, misuse of EU structural funds, etc.

Such 'cultural' explanations – which can be found both in central countries and, to a certain extent, in peripheral countries – reproduce the old dogma of 'blaming the victim'. In line with our theoretical model, it is not the structural problems of the eurozone and the global financial and economic system that are seen as the source of the problem, but rather its victims, the populations of the indebted economies themselves. If not because of certain 'cultural characteristics and habits', such as alleged laziness,[97] non-productivity ('with easy jobs and retirement at 42'[98]), corruption, wasteful spending, inefficiency and lying,[99] a supposed 'Mediterranean mix of indiscipline, extravagance and outright corruption',[100] it is because they are irresponsible and ignorant for choosing the wrong political representatives.[101]

This rhetoric has a clear underlying political interest: to reinforce the arguments in favour of the imposed social cuts. The euro crisis forced central countries to 'help' the periphery. Two things must be said about this aid: first, that the EU proved incapable and unwilling to deal with the crisis as such. Only when the crisis proved to transcend the particular case of Greece – and banks in core countries could be in danger – was a 'solution' found to contain it.[102] The bailouts can never be seen as a gift; they were not designed to guarantee the

96 Bohle 2010; Lapavitsas 2010; Mylonas 2012.
97 Bohle 2010.
98 Ibid.
99 De Grauwe 2010; Lapavitsas 2010.
100 Bohle 2010.
101 Hadjimichalis 2011.
102 Ibid.

ability to pay civil servants' salaries and social expenses. They were designed temporarily to bail out countries with solvency problems in order to guarantee the solvency of debt held by German and French banks.[103] The 'aid' allowed Germany and France to design an indirect bailout mechanism.

The financial 'aid' was portrayed and widely understood as a transfer of working-class taxpayers from core countries to corrupt peripheral states and their 'lazy and lying' populations. In reality, it was a transfer mainly from working class taxpayers in these core countries, in the form of state guarantees, especially to the banks in these countries. By bailing out the peripheral states, it forced German and French workers to bail out their own banks – not directly, as in the 2008–2009 bank bailouts, but through the mediation of Greece and the other PIGS.[104] Austerity was thus legitimised through a type of collective cultural guilt. Right-wing politicians from peripheral eurozone countries reproduced this picture in their electoral campaigns during the crisis: 'The Troika intervention was *our* fault'; '*We* were living beyond our means'.[105]

The forms of legitimation mentioned above are not necessarily linked to the democratic legitimation of capitalism. Forms of neoliberalism, depoliticisation, and culturalisation of politics occur in authoritarian regimes and dictatorships. The first implementations of neoliberalism were in fact introduced in authoritarian regimes in the neocolonial world, such as the experiences of the Chicago boys in Chile after Augusto Pinochet's military coup in 1973.[106] Only later, with Margaret Thatcher's conservative victory in the United Kingdom in 1979, did the neoliberal revolution reach democratic states. In the next paragraphs we will analyse the traditional methods of democratic legitimation. The first two are also traditionally considered as two different 'dimensions' of democratic legitimation: formal, procedural, or input methods of democratic legitimacy and substantive or output methods of democratic legitimacy.

2.4 Formal Democracy

The formal perspective has been dominant in neoliberal discourse on democracy. The theoretical background of formalist rhetoric is based on Joseph Schumpeter's minimalist model of democracy. Unsatisfied with the classical republican model of democracy based on Rousseau's 'general will', Schumpeter

103 Lapavitsas 2010.
104 Douzinas and Papaconstantinou 2011.
105 Van Vossole 2016a.
106 Fourcade-Gourinchas and Babb 2002, pp. 545–49.

tried to constitute an 'applicable model of democracy'.[107] He did this by reducing democracy to the method of electoral competition. Instead of an end in itself, democracy becomes merely a method for legitimising policies. Policies are legitimised through a form of market mechanism: as an aggregate of consumers, citizens decide through a competition of votes between different political players. The role of the people is to 'produce a government', acceptance of leadership is the true function of voting. According to Schumpeter, such an approach leaves room for the vital role of leadership; it theoretically allows group volitions to be formed and represented by leaders competing for votes; votes are an electoral incentive for good governance.

In his more recent defence of this approach, Przeworski defines democracy as 'a system in which parties lose elections'.[108] The minimalist approach presupposes regime and policy change and conflict between interests without violence and bloodshed. The mere prospect of a change of government results in a peaceful nature in the regulation of conflicts. It is therefore implicit in the formal view of democracy that elected representatives regularly face re-election or removal at the end of their term, and that fear of removal will motivate representatives to act responsibly and to respond to the wishes of the public.[109] Voting also legitimises coercion; it constitutes the 'flexing of muscles', as the majority represents a power relationship and coincides with the physical strength of citizens. The electoral process generates information about this power relationship.[110]

Formal democratic discourse therefore legitimises policies purely on the basis that those who carry them out have been democratically elected and are supported by a parliamentary majority. It limits democracy to voting procedures, the rule of law, freedom of speech, etc., thus restricting democracy to the electoral act by which citizens every four or five years have the right to choose their representatives from among recognised political parties. This perspective neglects the democratic substance of government activity between elections.[111]

The elected representatives then have the right to conduct 'responsible' policies that respect the rules of pre-determined international treaties, with their area of power increasingly limited by the primacy of the market in ever lar-

107 Schumpeter 1976.
108 Przeworski 1991, p. 10.
109 Jacobs and Shapiro 1994, pp. 10–11.
110 Przeworski 1999, p. 39.
111 Jacobs and Shapiro 1994, pp. 10–11.

ger areas of social life. In the case of European countries governed by the Troika, these limitations were taken to the limit, through the limitation of political sovereignty by globalisation, the agreements with the Troika, and the power of financial markets due to their influence on the finances and debt of states. The elections legitimised these executive policies until the end of the legislature. Substantial resistance against these policies that goes beyond symbolic protest and attempts to influence policy is therefore accused of failing to respect democracy.

2.5 Substantive Legitimation

The substantive view of democracy criticises the narrowness of the minimalist perspective. Macpherson defines the substantive view of democracy as 'a quality pervading the whole life and operation of a national or smaller community, or if you like a kind of society, a whole set of reciprocal relations between the people who make up the nation or other unit'.[112] For Box, Marshall, Reed and Reed:

> substantive democracy may be summarized as a setting in which people may, if they choose, take part in governing themselves with a minimum of interference or resistance (for example, from economic or other elites, or administrative 'experts'), and without being required to assume in advance a uniform or universal set of constraints.[113]

The classic approach to substantive democracy is republican, based on the participation of citizens in the administration of their community and the construction of common interests. Adams, Bowerman, Dolbeare and Stivers argue that the separation of the procedural and the substantive leaves unanswered questions about 'outcomes, people's living conditions, and the realization of the political potential of all people that have made democracy a politically explosive concept in the past'.[114] Box et al. consider this republican form of substantive democratic discourse as intrinsically opposed to neoliberal policies – or New Public Management – because it attempts to collapse the sphere of republican participation in government. Through neoliberal discourse, we are relegated to representing the democratic pole within a tension between

---

112 Macpherson 1977, pp. 5–6.

113 Box, Marshall, Reed and Reed 2002, p. 611.

114 Adams, Bowerman, Dolbeare and Stivers 1990, p. 220.

bureaucracy and democracy. Neoliberal discourse appeals to the general public and those in government whose job it is to make government 'run better' and 'cost less'.

Jakobs and Shapiro's approach to substantive democracy, on the other hand, is empirical. Substantive democracy is based on public opinion polls. Policies are substantively democratically legitimate when they reflect public opinion. Substantive democracy refers to the extent to which public opinion is reflected in decision-making between elections. Within this approach, there are two dimensions of substantive legitimacy, depending on whether the change in public opinion occurs after (leadership) or before (responsiveness) a change in policy. Substantive democratic legitimacy can therefore be achieved by policies that reflect public opinion or by public opinion that reflects policymakers who mobilise the public in support of their policies through superior skills and knowledge.[115]

The empirical approach is the only one of the two that allows for some kind of substantive democratic articulation with austerity. In the neoliberal era, with a balance of powers strongly in favour of capital, the substantive legitimisation of the system could be partially provided by higher growth rates resulting from globalisation and market liberalisation.[116] According to neoliberal economic thinking, austerity ultimately provides the basis for growth and individual wealth. The basic idea is: 'while politics shrinks, the economy grows'.[117] People are offered a piece of capitalism, and everyone is approached as a shareholder or rentier, so that even as rates of exploitation increase and social benefits are reduced, they can get a share of the profits it creates.[118] Typically, this specific substantive legitimacy is projected into the future.

The policies of the Memorandum brutally affected areas considered substantive elements of democracy, such as the welfare state. Furthermore, the Troika included a reduction of the state and its budget, a reduction of voters' sovereignty through foreign and European control over policies, and privatisation of important public services. External supervision by the Troika, tighter control by the European Commission over national budgets and increasing dependence on the ECB for financing led to a decrease in the room for manoeuvre for national political actors and a substantial legitimisation of their decisions. The consequence is not only that democratic institutions themselves are de-substantiated; what is perceived as democracy can lose its legitimacy.

115 Jacobs and Shapiro 1994.
116 Paterson 2010.
117 Bello 2006, p. 16.
118 Graeber 2012, p. 376.

2.6 Exception as a Rule

A third way to legitimise austerity within a democratic discourse is to portray the situation as a temporal exception to the rule, in order to protect the democratic rule. As we have argued previously, the crisis is used as a political opening to impose exceptional measures that would be difficult to achieve in a context of normality. According to this democratic exceptionalism, a practice or situation is democratic as long as it is necessary to preserve or found a democratic state. These extraordinary policies 'can be prior to and below instituted politics, within it, and on its fringes'. This founding moment – linked to the concept of 'legitimacy' in the work of Weber and Schmitt – precedes a moment of 'institutionalized politics or normal law-making'.[119] It is a legitimisation that is, by definition, on the borders of democracy itself.

Schmitt famously stated that sovereignty was defined by those who decide on the state of exception.[120] The state of exception is the state in which normal constitutional politics finds itself in a situation of crisis, requiring sovereign intervention to restore the rule of law. It is based on the original Roman interpretation of dictatorship. The state of exception and sovereign powers are thus legitimised to restore the rule of law – in our example, democratic normality.[121]

This concept of exception has been a fundamental principle for the implementation of neoliberal policies. Since the 1980s, right-wing dictatorships in Latin America have been the first laboratories for neoliberal policies. These first experiences did not need to worry about the articulation between neoliberalism and democracy. In *The Shock Doctrine*, Naomi Klein explains how the triumph of global free market ideology was achieved at the expense of democracy, not through it. Economic and financial shocks were used to force Third World countries to implement the so-called Structural Adjustment Programs (SAPs) of the IMF and the World Bank. Social and economic disasters were the opportunity to implement SAPs that included privatisations, trade liberalisations, but also some form of liberal democracy, in order to access the necessary credit lines.[122]

But the discourse of exception would be essential in democratic regimes. The exception serves as a transcendental and legal basis for reconfiguring the power relationship between those elected (members of parliament, union rep-

119 Kalyvas 2008.
120 Schmitt 1986.
121 McCormick 1999.
122 Klein 2008.

resentatives) and those not elected (financial markets, international financial institutions).[123] Southern Europe's austerity measures were the latest adaptation of this exceptional neoliberal approach to democracy.

Austerity creates and deepens its own exceptional situation at the political level. In *Linhas vermelhas: crítica da crise-como-política* (Red Lines: Critique of Crisis-as-Politics), José Manuel Pureza states that the debt crisis in Portugal has turned into a politics of crisis. The devaluation of labour through cuts in wages, pensions and public services was legitimised 'through the invocation of a lasting state of exception called ... crisis'.[124] In their analysis of the conflict between the Constitutional Court and the Portuguese Government over austerity measures, Ferreira and Pureza show how exceptionalism is a legal and rhetorical use of the crisis as a political strategy for the liberal transformation of society and the economy. The Passos Coelho government called judges who obstructed measures deemed necessary for 'economic rationality' 'constitutional activists'. This naming opens the doors to extra or supra-constitutional values that guide austerity policies.[125]

2.6.1 There Is No Alternative

Since the beginning of the euro crisis, policymakers and opinion makers have used the speculative pressure of financial markets, European laws and procedures, the Troika, and neoclassical economic theories portrayed as economic 'laws' to create an exceptional situation that discredits all political alternatives to austerity. Accompanying austerity policies, austerity discourse emerges as a radical form of neoliberal discourse that 'eclipses the possible political alternatives and implies the denial of the primacy of the political'.[126] The austerity discourse thus delegitimises alternative perceptions of reality through permanent coercion and the internalisation that there are no alternatives.[127]

There is no alternative, or TINA for short, became iconic as a catchphrase of former British Prime Minister Margaret Thatcher, who used it to legitimise the sweeping economic reforms of the 1980s, which included the privatisation of public services, breaking the miners' strikes, and the failed introduction of the poll tax. Since the 1980s, TINA has become the symbolic cornerstone for

123 Ferreira 2012, p. 67.
124 Pureza 2015b, p. 96. Our translation. In the original: '*alicerçado na invocação de um estado de exceção duradouro chamado ... crise*'.
125 Ferreira and Pureza 2013, pp. 260, 271.
126 Borriello 2017, p. 242.
127 Ferreira 2012, pp. 44, 60–5.

legitimising the neoliberal doctrine that became hegemonic in the form of the Washington consensus in the 1990s.[128] During the euro crisis and the accompanying austerity, the symbolic catchphrase 'There is no alternative' entered the public debate as an unquestionable 'fact', used by policymakers to legitimise austerity measures.

Concrete examples of TINA discourse were very frequent in the public sphere during the crisis in Portugal. The media itself played an important role in imposing this consensus. Caldas and Almeida analysed the speeches of the Portuguese economic press during the crisis period. Recurring themes in the narratives of the crisis were guilt, inevitability and sacrifice: 'The State, first and foremost, but also families and companies – that is, 'we' – had spent beyond our means'; 'We spent beyond our means. We got into debt. Now, creditors are demanding savings and spending cuts. There is no point in accusing them. Resisting them. We need them. We have to obey'.[129]

On 14 October 2011, Marcelo Rebelo de Sousa, then a television commentator, former president of the PSD, and future president of the Republic, stated, 'In the situation we have reached, there is no alternative to control the deficit and public debt'.[130] A month later, the Minister of Parliamentary Affairs said he understands the frustration of the Portuguese people, but argued that 'there is no alternative' to the path the Government is following. Minister Relvas stated, 'Over the last few years we have spent what we had and what we didn't have, we have let unemployment soar, we have let the debt increase and the measures that are being taken are reformist measures that have one objective: to correct the course that has been followed over the last few years'.[131] He repeated this the following month when asked about the installation of new tolls in motorways: 'the Portuguese have to understand that the Government has no alternative to introducing tolls, as it is obliged to pay the debts that others

128 Harvey 2007, p. 13.

129 Caldas and Almeida 2016, pp. 6–7, 24. Our translation. In the original: '*O Estado, antes do mais, mas também as famílias e as empresas – isto é, "nós" – haviam gastado acima das nossas possibilidades*'; '*Gastamos acima das nossas possibilidades. Endividámo-nos. Agora, os credores exigem-nos poupança, cortes na despesa. Não vale a pena acusá-los a eles. Resistir-lhes. Precisamos deles. Temos de obedecer*'.

130 Marcelo Rebelo de Sousa 2011. Our translation. In the original: '*Na situação a que chegamos, não há nenhuma alternativa para controlar o défice e a dívida pública*'.

131 Governo Reitera 2011. Our translation. In the original: '*Nós ao longo dos últimos anos gastámos o que tínhamos e o que não tínhamos, deixámos disparar o desemprego, deixámos aumentar a dívida e as medidas que estão a ser tomadas são medidas reformistas e que têm um objetivo: corrigir o rumo que foi sendo seguido ao longo dos últimos anos*'.

have assumed ....difficult times, but there is no alternative'.[132] The same rhetoric was repeated by the then President of the European Commission, José Manuel Durão Barroso, who expressed his confidence in the 'wisdom' and 'common sense' of the Portuguese people: 'People may disagree with this or that measure, but deep down they know that there is no alternative to a path of budgetary consolidation and structural reforms. The overwhelming majority of the people know this'.[133] The same message is given by the government to the 'social partners'; the executive 'reinforced' that 'there is no other path than austerity'.[134]

This rhetoric is reinforced by economists who support government policies: 'But is there any alternative to austerity?' This is how Teodora Cardoso, president of the Public Finance Council, begins her response to a question from PS deputy João Galamba. For her, there is no other way forward, warning that 'Any alternative to austerity implies more financing. And more financing implies more debt. ... Anything that means increasing debt means worsening the economy's problem'.[135] In *Jornal de Negócios*, economist Vítor Bento stressed that 'There is no alternative to austerity' as in Portugal 'since 1995 we have been increasing the gap between internal expenditure and the income we have, which means that this difference can only be maintained as long as there is someone to finance this difference with external money'.[136]

3 Critical Discourse Analysis of Two Policymakers

Inspired by the work of Foucault, Antonio Gramsci, Althusser, as well as Habermas' theory of communicative action, critical discourse analysis (CDA*) is one

132 Lusa 2011. Our translation. In the original: '*os portugueses têm de perceber que o Governo não tem alternativa à introdução de portagens, já que é obrigado a "pagar as dívidas que outros assumiram"* [...] *"tempos difíceis," mas "não há alternativa"*'.

133 Lusa 2011. Our translation. In the original: '*As pessoas podem discordar desta ou daquela medida, mas no fundo sabem que não há alternativa a um caminho de consolidação orçamental e reformas estruturais. A esmagadora maioria das pessoas sabe isso*'.

134 Governo Reafirmou 2012. Our translation. In the original: '*alguns parceiros sociais explicaram que o executivo reiterou que não há outro caminho se não o da austeridade*'.

135 Redação/VC 2012. Our translation. In the original: '*Qualquer alternativa à austeridade implica mais financiamento. E mais financiamento implica mais dívida.* [...]. *Tudo o que signifique aumentar a dívida significa agravar o problema da economia*'.

136 Laranjeiro 2013. Our translation. In the original: '*Não há alternativa à austeridade* [...] *desde 1995 temos vindo a aumentar o "gap" entre a despesa interna e o rendimento que temos, o que significa que essa diferença só se consegue manter desde que haja quem financie, com dinheiro externo, essa diferença*'.

of the most common schools for analysing language as a social practice.[137] Its intrinsic relationship to crisis and critique, its assumption of political commitment and the fact that its seminal work, Fairclough's *Language and Power*, is a study of neoliberalism and Thatcherite rhetoric make CDA* the best methodology for our inquiry into the discourse of democratic austerity.[138]

According to Jan Blommaert, Norman Fairclough's *Discourse and Social Change* and Chouliaraki and Fairclough's *Discourse in Late Modernity* provide the most elaborate and ambitious attempt at a methodological model of critical discourse analysis.[139] In Fairclough's model, discourse is seen in terms of processes and changes in hegemony, including 'large-scale hegemonic processes such as democratization, commodification and technologization'.[140] Fairclough distinguished three dimensions of discourse: 1) Discourse-as-text, which focuses on linguistic cohesion and structure. One example is the use of the passive form of the verb, which obscures the political agent; 2) Discourse-as-discursive-practice, which focuses on how discourse is consumed, produced and distributed in the macro-conditions of society; and 3) Discourse-as-social-practice, which designates the ideological effects and hegemonic processes in which discourse operates, through the construction of alliances, the integration of classes through consent, the rearticulation of orders of discourse; it focuses on the struggle for hegemony and hegemonic discourse as part of social change, on the emergence of new orders of discourse, on struggles for normativity, as well as on attempts at control and resistance.[141]

Each of these three dimensions must go through three phases: description, interpretation, and explanation. The description phase focuses on the textual-linguistic characteristics of the material. The researcher adopts the participants' categories in his description, making his/her interpretative framework explicit. The interpretative phase concerns the way in which participants understand the discourse based on their cognitive, social, and ideological resources, through categories and criteria provided by the participants. This requires a degree of distance between the researcher and the participant: such interpretations display ideological framings: 'participants "reproduce" elements of social ideologies through interpretative procedures organized inter-

137 Blommaert 2005, p. 27.

138 The political commitment dimension of CDA* lies in the fact that CDA* looks at subversion within this dialectic of discourse: empowering the powerless, giving voice to the voiceless, exposing abuses of power and mobilising people for social change (Blommaert 2005, pp. 23–4).

139 Blommaert 2005, p. 30.

140 Ibid.

141 Blommaert 2005, p. 30; Fairclough 1992, p. 93.

actively in everyday life'. In the explanatory phase, the researcher uses social theory to reveal the ideological foundations of lay interpretative procedures. Social theory creates the necessary distance to move from 'non-critical' to 'critical' discourse analysis, transcending the limitations of lay consciousness about the ideological dimensions of discourse.[142]

3.1 Democratic Austerity Discourse as Text

Our textual analysis is based on interviews with two key actors in the implementation of austerity measures: Abebe Selassie, president of the IMF delegation in Portugal, and Maria Luís Albuquerque, Minister of Finance in the Passos Coelho government.[143] The interviews were semi-structured and therefore included more structured and unstructured parts. The structured component was composed of a list of topics, which took the form of precise questions, without a very rigid interview framework, allowing for new topics, which might lead to areas of research not previously considered.[144] Our interviews were conducted around four main questions: 'What is your opinion on the state of democracy in Portugal?'; 'What is the impact of the crisis on democracy in Portugal?'; 'How do you define democracy?'; and 'What is your opinion on the anti-austerity movements and those calling for "Real Democracy Now!"?'

As a political representative of the country, Albuquerque frequently used the 'we' perspective during the interview, blaming 'us', 'the country', for the existing problems. Albuquerque restricts her judgement on the state of democracy to the relationship between government and parliament, and between majority and minority in parliament. She claims that the state of democracy under the Passos Coelho's government was in 'good shape', 'because members of government were transparent in their communication with the parliament'. She

142 Blommaert 2005, pp. 29–30.

143 Interviews: 13/3/2013 Interview by Jonas Van Vossole with Mr. Abebe Selassie, president of the IMF-delegation in Portugal, and one of the high officials of the Troika. 3/3/2017 Interview by Jonas Van Vossole with Mrs. Maria Luís Albuquerque, member of parliament for the PSD. She was State secretary of Treasure (2011–13) and Minister of Finance (2013–15) during the Troika intervention. Getting access to elite interviews is usually a hard job which requires negotiation and strategy (Burnham, Lutz, Grant and Layton-Henry 2004, pp. 208–11). As I started this research in collaboration with the University of Ghent, and as an associated researcher of the Ghent Association for Studies on Parties and Representation, I presented myself as a Belgian researcher and economist associated to the University of Ghent. After many trials, the interview with Mr. Selassie was conducted during his mission in Lisbon in 2013. Mrs. Albuquerque only granted the interview after she had left office; she had refused several times before due to the political sensitivity of the questions.

144 Burnham, Lutz, Grant and Layton-Henry 2004, p. 12.

contrasts this with the subsequent Costa government. That government would have been much less democratic because of secret agreements between minority parties that would 'restrict parliamentary scrutiny'. The rules imposed by the Memorandum of Understanding during the crisis 'did not pose any obstacles to democracy' because 'the parties that negotiated the memorandum represented 85 percent of the members of parliament'; 'its programme and execution were, therefore, from the point of view of the popular vote, completely legitimate'. Some 'restrictions on national sovereignty in the agreement were consequence of a pre-bankruptcy situation; but they were necessary because bankruptcy would represent a real threat to democracy'. 'It was not the international institutions that forced us to accept the money, we created this situation'. The imposed reforms were 'necessary to correct the structural problems of the Portuguese economy and the rule of law'. Albuquerque states that Portugal is a 'Western democracy', which she defines as 'a representative system' of 'free elections' and 'checks and balances'. She thinks it is 'normal' that there is a 'reaction' in 'situations of crisis' because they create 'multiple victims'. It is important that policies pay attention to the most vulnerable. But 'some groups' advocate a 'rupture with the regime' and want to move towards a 'more direct form of democracy'. This is not our 'successful', 'Western model of democracy' that Portugal had for forty years and brought more 'peace, security, and prosperity'. This 'rupture of the regime', 'including what is designated as capitalism' is 'wrong and dangerous'.[145]

Abebe Selassie frames things from a third-person perspective, as an external and objective analyst. If we summarise the interview concisely, Selassie 'frames things through an economic lens' but finds democracy to be 'in a relatively healthy state'. Portugal appears to be a 'very harmonious and consensual society', although the 'deep crisis' has 'put strain on the body politic' and on 'political discourse'. The 'institutions are still there'. The crisis is creating more 'differences between the parties' and there is 'a blame game going on', and 'it is not easy to see the path forward'. A 'broad-based consensus' remains for 'some elements of the program', which 'differentiates Portugal from other countries', such as Greece, 'which has a history of political violence' and this 'stands Portugal well'. An important aspect is the 'role of civil society', such as 'many church-related charities', 'Caritas', 'not very political community networks' that 'provide the fabric of support' – things that did not 'work in Greece and Spain'. The 'institutions', 'in terms of parliament, freedom of speech', 'constitutional court', 'checks and balances', 'remain in place'.

145 M.L. Albuquerque, personal communication, 3 March 2017.

Given the 'increases in taxes', 'user fees', 'unemployment', 'inequality'; the protests are 'understandable', but in the 'deep economic crisis', 'the measures were unavoidable'. 'We have been asked for technical assistance'. 'It's for the government to have the political debate, it's the parliament's and government's will'. The government was 'democratically elected', so it is not technocratic. But whether 'it's a technocratic or a democratic elected government', you have 'very limited budgetary tools, policies, to overcome the crisis'. 'There is no way out'.[146]

3.2 The Discursive Practice in the Interview

While both Maria Luís Albuquerque and Abebe Selassie played a prominent role in the implementation and legitimisation of austerity measures, the context of both interviews is different. There is, of course, a time difference between the two interviews: the interview with Selassie was conducted on 13 March 2013 at the Ritz Hotel in Lisbon. Selassie was in Lisbon as part of the seventh evaluation of the implementation of the measures agreed in the Memorandum of Understanding. The interview with Maria Luís Albuquerque was conducted on 3 March 2017 at the Portuguese Parliament premises; it was made after a change in government and government policies, when she was no longer Minister of Finance in the PSD/CDS-PP government led by Passos Coelho, but rather one of the key figures in the opposition to the so-called *Geringonça* government led by António Costa.

The political role of these two figures is also relatively different. Abebe Selassie is a 'foreign technician' and a high-level international official. He is not a direct actor in the Portuguese political game; since he does not need to be re-elected, there is no need for any form of substantial democratic legitimacy. He admits to having very little direct knowledge of Portuguese politics and history. He is a representative of a foreign international institution. His sole mandate is to control the implementation of the technocratic structural measures included in the Memorandum of Understanding, guaranteeing the financial stability of the government budget, in order to ensure the sustainability of the troika's financial investments.

Maria Luís Albuquerque was Secretary of State for the Treasury in the Passos Coelho government since 2011 and became Minister of Finance in the same government on 1 July 2013, after a government crisis that led to the departure of former Finance Minister Vítor Gaspar in June 2013. Both Gaspar and Albuquerque refused to be interviewed in 2013, when Selassie's interview was

146 A. Selassie, personal communication, 13 March 2013.

granted. This probably occurred precisely because of their different roles in the political process. Albuquerque was not just a technocrat – although, as we will see, she is an economist and was a university professor previously and uses a similar discourse. She was, first and foremost, an elected politician who was under more direct democratic scrutiny than Selassie, at a time when the government was heavily criticised. Albuquerque only gave the interview in March 2017, more than a year after leaving the government and now firmly in opposition as a parliamentarian for the PSD. When she finally admitted her availability for the interview, she stated that 'not holding government positions certainly makes my answers easier'.[147]

During the interview, Albuquerque was much more comfortable with her own speech. She articulated her answers in a coherent political discourse, she was confident and answered without having to think too much, and her answers were extensive and more factually based. Selassie's answers were short, with many long pauses, admitting a lack of knowledge. He questioned several times whether he was the right person to answer the questions. Selassie's factual basis was more technical and economic – in this technical area of knowledge, his parallel answers were much more exhaustive.

3.3 Democratic Discourse as Social Practice: Explanation

As we have seen, both interviewees had different social roles in the implementation of austerity measures. These differences are reflected in the way they frame their answers: when asked about the 'state of democracy', Maria Luís Albuquerque focuses mainly on the parties that, at the time of the interview, were part of the new government agreement, but which at the time of the Troika were in opposition. She focuses on the 'parliamentary debate' and the 'disrespect for the parties that today [2017] make up the opposition and the use of the majority's force to block minority rights', as opposed to the 'attitude of great respect' and 'transparency' to describe the situation during the PSD-CDS government. She warns the majority that 'majorities are circumstantial'.[148]

She focuses on the role of the radical left – both the Communist Party and anti-austerity movements – as the greatest dangers to democracy. Democracy is presented as synonymous with 'the regime' and 'what is called capitalism'. She calls the PCP 'totalitarian' and claims it is as dangerous to democracy as the far-right parties of Eastern Europe. She claims that the only reason this is not

147 M.L. Albuquerque, personal communication, 3 March 2017.
148 Ibid.

recognised by the general public is because Portuguese democracy is generally left-leaning, because it was born out of a movement against Salazar's far-right *Estado Novo* dictatorship.[149]

When asked about the 'state of democracy', Selassie considers that it is 'relatively healthy', that 'in normal times', Portugal 'seems like a very harmonious, very consensual society'. There is even a 'broad based consensus ... for some elements of the program', which he considers to be 'something that stands Portugal well and probably differentiates it from other countries'. He acknowledges that the 'economic crisis is putting a strain on political discourse', creating 'more differences between parties'. But 'the institutions are still there'.[150]

Common elements in Abebe Selassie's and Maria Luis Albuquerque's definitions of democracy include this focus on institutional characteristics. Albuquerque's discourse focuses on 'representative government', 'free elections', 'checks and balances', 'transparency', 'government', 'democratic alternation', 'majorities and minorities', 'law', 'democratic rights', 'parliamentary debate', 'parliamentary control', 'democratic choice of representatives', 'electoral mandate', 'parties', 'program', 'power', 'institutions', 'pillars of the democratic regime', 'Western democracies', and 'capitalism'.[151] Selassie's discourse is less extensive and focuses on 'institutions', 'constitutional court', 'checks and balances', 'parliament', 'parties', 'peaceful', 'freedom of speech'.[152] Characteristics such as 'social welfare', 'social rights', 'inequality', 'participation', etc. are absent from his argument.

Regarding social movements that oppose austerity policies with the ideas of 'real democracy', Albuquerque begins by recognising that it is important to protect the most vulnerable people in society, but 'movements that advocate a break with the regime ... where I include what is called capitalism ... and want to move from a representative democracy to a more direct form of democracy' are 'wrong and dangerous', she says. Some propose 'alternative models within a revolutionary logic, in some cases alternatives that have proven very bad in the past, and in other cases you can't even understand what they are proposing – they are against everything, and in organized societies, this is a path that can be very dangerous'.[153]

What struck me immediately in Selassie was his lack of knowledge and personal connection with the political and social situation in the country. The

149 Ibid.
150 A. Selassie, personal communication, 13 March 2013.
151 M.L. Albuquerque, personal communication, 3 March 2017.
152 A. Selassie, personal communication, 13 March 2017.
153 M.L. Albuquerque, personal communication, 3 March 2017.

technical background of these highly qualified officers of international institutions allows such ignorance of social reality to be considered acceptable, as it translates the problems of countries into what are considered objective economic statistics. At the same time, there was a kind of self-censorship on sensitive issues, such as the structural problems of the eurozone, expressed through silences.

This brings us to the following intertwined elements that underpin discourses on the democratic legitimacy of the Troika and government policies: depoliticisation, formal legitimisation, and exceptionalism.

3.3.1 Depolitisation

According to the IMF official, the crisis was a consequence of the 'drying up of financing flows' and the policies were designed to meet the need to 'reduce their imbalances'. At the same time, the austerity programme is portrayed as a form of aid to 'try to provide temporary funding' to ease the pain. Simultaneously, the 'programme sought to protect minimum levels of benefits, minimum pension levels' and it 'ensures … that social protection is at the core helping the poor'. Portraying the antisocial character of austerity would therefore be 'unfair'. He claims that political debate is too much 'a bit of a blame game'.[154]

At the same time, Selassie portrays the role of the Troika as that of an apolitical, good-governance advisor: 'we form judgments about what is reasonable and what is unreasonable'. The Troika only provides 'technical assistance' and gives 'advice' on 'what kind of financing exists'. This also means that the political decision is restricted to 'how you get there', which is 'ultimately a decision that has to come from here (the national government)', as long as 'it is reasonable'.[155]

According to Albuquerque, the loss of sovereignty as a result of the austerity programme 'was a consequence of pre-bankruptcy'. It was the only 'alternative to a situation in which the country lost its capacity to finance itself'. This would have been the 'real threat to democracy'. She blames 'political errors' – as opposed to good governance – for leading the country 'to such a situation'. The mistakes of the austerity programme, if any, were 'committed in good faith'.[156]

154 A. Selassie, personal communication, 13 March 2013.
155 Ibid.
156 M.L. Albuquerque, personal communication, 3 March 2017.

3.3.2 Formal Legitimation

Selassie admits that the crisis and the need for austerity 'puts a strain on the political discourse' and 'puts a strain on the body politic'. Policies are constrained by 'very limited budgetary instruments'. However, to his surprise 'the institutions are still there'; 'The democratic institutions remain in place; if we think in terms of parliament, freedom of speech, constitutional court control, checks and balances'. It is 'normal' that people protest, but as long as the 'numbers are endorsed by parliament', there is no problem. He even seems surprised by 'how broad-based consensus there has been', acknowledging that this is 'something that stands Portugal well'.[157]

There is no problem of democratic legitimacy, which he considers 'relatively healthy'. Furthermore, 'the adoption of the fiscal compact ... and, of course, the annual budget, are approved and ratified by parliament'. As long as 'the government [is] democratically elected', according to this official, we cannot see an opposition 'between technocracy and democracy'.[158]

Albuquerque argues that the 2011 elections took place after the first agreements on the adjustment programme and that the parties – PS, PSD, and CDS – that supported the programme had the support of 85 percent of the members of parliament. According to her, this 'means that, from the point of view of the popular vote, the programme and its execution were legitimate'. The relationship between government and parliament forms the basis of her arguments about democracy: her government has always shown 'respect for parliament', 'members of the government were accountable to parliament', etc.[159]

3.3.3 Austerity as an Exception

In the discourse of Abebe Selassie, there is no exceptional way to legitimise austerity measures. On the contrary, the measures are framed as consensual and the social protests as normal: the 'institutions are still there', despite the crisis, and society is relatively calm and peaceful. The situation contrasts with countries where the situation is much more explosive, such as Greece. Comparisons between resistances are attributed to differences in 'culture'.[160]

While Mrs Albuquerque criticises social movements that advocate a 'rupture with the regime', she nevertheless legitimises her own policy based on the

157 A. Selassie, personal communication, 13 March 2013.
158 A. Selassie, personal communication, 13 March 2013.
159 M.L. Albuquerque, personal communication, 3 March 2017.
160 A. Selassie, personal communication, 13 March 2013.

framework of exception: as the crisis is an exceptional situation that requires emergency measures, the suspension of normal rules, of some kind of sovereign powers, and external intervention are legitimate to restore democratic normality. She frames the situation as one of 'extreme difficulty', a situation of 'near default' in which 'the loss of the country's capability to finance itself autonomously was a real threat to democracy'; a situation in which 'democratic values are challenged'. From the perspective of the exception, it is the previous normal situation that is defined as problematic: 'The political errors made in the past, which left the country in this situation, were the real threat to democracy'. The implementation of the programme that 'puts limits to liberty and degrees of freedom of decision making' is necessary 'to get a clean exit'. Those who disagree 'just do not assume the responsibility'.[161]

Moreover, she argues that her government efficiently used this exceptional situation to do 'many other things: put into practice many other reforms that, according to us, are fundamental to correcting structural problems in the economy and the rule of law in Portugal'. She therefore states that the crisis opens up opportunities for sovereign powers. The exception creates the possibility, not only of restoring normality, but of creating a fundamentally different norm.[162]

4 An Austerity Definition of Democracy in Crisis

The implementation of austerity measures was not accompanied by a discursive abandonment of the idea of democracy by political decision-makers. Throughout the crisis period and in interviews, policymakers generally claimed democratic legitimacy for these measures and defended them against criticism. Realising the need to legitimise the application of harsh austerity measures with a democratic discourse, political decision-makers entered into a discursive (political) exercise of trying to articulate discourses on democracy with the need for austerity. The result was the 'democratic discourse of austerity': the discursive way of articulating the meanings and practices of democracy with austerity reforms in the context of the Portuguese crisis between 2011 and 2015.

We analysed the basic concepts of hegemony, austerity, and neoliberalism, and how these are legitimised through the depoliticisation and culturalisation of political problems. Arguments are then articulated through their

161 M.L. Albuquerque, personal communication, 3 March 2017.
162 M.L. Albuquerque, personal communication, 3 March 2017.

discursive incorporation into the formal and substantive democratic dimensions of democracy. The elements of depoliticisation and formal democratic legitimisation are predominant. Depoliticisation can be found in technocratic arguments, in 'economist' discourse, in the framing of 'exceptionality', in the use of the concept of 'good governance', in the transfer of responsibility to other/external actors (to the Troika, national governance of financial markets), in the irrationalisation of any political alternative. On the one hand, power and policies are repeatedly legitimised on the basis of formal democratic procedures, particularly on the basis of law, elections, parliamentary majorities, ratified treaties, and constitutional judgments. The substantial elements, on the other hand, are very limited, as the 'circumstances' of the crisis do not allow for such legitimisation.

This perspective very much resembles the traditional, neoliberal paradigm of democracy. The austerity model of democracy reflected the liberal-democratic model that has been hegemonic since 'the end of history' in the 1990s. While the acceptable political spectrum is narrowed by the 'golden straitjacket'[163] of financial markets, this form of democracy is presented as both universal and non-ideological. It fits into the post-political and post-democratic[164] and low-intensity[165] form of the democratic ideal.

At the same time, it strongly reflects the exceptionalism that is closely linked to the crisis perspective. Exceptionalism and crisis not only legitimise the application of austerity measures that would clash with existing normativity in the formal and substantive dimensions of democracy. Exceptionalism also legitimises the 'necessary' transformation of society and democracy towards a new normal, giving decision-makers sovereign powers that supersede existing democracy.

---

163 Friedman 2000, p. 16.
164 Mouffe 2005; Swyngedouw 2007; 2014.
165 Santos and Avritzer 2005.

CHAPTER 5

Democratic Alternatives

The economic and financial crisis that affected Portugal in 2011 left representative democracy in a serious crisis of legitimacy. Large demonstrations and other forms of protest shook the country between 2011 and 2013. We begin with a chronological description and discussion of the main protest movements that questioned austerity policies. Then I will discuss the interviews with activists that were collected at these demonstrations. Sixty-seven short interviews with activists and protesters focus on their perspectives on the state of democracy in Portugal, how they perceived the influence of the crisis in Portugal, and how they conceived their ideas of democracy. In these interviews, one observes a complete rejection, on the part of the activists, of the state of liberal democracy at the time. The main reasons for this rejection are the perceived lack of social rights, accountability, legitimacy, freedom of speech, sovereignty, participation, and respect for the constitution.

Secondly, the delegitimisation of the existing structures and ideas of the current democratic hegemony is manifested in the emergence of alternatives to the traditional representative form that has governed Portugal since the 1976 constitution. A wide range of different conceptions of democracy emerge. We distinguish and elaborate three more-developed democratic conceptions found during this research: the autonomist movement of the *Acampadas*, the Occupy movement influenced by the Spanish 15M; the radical trade union democracy in which the Lisbon Dockers' Union assumed the leadership; and the left-wing parliamentary alternatives presented by the PCP and the Left Bloc. Finally, we will discuss the possible connections between these discourses and the possibility of a unified alternative.

1 From Crisis to Protest: An Overview

Protest is a practice of delegitimisation. Widespread protests are often the most visible sign of the delegitimisation of a system as a whole. Austerity policies were met with a long wave of protests. These protests have been widely analysed on an international scale, where they are often compared to the Arab Spring, Occupy Wall Street and the various anti-austerity protests in the context of the euro crisis. José Soeiro, Camargo, Fonseca, Accornero and Pinto and Baumgarten provide a chronological perspective of how these different organ-

HTTPS://DOI.ORG/10.1163/9789004766235-007

isations developed over the period 2011–13, and how the focus of mobilisations shifted from more spontaneous forms of action and protest to actions organised by the more institutionalised sectors of the left.[1]

The demonstration of 12 March 2011 by *Geração à Rasca* against PEC IV, the fourth austerity reform of the PS government led by José Sócrates, was the first gigantic moment of these protests.[2] The demonstration was called under the slogan of being 'democratic, secular, non-partisan, and peaceful'. It was a relatively spontaneous movement, not mediated by any organisation, called by four young activists, against the precarious working conditions of young people in the context of rising unemployment and emigration.[3] It brought together groups that were previously difficult to mobilise, such as young people in vulnerable situations. Its focus on issues of representative democracy, precariousness, and criticism of the political caste found a broad echo in various social organisations (feminist, LGBT, etc.), organised sectors of the left (including the Left Bloc), and even sectors of the right and the far right.[4] According to Soeiro, its programmatic 'fluidity' or 'inclusiveness' contributed to its mobilising strength, as well as to its political fragility – its echo on the far right was considered uncomfortable by the organisers themselves. It managed to become one of the biggest demonstrations in Portuguese history. But its effectiveness in influencing the political course depended on the redefinitions made in the political field based on power relations between institutional agents.[5] The broad social climate of protest against further austerity, as well as the lack of parliamentary support – following Pedro Passos Coelho's declaration that the PSD would no longer tolerate austerity – ended up leading to the fall of the PS government in less than two weeks.[6] New elections in June would eventually bring to power a new right-wing PSD-CDS government led by the same Pedro Passos Coelho as Prime Minister. As research shows, the victory of the PSD and CDS should not be seen as support for more right-wing neoliberal policies.[7] It

1 Accornero and Pinto 2015; Baumgarten 2013; Camargo 2014; Fonseca 2016; Soeiro 2014.
2 Camargo 2014.
3 Fonseca 2016, pp. 165–68.
4 Fonseca 2016; Soeiro 2014.
5 Soeiro 2014.
6 Camargo 2014, p. 137. Pedro Passos Coelho, then leader of the opposition, and the future prime minister, justified the vote of no confidence in the Sócrates' government, based on its opposition towards PEC IV, which he considered a 'set of new grievous and extremely unjust measures'. See: Lourenço 2011. Our translation. In the original: *'novas medidas gravosas e extremamente injustas'*.
7 Freire 2016; Freire et al. 2015; Magalhães 2014.

was, instead, the result of an electoral rejection of the incumbent government's performance and four consecutive austerity programmes.

Meanwhile, in Spain, young people took to the streets in large numbers on 15 May 2011, under the slogan *'Democracia Real Ya!'* (Real Democracy Now!). Influenced by the Arab Spring, the *'Indignados'* – as they called themselves – protested against rampant unemployment, especially among young people, and corruption in the political system. As a consequence of the demonstrations – and influenced by the events in Tahrir Square, Cairo – some of the participants began camping in Puerta del Sol (*Acampada del Sol*) in Madrid.[8] This form of prefigurative protest, which focused on democratic and participatory decision-making in assemblies and on solidarity-based coexistence, while also reclaiming and occupying public space, inspired other cities in Spain and across Europe, including Portugal.[9]

In Portugal, similar camps, or *Acampadas*, have sprung up in several cities, particularly in Porto, Coimbra, and Lisbon. These, however, never reached the strength of the movement in Spain.[10] The *Acampada do Rossio* in Lisbon began on 20 May with 37 people sleeping in tents in Rossio square, a practice that lasted 12 days.[11] According to Camargo, most participants had a high level of education, but the crisis frustrated their prospects for a decent future. At its peak, more than 500 people participated in the assemblies.[12] After frictions between the organised political left and anarchist-leaning activists, the *Acampada do Rossio* quickly split. Parallel to this, *'Indignados Lisboa'* was formed, but both had reduced expression, at least in numbers. Most participants were young, precarious and unemployed, or students.[13]

Although the *Acampadas* did not have a clear political conclusion, they regrouped a new layer of activists and opened up some new political spaces.[14] On 10 July, members of the *Acampadas* organised an international meeting in Lisbon with 130 activists, which resulted in the organisation of the 'Global Day of Action' on 15 October. This included actions and demonstrations organised in 961 cities in 82 countries.[15] To organise this demonstration in Portugal, a platform with the same name, *15 de Outubro*, was launched, with representatives from a vast range of social organisations.[16]

---

8 Camargo 2014.
9 Soeiro 2014.
10 Ibid.
11 D. Fonseca 2016; Soeiro 2014.
12 Camargo 2014.
13 Soeiro 2014.
14 Camargo 2014.
15 Soeiro 2014.
16 Camargo 2014.

While at an international level the date of 15 October 2011 gained prominence through the appeal of Occupy Wall Street in the USA, in Portugal participation in the 15 October demonstration was reinforced by the announcement of new austerity measures in the first government budget presented by Pedro Passos Coelho. The measures included cutting two months of salaries for civil servants.[17] The 15O, as it used to be called, was the first major mobilisation after the Memorandum of Understanding signed between the Troika and the PSD, PS, and CDS parties on 17 May 2011.[18]

There were local demonstrations in the cities of Angra do Heroísmo, Braga, Coimbra, Évora, Faro, Ponta Delgada, Santarém, and Porto, among others. In Lisbon, the demonstration mobilised around 100,000 people.[19] Behind the motto 'we are the 99 percent', three key ideas were defended in the 15O manifesto: participatory democracy, transparency in political decisions, and the end of precariousness in people's lives. According to Camargo, amid the success of the mobilisation, weaknesses emerged in the platform. A violent confrontation between different political strategies of the participating organisations, particularly some trying to control the platform by imposing a majority, led to the practical end of the platform between organisations as such, which became particularly evident in the demonstrations of the second general strike of 22 March 2012.

On 24 November 2011, the CGTP and the UGT called the first general strike against the austerity measures of the Passos Coelho government. It was only the seventh general strike since Portugal's redemocratisation in 1974, and only the third jointly called by the two trade union confederations. In addition to the successful participation, the strike was particularly relevant due to the fact that it was supported by an appeal from Platform 15O. This explicit participation of social movements led to the first organisation of a demonstration coinciding with the general strike in front of the *Assembleia da República* – the Portuguese parliament. According to Soeiro, this was a clear sign of a first concrete alliance between the 'old' and 'newer' social movements.[20] The tension between unions and new social movements has been structural throughout the protests.[21]

When the CGTP called a new general strike for 22 March 2012 – this time excluding the UGT – it took the initiative of launching a demonstration on the day of the action, the first time it had done so. According to Fonseca, this

---

17 Soeiro 2014.
18 Fonseca 2016.
19 Soeiro 2014.
20 Soeiro 2004.
21 Fonseca 2016.

was a consequence of the success of the previous mobilisation, added to the fact that if the CGTP did not organise one, the demonstration would be organised anyway.[22] In fact, Platform 15O, which had organised the demonstration on 24 November, had already called for a demonstration in the same place and following the same route as the CGTP. The left organised in Platform 15O was divided over the issue. The radical left-wing party MAS, *Movimento Alternativa Socialista*, accused the CGTP of organising the demonstration only to control the grassroots movement inspired by social movements, control the loudspeakers, and avoid any dynamics outside their own control. *Precários Inflexíveis* (PI), a social movement around young precarious workers – and close to *Bloco de Esquerda* – and UMAR, a feminist organisation, two of the most important organisations of Plataforma 15O, abandoned the call for a separate demonstration and wanted to join the CGTP demonstration as a matter of class unity. MAS accused them of opportunism and betrayal. To make matters worse for the idea of a unified struggle against austerity, the social movements PI and UMAR ended up being physically banned from the union demonstration by the confederation's security when they tried to join it with their own banners.

After the internal strife within *Plataforma 15O*, some of the protagonists involved in the previous mobilisations launched a separate platform to organise a new demonstration called *Primavera Global* (Global Spring) on 12 May 2012, to mark the anniversary of the *Indignados* movement in Spain. The protest took place in Braga, Coimbra, Évora, Faro, Porto, Santarém, and Lisbon, although with considerably fewer people.[23]

During the summer, a group of 29 activists launched a new call for a demonstration, under the slogan 'Damn the Troika, We Want Our Lives Back' (*Que Se Lixe a Troika, Queremos nossas vidas de volta*). This demonstration was launched as a critique of the Troika's foreign political intervention and as a call for human dignity and to end austerity. The statement calling for mobilisation said, 'The austerity they are imposing on us destroys our dignity and our lives, it does not function, and it destroys democracy'.[24] Different tendencies from the previous nucleus of anti-austerity activists remained, but a more 'reformist' stance prevailed, which emphasised the need for healthy relations with the CGTP and the political left.[25] The organising group of *Que Se Lixe a Troika*,

22 Ibid.
23 Soeiro 2014.
24 Manifestação 2012. Our translation. In the original: '*A austeridade que nos impõem e que nos destrói a dignidade e a vida não funciona e destrói a democracia*'.
25 Fonseca 2016, p. 286.

which included representatives from several left-wing organisations, including the PCP and the *Bloco de Esquerda*, would have a strong impact, materialised in the largest demonstrations since the beginning of the protests, with more than a million participants in around 30 cities in the country.[26] The success of the mobilisation was due in part to the announcement of changes to the Single Social Tax (TSU) by the Passos Coelho government. This tax reduction for companies was financed by an increase in workers' contributions and provoked widespread social outrage, including among traditionally right-wing sectors.[27]

From then on, the same group, QSLT, took the lead in organising impactful protest actions. These included the cultural demonstrations, coordinated internationally at the 'Global Noise' event on 13 October 2012, and the demonstration '*Que se Lixe a Troika! O Povo É Quem Mais Ordena!*' on 2 March 2013, which mobilised more than 1.2 million people in Lisbon and more than 20 cities, according to the Left Bloc. The last demonstration was the culmination of a longer period of symbolic actions called '*Grandoladas*', which involved interrupting public appearances by politicians by singing '*Grândola, Vila Morena*', the signature song of the 1974 Carnation Revolution.[28]

The impetus for stronger collaboration was evident in October 2012, when M12M leaders joined others close to the CGTP, the PS, and the *Bloco de Esquerda* in organising a Congress of Democratic Alternatives (CDA).[29] The initiative involved MPs from the Left Bloc and the PS, former President Mário Soares, former CGTP leader Carvalho da Silva, and several public intellectuals. On 5 October, 1,700 people from diverse academic, political, and social movement backgrounds gathered in the Aula Magna of the Rectory of the University of Lisbon with the aim of proposing a participatory and transparent alternative to austerity and debt, reducing external economic dependence, valuing labour, protecting the environment, and reducing inequalities. The CDA organised several important conferences and published reports on political alternatives in 2013 and 2014. In 2015, it would organise the 'Governing on the Left' conference, seen by some as the basis of the left-wing coalition that would support the PS government in 2015.[30]

Meanwhile, union initiatives faced police violence and legal restrictions. The European general strike called by the European Trade Union Confedera-

26 Soeiro 2014.

27 Ibid.

28 Camargo 2014.

29 Accornero and Pinto 2015b.

30 Sabariego and Matos 2018.

tion for 14 November 2012 and supported by the CGTP, the *Precários Inflexíveis*, the Students for the Strike, the remnants of *Plataforma 15O*, the Dockworkers Union, and the *Movimento 12 de Março*, ended in police violence.[31] The last major standoff between unions and the government – excluding the dockworkers' struggles – was the CGTP *'Ponte-a-pé'* (Walk the Bridge) demonstration on 19 October 2013. The government banned the demonstration for alleged security reasons, and the unions were eventually forced to back down. From then on, the unions' hope for political change was channelled into the elections.[32]

2 Questioning the Protestors

During the period of these protests, I conducted a series of interviews to examine the evolution of individuals' perspectives on democracy.[33] The study also incorporated extensive personal involvement in various protest activities and assemblies, adhering to Participatory Action Research (PAR) methodologies.[34] In addition, in-depth qualitative interviews were conducted with key figures from social movements, trade unions and political parties to explore their perspectives on democracy.[35] These interviews aimed to understand the participants' ideological views and narratives about democracy, analysed through a dialectical-relational critical discourse framework.[36]

2.1 The State of Democracy

While negative judgments about government policies among protesters were to be expected – given that opposition to austerity policies was the main reason for their presence – the extent to which these negative judgments were projected onto the concept of democracy itself was surprising. Interviews revealed that the vast majority of protesters considered democracy to be non-existent or in a severely degraded state. The former described it with terms such as 'laughable', 'a fiction', 'beheaded', 'failed', 'dictatorship', 'no practice', 'decadent', 'a lie', 'a hypocrisy' and 'a farce'. Others characterised it as being in terrible condition,

31 Soeiro 2014.
32 Van Vossole 2020.
33 For a more detailed description of the methodology and results, see Van Vossole 2021.
34 McIntyre 2008.
35 Yin 2011, pp. 134–40.
36 Fairclough 2013.

using descriptions such as 'sick', 'very sick', 'degraded', 'weak', 'bad', 'questionable', 'undemocratic', 'a misery', 'not for the people', 'a robbery', 'threatened', 'not what I wanted', 'damaged', 'masked', 'deteriorated', 'mostly formal', 'degenerate', and 'wounded'.

Only a small minority of the protesters interviewed (fiveof 67) distinguished between 'the deplorable state of the country' and the state of democracy. These individuals argued that 'there are still elections', 'people have the right to express themselves', 'democracy is the best system, despite its weaknesses', 'formally, things work well', and 'the alternative is totalitarianism'. However, even this minority believed that democracy 'should be improved', 'politicians should keep their promises', and 'there should be more participation'.

A wide array of reasons justified the negative judgment in the protesters' discourses. These could be ranked, from most to least mentioned, into the following, often overlapping, categories: 1) Lack or deterioration of social and labour rights, which includes the failure to provide health care and education, attacks on workers' rights, declining wages, widespread injustice, and the belief that democracy serves only the rich. 2) A lack of political and financial accountability, characterised by representatives who do not listen and do not fulfil electoral promises, widespread incompetence and corruption, reducing politics to mere theatre. 3) The government's lack of popular legitimacy to implement austerity, as manifested in the protests. 4) Lack of freedom of expression and information, stemming from promiscuity between politicians and media editors, media dominated by economic interests and fear of repression in the workplace. 5) Lack of national sovereignty, as policies are designed by unelected transnational organisations such as the European Commission, the International Monetary Fund, and the European Central Bank. 6) Lack of participation, with low electoral turnout, absence of participatory mechanisms and absence of popular mobilisation in the streets. And finally, 7) a lack of respect for the constitution, which is set aside to balance the budget.

2.2 Perception of Change

When asked about a possible change in their opinion about the state of democracy, most respondents attributed this change to austerity measures, the intervention of the Troika and the financial crisis of recent years. Consequently, the issue of democracy became politicised in the context of the crisis, using the pre-crisis situation as a comparative reference. Another frequently mentioned milestone, especially among older protesters, is the Portuguese Revolution of 25 April 1974, which is associated with the establishment of social rights and serves as a cornerstone of Portuguese democracy. Some even describe the perceived loss of democracy as a regression to the pre-revolution era, with one protester commenting, 'All that's missing is the PIDE' (secret police).

Almost two-thirds of the protesters interviewed acknowledged that their perspective on democracy had changed for the worse in the recent period due to the crisis or austerity measures. For example, Alfredo, 68, criticised external control over Portugal, and Laurentino, 47, highlighted the unequal social impact of the crisis. Among the minority of respondents who stated that their perspective on democracy had not changed, about half had a positive view of the state of democracy and reproduced the once hegemonic liberal-democratic narrative, stating that institutions remained in place and functioned well. Marta, 31, was one of them and declared, 'We still have the rule of law. Our civil rights remain, they are respected'. The other half responded that their perspective on democracy had not changed because they already had a negative judgment before the crisis began; at best, austerity policies confirmed their pre-existing judgment. João, 44, declared that 'nothing has really changed. Democracy is a farce, as it always has been'.

The attempt to understand whether it was people's perspectives or their material realities that changed highlights the relationships between infrastructure and ideology: some individuals retained their theoretical or idealistic views of democracy but understood that there had been a fundamental change in its state. For example, Ana, 38, noted that her perspective on democracy remained unchanged, but that the actual state of democracy had worsened, making it increasingly difficult to achieve the democratic ideal. Likewise, Francisco, 51, distinguished between his enduring belief in democracy and his disillusionment with its current state. Others reflected on how their consciousness evolved due to the crisis, often attributing this change to their own studies or experiences, suggesting that the crisis had a pedagogical role.

2.3 Redefining Democracy

After explaining why 'this is not democracy', a considerable number of responding protesters seemed to have difficulty explaining what democracy actually is: 'I can't answer that question', 'That's a difficult question', 'That's a complex question', 'I have to think', and 'I'm not the best person to answer that question' were some of the responses. This means that while people reject the current state of democracy, confusion prevails and there is not necessarily a clear idea of how it should or could be different. This could be interpreted as a reflection of a disappearing hegemony, a feeling of emptiness, in which no alternative is ready to fill its place.

Some respondents managed to define a different ideal of democracy, but were unable to connect it to contemporary reality. In defining democracy, many used conditional language: 'Elected people who *would* respect the opinion of the people', 'The people *could* choose representatives who *would* make decisions and defend the interests of the people', 'I *would* define democracy as a political system that gives equal voice to everyone', and 'supposedly it *should* be exercised by those who were democratically elected'. Others provided a straightforward definition, followed by a caveat: 'Democracy is the government of the people, in theory. But what is happening is that those elected do not represent the interests of the people, but of an elite'.

Some people defined democracy in abstract terms of state, system, and institutions without the (self-)identification of the subjects of democracy, but the overall majority of respondents defined democracy in terms of the power of 'the people' (60/67 respondents), 'we' (18/67), 'persons' (11/67), 'citizens', or 'population' (2/67). Surprisingly, however, taking into account the criticism of liberal democracy in the responses to the first question and the reasons for this rejection, only one in four participants specifically referred to any form of substantive content in their definition of democracy. One would expect more answers like 'Democracy is us all being equal, everyone having food, everyone having shelter', 'Democracy is our well-being', 'Democracy is a welfare state in which the general population chooses who governs', 'Democracy should be equal to better living conditions for us, living in health and peace'. Half of the respondents define democracy by referring to its formal aspects, without mentioning political outcomes or substantive dimensions. Democracy is described as 'participation and representation', 'elected authorities who respect the views of the people', a 'political system that allows all citizens to have an equal voice', and a 'rule of law where people have rights and obligations'. One respondent began his definition with 'I'm not going to get into an extremely political definition' and simply stated that democracy is the 'right to vote'. This indicates that the wide range of reasons people gave for the absence of democracy in the first question – such as social rights, participation, mobilisation, and freedom of expression – are hardly reflected in their positive definitions of democracy. This suggests a similar 'void' or social disarticulation in their discourses, a consequence of the decline of the hegemony of liberal democracy.

Although the sample is too small for statistically significant conclusions, a comparison over time reveals another interesting pattern. In 2012, 46 percent of respondents denied the existence of democracy, a number that fell dramatically to 7 percent in 2013, while the 'bad state' category rose from 49 percent to 77 percent. This shift suggests a transition from radical rejection to a more conformist narrative. This may be due in part to the different nature of the protests: the 2012 demonstrations were more confrontational and focused on concrete cuts, while the 2013 protests were more symbolic, including the 25 April memorial march and the *Que se Lixe a Troika* demonstration. It seems that during the initial peak of the protests, there was a clearer rejection of the state of democracy, while during the decline, with no immediate concrete alternatives, people's judgments became less radical.

3 From Protest to Democratic Alternatives

The statement that 'there is no alternative' symbolises the legitimisation of neoliberal democratic hegemony for more than three decades and raises the question: is democracy without alternatives even possible?[37] One of the demonstrations of the *Que se lixe a Troika* movement – on 26 October 2013 – carried the slogan 'There are no dead ends'. From a theoretical perspective, a crisis inherently implies the existence of alternatives, as it is defined by the acute need for external intervention or decisive action. Throughout this research, we came across several alternative democratic discourses and practices that positioned themselves as responses to the hegemonic form of democracy in crisis. We limit ourselves to what we could describe as three main forms that we found: the *acampadas*, union democracy, and parliamentary alternatives.

In no way do these 'alternative models' exclude other forms of democracy, nor do they prevent the overlapping of elements and discourses between them. As we will see, these empirical 'models' overlap with different theoretical perspectives that we find in democratic theory and in the history of the development of democracy. The models were enriched with some more extensive interviews. In addition to the questions used in the shorter interviews about the personal definition of democracy, its state and evolution, more specific questions were used, targeting in particular the alter-ideological conception of democracy issues. For example: 'How do you think "the other side" views democracy?' or 'Do the concrete actions of the other side in the social conflict influence democracy?' In these interviews we address the narratives involving 'democracy' around specific cases (*grandoladas*, Constitutional Court), but also those about recent elections and the high levels of abstention. These conversations, held with two activists from the Coimbra Popular Assembly, two trade union leaders – António Mariano, president of SEAL (Dockers Union)

---

37 Harvey 2005, p. 13.

and Mário Nogueira, president of FENPROF (teachers' union federation) – and two left-wing MPs – José Soeiro (BE) and Miguel Tiago (PCP) – were conducted as semi-structured interviews, allowing for some flexibility in the questions.

3.1 The *Acampadas*

The Portuguese *acampadas*, or encampments, characterised by the occupation of public space,[38] resembled the global Occupy movement.[39] They were inspired by the Spanish *Indignados* movement and the Arab Spring, through active communication and the emergence of transnational activist networks.[40] The *acampadas* have become the most symbolic form of protest against austerity in Portugal.[41] Although the *Geração à Rasca* protest – significant as an independent and largely spontaneous initiative that marked the end of a 35-year period during which unions were the sole organisers of mass demonstrations[42] – occurred nine weeks before the 15M occupation of Puerta del Sol in Madrid, it was only after inspiration from the *Indignados* that experiences similar to those in Madrid were replicated.[43] While at the beginning the protests framed social discontent in terms of lack of employment, lack of future prospects, housing, etc., 15M and 'Real Democracy Now!' in Spain posed the problem of austerity and economic difficulties as a question of democracy and transformed the protest into a 'democratic practice'.[44] Protesters occupied Rossio Square in Lisbon in May 2011 to demand true democracy, and the movement spread across Portugal, leading to the establishment of popular assemblies in some of the main cities, including Porto, Angra do Heroísmo, Braga, Évora, Faro, Ponta Delgada, and Coimbra.[45]

The Popular Assembly of Coimbra is a concrete example. Almost a hundred people gathered in *Praça 8 de Maio*, a central square in front of Coimbra City Hall, on 20 May 2011. Inspired by the practices of collective discussion in Madrid, the participants quickly concluded that they wanted more than just to show solidarity with the *Indignados* in Spain: they wanted to implement a 'real democracy', based on direct participation and consensus-based decision-making,

38 Pickerill and Krinsky 2012.
39 Castañeda 2012.
40 Baumgarten and Díez García 2017; Díez García 2017.
41 Baumgarten and Díez García 2017.
42 Accornero and Pinto 2015a, and 2015b; Baumgarten and Díez García 2017; Estanque et al. 2013.
43 Baumgarten and Díez García 2017.
44 Baumgarten and Díez García 2017.
45 Alípio et al. 2013; Soeiro 2014.

'different from the one that is reduced to one vote every four or five years, a democracy that is authentically of the people and for the people'.[46] The participants decided to meet every afternoon in that same square: the *Acampada de Coimbra* was born. From 25 May to 5 July, *Praça 8 de Maio* was permanently 'occupied' – a symbolic and permanent presence in public space, rather than a blockade – with hundreds of people participating in many activities and debates and dozens of people participating in the night camp. Participation began to decline in June. By the end of June, it was becoming almost impossible to maintain the night occupation and on 5 July it was decided to break up the camp and reorganise. Instead, from then on, weekly assemblies would be held. In February 2012, the name would finally be changed to *Assembleia Popular de Coimbra* [Popular Assembly of Coimbra].[47]

In the evolution of the Coimbra *acampada*, we observe the transformation of economic awareness into democratic practice. The *acampada's* founding manifesto declared its commitment to 'the struggle for freedoms repressed by the economic system'. 'We have reached a limit and we can no longer tolerate a few lining their pockets and living like kings while the others, the majority, have to tighten their belts'.[48] The interviews elucidate the importance of the crisis in promoting a change in consciousness towards emancipatory potential. For example, CD noted: 'The crisis has led many people to ask themselves why they felt oppressed. In this sense, the crisis is a bath of democracy: people get involved, pay more attention and can discern more easily. … The crisis can be positive, although this is ambiguous, as it can also breed hatred'. Similarly, CVB stated that 'for the government, the crisis was an excuse to steal democratic power from the people', but 'on the other hand, the crisis led to a wave of numerous social movements and increased political participation. If people had not been confronted with the extreme situation of the crisis, they probably would not have participated in demonstrations … Confrontation with extreme situations raised the level of consciousness, and this could have been positive if it had been further developed'.

3.1.1 Real and Prefigurative Democracy

Rather than representing a defined model or programme, 'real democracy' implies a practice and a critique of existing forms of representative democracy. It involves an open discussion process characterised by 'a community always

46 Alípio et al. 2013, p. 359.
47 Alípio et al. 2013.
48 Manifesto Primavera Global 2012.

in the making, being nothing but the sum of actions of its members'.[49] This form of democracy is not guided by specific goals but rather defined by what it opposes: a shared scepticism towards the state, bureaucracy, party politics, representation, hierarchies, and power in general.[50] It values a democracy of assemblies based on participation, immediacy, diversity, and 'horizontality'.[51] Decisions within this structure were made during daily and later weekly assemblies, based on consensus rather than voting. This approach is aligned with the idea of creating an inclusive space for democratic participation, where all individuals' ideas and opinions are fully considered.[52] The voting process is rejected because it is perceived as exclusive, oppressive towards minorities, and individualistic, as it quantifies individual opinions.

To constitute an alternative to liberal representative democracy in crisis, democracy should be transformed through the practices of citizens themselves; participation itself is the pedagogical basis for real citizenship and real democracy. The horizontal nature of this democratic practice meant that the *acampada* rejected formally elected representatives or leaders, whether they came from 'parties, unions' or 'other representatives who want to make decisions in our name', although some activists have naturally assumed such roles, taking on most of the initiatives and leading the debates.[53] Assemblies often took long hours to make decisions, when they came to make decisions at all. Participants preferred inaction to making decisions that went against the will of any individual participant. This non-exclusionary approach also ensured that democratic decision-making was interconnected with other aspects of life.

Since personal circumstances, such as motherhood or hunger, should not be a reason for exclusion in the deliberative process, democracy must be accompanied by practices of solidarity and alternative economies, sharing, and mutual aid. Initially focused on creating spaces for free debate and expression, occupation of the public sphere, deliberation, and participation, the movement ended up imagining itself as a genuine prefigurative form of social alternative in the midst of the social crisis. In addition to the popular assemblies, participants organised a free forum and frequently held debates and workshops, cultivating a complete 'alternative society' with spaces for studying, sleeping, cooking, a public library, and a children's area. This configuration prefigured

49 Rohgalf 2013, p. 155.
50 Rohgalf 2013.
51 Rohgalf 2013, p. 152.
52 Alípio et al. 2013, p. 359.
53 Assembleia Popular de Coimbra 2011; Alípio et al. 2013.

an alternative society that rejected capitalist profit, operating instead based on principles of solidarity, autonomy, and decentralisation.[54] Political discussions were integrated with shared community meals, and plans were developed for community gardens.

Because it is centred on horizontal procedures, the Occupy movement is often associated with anarchism and council communism, insofar as it is 'premised on opposition to externally imposed hierarchy'.[55] The core of anarchism is the teleological pursuit of individual freedom, in which the individual is seen as possessing intrinsic moral worth, a view that was most clearly expressed by one of its leading theorists, Mikhail Bakunin. Anarchism is anti-state and anti-government. Anarchists regard the state as 'the primary perpetrator of coercion and the most egregious example of externally imposed hierarchy'.[56] Gibson argued, however, that the Occupy movement was anarchist in its praxis, expressed particularly in its pursuit of direct democracy and refusal to engage with state capitalist institutions, rather than ideologically. Activists in the movements as such rarely referred to anarchist theory or theorists, unlike socialist activists involved in the movements. The Occupy movement refused to formulate a pre-determined programme for social change or to make reformist demands on the *statu quo*.[57]

As a consequence, the lack of concrete proposals, and with it a very poorly elaborated discourse on what exactly democracy would be, is one of the main characteristics of the entire Occupy movement.[58] Even though the entire *acampada* movement was built around the slogan 'Real Democracy Now!', in the specific case of Portugal, the only reference made by the Coimbra Popular Assembly to democracy is relatively vague. For example: 'We believe that the struggle for the "public" and the "common" can sow the seeds for a new democracy. An inclusive democracy, where the values of self-determination (or autonomy), equality, and freedom are the guiding principles for building a society for all'.[59]

---

54 Alípio et al. 2013.

55 Gibson 2013, p. 339.

56 Gibson 2013, p. 340.

57 Gibson 2013, p. 346.

58 Pickeril and Krinsky 2012; Rohgalf 2013.

59 Assembleia Popular de Coimbra 2011. Our translation. In the original: '*Acreditamos que da luta pelo "público" e pelo "comum" poderão ser lançadas as sementes para uma nova democracia. Uma democracia inclusiva, onde os valores da autodeterminação (ou autonomia), da igualdade e da liberdade sejam as linhas condutoras da construção duma sociedade para todas e para todos*'.

About what this alternative democracy would be, CD, a member of the Coimbra popular assembly, is afraid of saying 'silly things'.[60] She vaguely defined democracy as, 'a state in which the community can choose its future on the basis of a system of representation; but real democracy must allow more freedom of choice than we have now. Real democracy does not create political careers'. According to CVB, another activist, 'we need another form of democracy' because the 'party system is exhausted, perverted to such an extent .... The parties we know are so deformed that it is impossible to trust them'. 'Markets rule and governments only control a little, we never vote for the people who make the real decisions'. This other form of democracy is defined as 'everyone has the same power ... being equal, effectively equal'.[61]

The *acampada* movement and the idea of 'real democracy' have often been associated with the idea of prefiguration. Prefiguration is a term used by activists and scholars to describe a protest practice that embodies the changes activists want to see on a larger scale.[62] According to Darcy Leach, prefigurative politics is based on the premise that the ends a social movement achieves are fundamentally shaped by the means it employs; therefore, these means must embody or 'prefigure' the type of society that the movement aims to create.[63] This involves enacting the ultimate values of an ideal society within the very methods of struggling for that society.[64]

Prefiguration is driven by more than a commitment to moral action; it serves as an alternative to both vanguardist and reformist strategies of social change. Rather than relying on a revolutionary vanguard to seize existing power structures and impose change on behalf of the masses, or on trade unions or social democratic political parties to enact reforms within the existing system, a prefigurative approach seeks to create a new society 'in the shell of the old' by developing counter-hegemonic institutions and modes of interaction that embody the desired transformation. This strategy is based on the principle of direct action, whereby individuals directly implement the changes they seek, rather than relying on others to make those changes on their behalf.[65]

Rather than presenting a coherent programme or discourse, the democratic alternative in prefiguration consists of practicing or performing democracy. This involves creating a practical example of what democracy actually looks

60 CD, personal communication, 19 February 2015.
61 CVB, personal communication, 26 February 2015.
62 Maeckelbergh 2009; Rohgalf 2013.
63 Leach 2013.
64 Maeckelbergh 2009, p. 67.
65 Leach 2013.

like through citizens' assemblies and embodied experiences, thus making 'the people', the often invisible sovereign of modern democracies, visible and tangible.[66] When formal institutions appear to fail, prefigurative initiatives are alternative strategies that seek autonomy beyond nation-states, international financial institutions, global corporations, and neoliberalism, while also going beyond the institutionalisation of social movements and their reproduction of authority and oppression.[67] According to Maeckelbergh, prefiguration functions as an alternative to the 'possible legitimization of terror in the idea of a dictatorship of the proletariat that would supposedly end exploitation and suffering'.[68] In contrast, prefiguration allows no tactical deviations from its own ideals: '[I]nstead, the struggle and the goal, the real and the ideal, become one in the present'. It enacts the supreme values of an ideal society through the very means of fighting for that society. Prefigurative tactics thus eclipse the opposition between means and ends, and between the struggle and the goal of emancipation.[69]

Judith Butler characterises prefiguration by its 'performative power to lay claim to the public in a way that is not yet codified into law, and that can never be fully codified into law'.[70] Inspired by Hannah Arendt's analysis of the Greek polis and the Roman republic in *The Human Condition*, Butler emphasises this performativity – more than deliberation – as a key aspect of contemporary prefigurative democracy. The public place, the site of democratic confrontation, is a 'space of appearance'; as Arendt describes, 'the Polis is the organization of the people as it arises out of acting and speaking together'.[71] Morgan Gibson sees this performativity as a practical reenactment of anarchic social forms where 'individuals and communities should simultaneously decide upon and live (prefigure) social arrangements, rather than having them imposed from without or after a revolutionary moment'.[72] This approach avoids involvement with the State and the formulation of demands in pursuit of social transformation.

Prefigurative politics has roots in religious traditions. In early Christianity, prefiguration served as a form of 'phenomenal prophecy', where acts of faith and good deeds prefigured salvation or life after death. The way people

66 Rohgalf 2013.
67 Soares 2017, p. 527.
68 Maeckelbergh 2009, p. 67.
69 Rohgalf 2013.
70 Butler 2011, p. 4.
71 Arendt 2013; Butler 2011.
72 Gibson 2013, pp. 342–5.

lived their lives was seen as 'something real and historical which announces something else'.[73] One of the major shifts in human emancipation and social criticism in modernity was the transition from religious criticism to social criticism – a transition from criticism of the kingdom of heaven to addressing the social misery of material life.[74] In this context, prefiguration gained a new political meaning.

Prefiguration is an integral part of Marx's theory of socialism and praxis, rooted in his conception of power, human needs and consciousness, and their interaction in human activity. Thus, the political agent of change, the organised working class, is formed within the structure of the capitalist system through its internal dynamics and its political practices oriented towards immediate social needs and political emancipation. These collective methods of struggle, including camaraderie, equality, and democratic participation, prefigure the communist society that aims to replace capitalism. Raekstad argues that this strategic conception of organisational structures gives us a promising approach to fostering dialogue between Marxist and anarchist critiques of capitalism.[75] A critical part of revolutionary socialist strategy is to develop organisations that embody the structures of deliberation and decision-making that the future society must contain.[76]

Political praxis, with its intrinsic relationship between thought and action, is a crucial element of traditional class-based politics, where the concept of the mass strike occupies a central position. A mass strike involves expanding the economic struggle of workers for specific demands in a particular corporation to eventually encompass an entire sector and society as a whole. In doing so, it transcends the inherent separation[77] between the private and political spheres in capitalism. This transcendence allows the struggle to adopt more political demands, with the potential to become revolutionary or insurrectionary. As Rosa Luxemburg has described, a strike may initially appear to be 'a mere economic struggle for wages', but through the government's response and social democratic agitation, it can become 'a political phenomenon of the first rank'.[78]

As Rosa Luxemburg suggests, the mass strike constitutes a complex historical and political process that takes shape in relation to the social scenario

73 Auerbach 1984, p. 29; Raekstad 2017.
74 Marx 1977.
75 Raekstad 2017.
76 Ibid.
77 Wood, 2016.
78 Luxemburg 2007.

in which it is inserted.[79] A mass strike is not artificially 'made', nor randomly 'decided', nor 'propagated', but is a historical phenomenon that, at a given moment, results from social conditions with historical inevitability.[80] During this process, collective political learning takes place, and the course of events requires the creation of parallel political structures for decision-making, as well as some form of economic organisation and planning. A sustained strike requires strike committees to collaborate at a higher level to organise security, food distribution, garbage collection, and health services. In this way, not only a form of dual power emerges, but an entire structure of parallel institutions, economy and laws, expressing the interests of workers, prefigures a more egalitarian society to come.

The politics of prefiguring a new society rather than making demands on the state, and the importance of ritualising and institutionalising protest, were undoubtedly major distinguishing elements of the *Acampadas*/Occupy movement as an alternative democratic practice after the global financial crisis.[81] As in other countries, in Portugal there have been prefigurative initiatives for decades; recent examples include social centres such as the well-known Fontinha School in Porto, eco-villages, and parallel currencies.[82] But, taking Rosa Luxemburg's analysis of the mass strike as a historical model for anti-capitalist prefigurative politics, how can we interpret contemporary movements characterised by ideas of prefiguration?

While the movement initially focused on creating spaces for free debate and speech, it gradually incorporated genuine elements of prefiguration. We have seen how the Occupy movement has often been linked to anarchist and council communist traditions within the working class. However, there are notable differences between the prefiguration of the historical labour movement and the contemporary prefiguration, which shed light on its potential and its problems.

A first difference lies in the role of democracy within the movement: in the historical labour movement, workers' democracy arose from a concrete need for collective organisation around specific demands. In contrast, contemporary prefigurative movements often treat democracy as an ideal, lacking concrete demands and a cohesive political programme. A second difference is the social composition of the movements: the labour movement consisted of an organised mass of workers, whereas today's prefigurative movements generally comprise a relatively small minority of young, highly educated students, unem-

79 Bonilla 2013.
80 Luxemburg 2007.
81 Butler 2011; Pickerill and Krinsky 2012.
82 Soares 2017, p. 522.

ployed individuals, and precarious workers. This organic disconnection from the production process is reflected in a third major difference: prefigurative historical goals and methods focused on taking control of the means of production through strikes, factory occupations, and picketing; they were organically anti-capitalist. Modern prefigurative movements, however, focus on the occupation of public space, discourse, and media attention. A fourth essential difference is the organisational structure: the first was based on collective organisations, such as unions and parties with political agendas. In contrast, contemporary movements emphasise the autonomy and opinions of participating individuals, who are expected to remain independent of any 'hierarchies' and formal organisations.

3.1.2 Post-protest and the Post-political

Regarding these differences, we can argue that contemporary forms of prefiguration, particularly in the Global North, are influenced by neoliberal hegemony, although they also mean that this hegemony is in decline. This hegemony profoundly impacts discourses, protest methods, and political organisation. Its emphasis on the method – democracy – rather than a political goal – such as socialism or communism – remains a consequence of neoliberal and post historical hegemony, reflecting the notion that 'there is still no alternative'. In this context, protest is reduced to a symbolic and moral statement rather than a political act capable of effecting change. Neoliberal influence is also evident in a general trend towards depoliticisation: a focus on consensus rather than conflict, on discussion rather than practical resistance, on citizenship rather than class, and a widespread rejection of parties and collective organisations or ideologies.

Contemporary prefiguration can be seen as part of a transition from traditional protest to post-protest movements, where aesthetic practices and changes in individual lifestyle are central. Post-protest movements born out of anti-austerity protests, such as the Portuguese '*Academia Cidadã*', emphasise cooperation and empowerment over direct confrontation. Activists have shifted the focus from collective action to individual or small group initiatives, often rooted in ecological and ethical concerns.[83] Post-protest movements prioritise individual behaviour and ethical consumption over collective political action, viewing personal lifestyle choices as deeply political. Two other forms of action are highlighted in this transition 'beyond protest': a push toward aesthetics and retreatism.

83 Fernandes-Jesus et al. 2018.

Decreus, Lievens and Braeckman argue that contemporary forms of prefiguration, which aim for symbolic efficacy through aesthetic and affective means, may have more in common with types of artistic activism – such as 'Reclaim the Streets' or the 'Yes Men' – than with traditional political protest.[84] 'Artivism', the blend of art and activism, uses performative and aesthetic means to challenge power relations and inspire action. While Mouffe emphasises that artistic practices play a role in the reproduction and 'disarticulation/rearticulation' that define hegemonic and counter-hegemonic politics[85] and there is always an aesthetic dimension to politics and a political dimension to all art, she also argues that no form of critical artistic practices, contrary to what some artivists believe, can bring about the end of neoliberal hegemony or carry out the necessary transformations to establish a new alternative hegemony.[86] The arts do not replace political practices – in the construction of a new order, the strictly political moment cannot be avoided, or in the words of the famous Portuguese protest song by José Mário Branco, 'The song is only a weapon / when accompanied by the struggle'.[87]

The turn to the arts and aesthetics mirrors the 'resistance' to industrial alienation that took the form of romanticism, which Schmitt fiercely criticised in the first half of the twentieth century.[88] Schmitt accused romanticism of accommodating itself to liberalism; its simple denial of modern technical rationality through aesthetics neglects the fundamental struggle of ideologies.[89] A contemporary refuge in the arts on the part of new protest movements could then, even if it opposed contemporary alienation, be just a reproduction of post-political liberalism.

The analysis of exodus as a form of reaction in the context of crisis is certainly not new. In his classic categorisation of behaviour in relation to social structures, Robert Merton classified the behaviour of such activists as 'retreatism'.[90] Retreatists neither accept the goals nor the institutionalised means offered by a social system, but at the same time they have given up on collective rebellion. The exodus, or 'withdrawal' among young people – as opposed to 'protest' – is also one of the behaviours that Habermas observed as empirical evidence of the legitimation crisis of late capitalism.[91] He attributed this to a

84 Decreus, Lievens, and Braeckman 2014.
85 Purakayastha 2014, p. 57.
86 Mouffe 2008.
87 Decreus et al. 2014; Mouffe 2013, p. 99; 2014.
88 Schmitt 1996; 2017.
89 McCormick 1999; Schmitt 2017.
90 Merton 1938, p. 676.
91 Habermas 1975a, pp. 91–92.

'reaction to an overloading of personality resources', a behavioural syndrome that Keniston observed and examined in 'alienated' individuals, as opposed to what he called 'young radicals'.[92] According to Döbert and Nunner-Winkler, the exodus of the 'alienated' was represented by 'hippies, Jesus-people, the drug subculture, phenomena of undermotivation at school, etc., a wide spectrum of behavioural potentials that cannot be explained by resorting to the trivial psychological assumptions made in economic theories of crisis (deprivation leads to protest)'.[93]

While we approach this retreat as a crisis of the system and a crisis of reaction, reproducing aspects of neoliberalism, some influential authors have promoted this exodus as a legitimate political strategy. In *Empire*, a popular work in the alter-globalisation movement, Hardt and Negri argued that, against postmodern imperial control, where power is diffuse and the enemy is increasingly difficult to identify, traditional forms of opposition lost their effectiveness.[94] After the failure of Soviet socialism, they placed their hopes in the 'multitude', a reconceptualisation of democracy beyond representation and sovereignty. As a post-working-class alternative, the multitude, a paradoxical unity based on differences, serves as a new way of 'being against' republicanism based on exodus and desertion, which they consider a powerful form of class struggle. Like the barbarians who overthrew the Roman Empire, capital depends on the multitude, but is constantly thrown into crisis by the multitude's resistance to its rule and authority. This refusal of the sovereign's authority, framed in terms of biopower, represents an exodus from oppression in search of freedom.[95] They describe this process as 'absolute democracy', an active politics capable of challenging the world imperial order.[96] Inspired by these ideas, post-*operaismo* theorists reject traditional political channels, such as parties and unions, defending a new model of organisation.[97]

Decreus et al. argue, however, that the exodus observed in the Occupy movements should be seen as part of a performance rather than a concrete strategy.[98] Often, the idea of an outside to the existing order has been enacted rather than genuinely pursued.[99] The *Indignados* and Occupy movements reflect a political landscape that has become increasingly complex, where clear

92 Keniston 1968.
93 Döbert and Nunner-Winkler 1973, p. 321.
94 Hardt and Negri 2003, pp. 210–16.
95 Hardt and Negri 2004, pp. 333–34.
96 Hardt and Negri 2004, pp. 90–1.
97 Mouffe 2014.
98 Decreus et al. 2014.
99 Decreus et al. 2014.

divides between hegemonic antagonists are less evident. They attribute this to two factors: the influence of neoliberal hegemony and its post-political societal representation, and the inherent complexity of issues such as financial capitalism and climate change, which highlight the challenge of identifying clear targets within these movements.

Swyngedouw's concept of post-political post-democracy includes elements such as the externalisation of problems inherent to global neoliberal capitalism, the elevation of an imaginary 'people' to a universal level, the disembodiment of a vague and nameless 'enemy', and the management of potential conflicts through consensual dialogue.[100] It offers a useful framework for examining depoliticisation in protest movement discourses. Although most of these movements presented explicit and traditionally left-wing and anti-capitalist political demands, such as references to the troika and austerity (AL, M12, QSLT), opposition to the 'law of the markets' (AL, IL, M12, AC, QSLT) and defence of the revolution of 25 April 1974 (M12M), the application of the post-political filter to the manifestos of *Geração à Rasca* and *Movimento 12 de Março* quickly reveals an emphasis on non-partisanship, the use of vague and non-ideological identities, and moralistic appeals.

Geração à Rasca self-identified as a 'generation' and, while highlighting the precarious working conditions, stated that it was not protesting against other generations, but ultimately included everyone: 'Unemployed, five-hundred-eurists, disguised slaves, subcontracted, temporary employees, false independent workers, intermittent workers, interns, scholarship holders, student workers, mothers, fathers and children of Portugal'.[101] The initial aim of emphasising the problem of precarious working conditions quickly became depoliticised: the manifesto does not mention capitalism, profits, or neoliberalism; instead, it refers to capitalists as 'employers' and uses management language, appealing to 'opportunities' to 'realize our potential' and to 'improve economic conditions' and 'economic success'. Condemns the 'waste' of 'efforts', 'investments', 'resources', and 'skills'. Ultimately, demands become depoliticised when the movement expects management solutions through dialogic policies. The manifesto states, 'We protest so that all those responsible for our current situation of uncertainty – politicians, employers and ourselves – act together for a rapid change of this reality, which has become unsustainable. … We protest for a solution, and we want to be part of it'.[102] *Movimento 12 de Março*, which evolved from *Geração à Rasca*, emphasised civic participation and democratic renewal.

100 Swyngedouw 2009, p. 613.
101 Manifesto 2011.
102 Manifesto 2011.

The manifesto criticised the democratic deficit and called for greater citizen involvement, but it also lacked a clear political or ideological structure. This approach reflected a broader social disillusionment with traditional politics.

It is remarkable the complete absence of references in the manifestos (GAR, M12M and QSLT) to traditional left-wing organisations, such as parties, unions, or even associations, as possible allies. It is all the more remarkable given that several participants, even in its leadership, were party members. It was less surprising that the same absence existed in the assembly movements (AL, IL, AC), where anarchist sympathies often strengthened the anti-party aspect of their discourses, particularly in the aftermath of struggles between organised left-wing militants (from Marxist parties and collectives such as BE, MAS, Rubra and SR) and disorganised activists and anarchists who were suspicious of any kind of organisation, particularly their organised colleagues in such meetings. This distrust ended up leading to the rupture between the *Acampada do Rossio/Lisboa* and the *'Indignados de Lisboa'* and reinforced the suspicion against political-party militants and the disbelief in the legitimacy of electoral democracy centred on parties. These movements rejected traditional political representation and emphasised horizontal practices and consensus decision-making, but their discourses often remained vague and depoliticised, focusing on corruption and poor governance.

This emphasis on corruption, combined with criticisms of inefficiency and governance, reflects a common post-political discourse indicative of a broader social disillusionment with traditional politics. Attributing 'bad governance' to 'corruption' and 'politicians' privileges' personalises and culturalises the crisis, legitimising the hypothesis of a 'corrupt culture' as its root cause, rather than the structural problems of capitalism. This approach externalises problems by focusing on the essential side effects of neoliberal capitalism, potentially obscuring deeper political-economic issues. Although movements are considered non-ideological, it is important to remember the well-known paradox about ideology: non-ideology is merely the semblance, formal distortion, or displacement of ideology itself. The power of ideology reaches its peak, its hegemonic position, when its subjects do not recognise it as ideology, but assume it as unquestionable truth or common sense.[103] 'Non-ideology' or 'apolitical position' is the predominant ideology of our time, reflecting the post-1989 belief that the grand narratives of the twentieth century are over. Consequently, resistance to neoliberalism has become more Fukuyamist than Francis Fukuyama himself. 'Politics' is blamed for the crisis and mismanagement, and associated

103 Žižek 2000, p. 185.

with corruption, careerism, and *'politique politicienne'*. Boaventura de Sousa Santos has argued that since the collapse of 'actually existing socialism' in 1989, anti-capitalist protest movements have resorted to rather vague demands for 'more democracy' due to the lack of 'real alternatives' to capitalism.[104] The slogan 'Real Democracy Now!' is emblematic of this phenomenon.

The analysis of six anti-austerity movements reveals how genuine grievances risk being co-opted by neoliberal discourses through common post-political themes such as vague self-identification, a focus on corruption, moralistic and managerial critiques, and calls for dialogue and cooperation with political elites. These factors make it challenging to articulate systemic policy alternatives. *Que Se Lixe a Troika*, the latest movement emerging from efforts to unify protests with broader parties and organisations, called for unified resistance against austerity and emphasised the need for a just society. Although it produced a more politicised discourse by clearly identifying the Troika and its collaborators as the enemy, it still displayed elements of depoliticisation, particularly in its focus on corruption and technocratic financial regulation.

The *acampada* movement was based on distrust in party politics and parliamentary representation. Its emergence signified not only the crisis of neoliberal democratic hegemony, but also that of its democratic opposition, while at the same time reflecting neoliberal hegemony. After months of mobilisation, the participants we interviewed were quite sceptical about the potential to configure the desired 'truly democratic' alternative. Although the experience could not be generalised, it nevertheless had a pedagogical effect on the participants, providing them with knowledge, deliberative capacity, and high political and civic awareness: 'Probably the popular assembly has more impact on those who participated in it than on society in general', concluded one of the participants. For prefigurative politics to once again become part of a viable post-capitalist alternative it probably needs to be rethought as a collective class project centred on economic power, as it originally was, rather than deliberation or discourse.

3.2 The Trade Union Alternative

While the rise of protest movements is often symbolised by the mobilisations of new activist groups, trade unions have played a central role in the resistance to austerity. Overall, this 'old' style of union politics provided most of the mobil-

---

104 Bonet 2010.

isation capacity.[105] Given their importance and the fact that most interviews were conducted during strikes or demonstrations organised by unions, themes related to unions appeared frequently in the respondents' conceptualisations of democracy. Fifteen respondents defined democracy in terms directly related to unions, focusing on practices of struggle and procedural aspects of democracy. This included participation in social struggles, strikes, demonstrations, and meetings. The lack of democracy was often attributed to restrictions on trade union rights, such as pressure against union organising, limitations on workers' meetings in the workplace, and restrictions on the right to strike.

In a concerned reflection on the state of democracy, one of the respondents, Manuel, 37, commented, 'One day, we won't even be able to organise a picket line'.[106] Similarly, Tiago, 50, said, 'There is repression; they try to stop people from organising meetings and strikes', while noting that the erosion of democracy is reflected in his lack of time for family life.[107] Trade union activity is often framed as a pillar of democratic legitimacy. Jorge, 66, emphasised this connection, stating, 'They [the government] do not represent the will and interests of the Portuguese people – this is expressed through demonstrations, rallies, strikes, and other forms of protest'.[108]

Other interviewees emphasised the substantive or outcome-oriented dimensions of union democracy, framing social and labour rights as the essence of democratic principles. The lack of democracy was often associated with the erosion of these rights, seen as hard-won in decades of union struggles. Nuno, 45, commented, 'On a daily basis, people are being robbed of things essential to their existence, basic and primary things like education, health and other aspects of the work sphere'.[109] Clara, 28, added, 'The government violates workers' rights and freedoms; this is not democracy'.[110] Similarly, Margarida, 56, expressed her perspective: 'Democracy should mean better living conditions for us: living in health and peace, living better, producing, working'.[111]

These union-related perspectives are consistently reflected in the views of two prominent union leaders interviewed for this research: Mário Nogueira, president of the teachers' union federation FENPROF, and António Mariano, president of the dockworkers' union SETC. Mário Nogueira defined democracy

105 Accornero and Pinto 2015c.
106 Manuel 2, personal communication, 14 November 2012.
107 Tiago, personal communication, 14 November 2012.
108 Jorge, personal communication, 27 November 2012.
109 Nuno 2, personal communication, 27 November 2012.
110 Clara, personal communication, 27 November 2012.
111 Margarida, personal communication, 26 October 2013.

as being rooted not only in representative governance, but also in the 'relationship with organizations representing workers' and in the extent to which it addresses 'the daily lives of people, in particular the most vulnerable, through public services such as health and education'. He highlighted the erosion of democracy due to the imposition of limits on collective bargaining and the decline in the quality of public services and wages.[112] Similarly, António Mariano articulated democracy in terms of citizens' rights, including employment opportunities, access to health and education, and the right to control one's own destiny and life. For Mariano, democracy is impossible as long as governments prioritise foreign and corporate interests over those of their populations. He argued that such policies undermine the sovereignty and dignity of citizens, effectively stripping democracy of its substantive meaning.[113]

Although unions lost their monopoly on social protest due to the emergence of the *Geração à Rasca* and the *acampada* movement, and were less emblematic, they continued to be the most powerful force against austerity, in terms of participation numbers, number of protests, and real impact on society and the economy. They organised national and regional demonstrations, as well as a record number of sectorial and general strikes. Although unions have lost a significant amount of influence and membership in recent decades, they have been able to draw on organised structures, broad social penetration, and a track record of past achievements. They played a crucial role in unifying struggles and mobilising the mass of the working class, particularly public sector workers, in the resistance against austerity.[114]

A considerable proportion of citizens who protested against austerity measures did so through trade unions. Unions not only mobilised their members and colleagues directly in their workplaces, through workers' committees and pickets; the national protests also mobilised many non-union citizens. Through these mobilisations and definition of the agenda, the unions determined their consciousness, demands, and forms of action. It is therefore not surprising that many of the protesters interviewed formulated their ideas about democracy through a union framework.

But the relationship between unions and democracy goes beyond this circumstantial coincidence. While rational choice theory, which views democracy as a historical accident in the pursuit of individual utility maximisation, views unions as market imperfections that are essentially undemocratic, and some postmodern theories view unions as mechanisms of domination that

---

112 M. Nogueira, personal communication, 28 September 2020.
113 A. Mariano, personal communication, 26 February 2015.
114 Accornero and Pinto 2015a, pp. 408–10.

are becoming increasingly superfluous, most democratic theories incorporate unions as a positive and essential part of democracy, in line with Geoffrey Wood's informative overview.[115] These include the Weberian perspective on the dynamics of bureaucratisation and representation and internal and external democracy in unions, theories of unions as social movements, and regulatory theories that promote more responsible and sustainable economic policies.[116]

Visser and Ebbinghauss consider that unions are among the main and most influential actors in democratic politics.[117] Within the framework of traditional representative democracy, unions are active agents that use different forms of pressure on governments, parliaments, and public institutions, and support and finance candidates, parties, and even referendums. But the democratic role of unions goes much further and was fundamental in the democratisation of society prior to universal suffrage.[118] According to the works of Visser and Visser and Ebbinghauss on European trade unionism, trade unions have historically played a crucial role in the labour movement to promote mass democracy, based on the universal emancipation of the working classes.[119] As the main organisations of the working classes, they were protagonists of rebellious mobilisations aimed at demanding rights for the most disadvantaged layers of society.[120]

In academic literature, trade union democracy is often associated with the concepts of economic democracy or industrial democracy, the latter coined by Webbs and commonly associated with the idea of 'industrial citizenship'.[121] Poole later broadly defined industrial democracy as 'the exercise of power by workers or their representatives in decision-making within their workplaces, along with a redistribution and adjustment of authority within the workplace'.[122] Industrial democracy is often contrasted with the more radical concept of workers' control.[123] Unlike industrial democracy, workers' control has anti-capitalist, if not revolutionary, implications, as it aims at workers' democracy within fundamentally transformed relations of production. This radical

115 Wood 2006, pp. 19–36.
116 Wood 2006, p. 35.
117 Visser and Ebbinghauss 2000, p. 6.
118 Costa 2011.
119 Visser 1995, pp. 37–8; Visser and Ebbinghauss 2000, pp. 4–6.
120 Ross and Martin 1999, p. 2.
121 Webbs 2003.
122 Poole 1979; Poole et al. 2001.
123 Gunn 2011; Stoleroff 2016, pp. 104–5.

vision often creates tension with trade unionism due to their potentially conflicting goals and strategies.[124] These different approaches reflect the ideological divisions within the Portuguese labour movement. Economic democracy, unlike socialism or workers' control, focuses on expanding workers' influence – primarily through union representation – over decision-making processes in capitalist economic structures. This includes mechanisms such as worker participation in management, worker ownership of shares, and profit sharing, aimed at increasing workers' participation in economic outcomes while remaining within the structures of capitalism.[125]

In the struggles to extend political democracy to the disfavoured classes, trade unions have developed historic alliances with political parties and served as a basis for different forms of democratic practices. The model of the German Social Democratic Party, founded in 1869, as a political voice of the working class and trade unions, influenced by the ideas of Karl Marx, is an important example.[126] This would eventually lead to the expansion of parliamentary democracy to include the votes and representatives of the working classes and trade unions. During the twentieth century, in many northern European countries, trade unions became central pillars of social democracy and the welfare state; examples of this are the role of trade unions in the co-management of companies in Germany or the social management structures in what Devos, Mus and Humblet call the neo-corporatist pacification democracy of Belgium.[127]

But trade unions, particularly revolutionary syndicalism at the beginning of the twentieth century, also left openings to go beyond parliamentary democracy.[128] Rosa Luxemburg stated that the class demands of the unions will eventually create the need to do so 'because every direct mass action in the period of open class struggle would be at the same time political and economic'.[129] She developed the traditional trade union method of mass strike as an alternative social, democratic, and pedagogical practice to go beyond parliamentary politics:

> It is true that these men [Bernstein, David, right-wing social-democrat parliamentarians] saw the desired civilising and mitigating of the class struggle in

124 Mandel 1973; Ness and Azzellini 2011.
125 Stoleroff 2016, pp. 104–5.
126 Costa 2011.
127 Devos, Mus, and Humblet 2011; Müller-Jentsch 1995.
128 Costa 2011.
129 Luxemburg 2007, p. 169.

> the light of petty bourgeois democratic illusions – they believed that the class struggle would shrink to an exclusively parliamentary contest and that street fighting would simply be done away with. History has found the solution in a deeper and finer fashion: in the advent of revolutionary mass strikes, which, of course, in no way replaces brutal street fights or renders them unnecessary, but which reduces them to a moment in the long period of political struggle, and which at the same time unites with the revolutionary period and enormous cultural work in the most exact sense of the words: the material and intellectual elevation of the whole working class through the 'civilising' of the barbaric forms of capitalist exploitation.[130]

With roots in radical republicanism, direct action, and anti-authoritarianism, principles that characterised the diverse landscape of Portuguese working class associations in the nineteenth century, the anarcho-syndicalist tradition in Portugal played a central role in the formation of the labour movement at the beginning of the twentieth century. The newspaper *A Batalha*, created in 1919, became the main organ of the anarcho-syndicalist movement, having a wide readership among workers and serving as a platform for the promotion of its ideals. This movement was institutionally represented by the *Confederação Geral do Trabalho* (CGT), which led numerous strikes and exerted significant influence during the First Republic (1910–1926). As in many other European countries, the anarcho-syndicalist tradition in Portugal ended up contributing to the creation of workers' parties, such as the Portuguese Communist Party (PCP), founded in 1921, which gradually distanced itself from anarchist principles in favour of Marxist-Leninist centralisation. Over time, severe state repression, particularly during the *Estado Novo* dictatorship (1933–1974), and ideological competition from Marxist organisations marginalised anarcho-syndicalism. Despite this, the ideals of direct democracy and self-organisation continued to resonate in segments of Portuguese labour activism, leaving a lasting legacy.[131]

In the period after the Second World War, the European trade union movement was marked by three phases; a period of strong mobilisation in the 1960s, a period of consolidation of negotiations and social agreements in the 1970s, and the emergence of neoliberal neo-Fordism from the 1980s onwards.[132] According to Boaventura de Sousa Santos, the historical development of trade

130 Luxemburg 2007, pp. 163–4.
131 Varela and della Santa 2023.
132 Ferreira 2004; Santos 1995a.

union practices in Portugal is somewhat different from the rest of Europe, due to its semi-peripheral position.[133] In Portugal during the 1960s, trade union activity was mainly restricted to clandestine and difficult organising during Salazar's far-right dictatorship. The 1970s were defined by the Portuguese Revolution, during which the frustrated dream of socialism gave way to the establishment of a liberal parliamentary regime.[134] The widespread mobilisation of industrial workers in 1974–1975, demanding fundamental democratic labour rights, organising workplace assemblies, creating workers' committees, and advocating the purge of managers who collaborated with the dictatorship regime, wage increases, and, in some cases workers' control – key elements of trade union democracy – stands out as one of the most defining aspects of the social revolution that initially drove Portugal's democratic transition.[135] The association of political and industrial democracy during this period opened an opportunity to 'apply the concept of democracy to a vast range of positive citizenship and class rights, pushing the limits of democracy beyond political representation and even formal rights to union representation and collective bargaining'. But the radical quest for workers' control eventually gave way to a paradigm of industrial democracy largely confined to distributive and redistributive issues.[136]

The Portuguese revolution of 1974 contrasts with Spain's 'smoother' transition to liberal democracy, which was negotiated between political representatives of the democratic opposition, which included the PSOE, the PCE and liberal sectors of the bourgeoisie, and remnants of the Franco regime. This difference explains why social pacts emerged earlier in Spain than in Portugal.[137] In the 1980s, when Portugal finally reached a point where social agreements and an embryonic welfare state could begin to consolidate, neoliberal reforms were already on the horizon. This period saw the implementation of the first bailout and structural adjustment programme under IMF guidance.[138] Subsequently, Portugal has relatively advanced social rights, but these workers' rights are continuously and massively violated.

After the 1974 Revolution, the *Intersindical Nacional*, later the *Confederação Geral dos Trabalhadores Portugueses* (CGTP-IN or simply CGTP), founded in 1970 and closely aligned with the Portuguese Communist Party (PCP), sought to

133 Santos 1995a.
134 Santos 1995a, p. 132.
135 Stoleroff 2016, p. 102.
136 Stoleroff 2016, pp. 104–5.
137 Lima and Artiles 2011, p. 390.
138 Santos 1995a, p. 132.

establish itself as the sole trade union confederation in Portugal. This vision of 'trade union unity' was rooted in the belief that a unified and centralised labour movement would be more effective in resisting capitalist exploitation and supporting the revolutionary transformation of Portuguese society. However, this perspective faced resistance from more reformist sectors of the labour movement, particularly those aligned with the Socialist Party (PS), who advocated for pluralism in the union scene. These more right-wing factions supported the creation of a rival trade union confederation, the *União Geral dos Trabalhadores* (UGT), in 1978, which reflected a more moderate and pro-European stance. The fight over the issue of the single central union became one of the central points of confrontation between the PS and the PCP during the years of the revolution. The end result was a dual confederal structure: the CGTP, more closely associated with the PCP but also including other sectors of the left – socialists, progressive Catholics, and the radical left – and the UGT, which has closer ties to the PS and PSD.[139] This division shaped the dynamics of labour relations in Portugal for decades. Between 1986 and 2008, the UGT signed all the social pacts, while the CGTP signed only six. Furthermore, almost all general strikes in Portugal were called exclusively by the CGTP, highlighting its continued role as an opposition force within the labour movement.[140]

In the decades following the revolution, trade union organising in Portugal moved away from its revolutionary and participatory roots, focusing primarily on defensive – and sometimes existential – struggles. These efforts prioritised maintaining employment, resisting privatisation, and preventing factory closures, rather than challenging corporate power or decision-making processes.[141] Union membership also declined significantly: between 1979 and 1985, 58.8 percent of wage workers were union members, but that number fell to just 22.4 percent in 1999.[142] Labour relations in Portugal were ranked among the least participatory in Europe, particularly in terms of workplace participation and direct democracy. By the late 1990s, unionisation rates had fallen by approximately 50 percent, falling to less than one-third of the workforce.[143]

When approaching the concept of union democracy, theorists often distinguish between internal and external democracy.[144] According to Boaventura de Sousa Santos, external democracy derives from the dual primary function

---

139 Lima and Artiles 2011, p. 390.
140 Lima and Artiles 2011, p. 392.
141 Stoleroff 2016, p. 106.
142 Lima and Artiles 2011, p. 390.
143 ILO 1997; Stoleroff and Naumann 1994; Sisson 2000; Stoleroff 2016, p. 103.
144 Harcourt and Wood 2004; Santos 1995a.

of unions: the struggle for social rights and collective bargaining with employers and the state.[145] Internal union democracy is based on close participation of members in decision-making, unity and solidarity, general assemblies, the election of shop stewards, and referendums on important decisions.

While some institutionalist, rational choice, and elitist literature argues that internal union democracy can be detrimental to broader societal democracy – suggesting that stronger unions can lead to 'excessive demands' or neo-corporatist tendencies – other perspectives, particularly those rooted in institutional and radical social theory, reject such a contradiction.[146] These approaches see internal and external democracy as deeply interdependent. Internal democracy concerns the decision-making processes within unions, including how leaders are elected, agendas are set, and struggles are organised, all of which are essential to safeguarding external democracy. Internal democracy also functions as a counterweight to the emergence of autocratic leadership and oligarchic privileges within union structures.[147] Furthermore, the active democratic participation of trade unionists ensures that unions do not become mere transmission belts for political parties, maintaining their autonomy and relevance.[148]

Unions serve as a 'voice' that articulates workers' interests and demands.[149] This collective voice allows workers to overcome their unequal individual positions when confronting employers in the labour market.[150] The main elements of this collective action include freedom of association, union organisation, collective demonstrations, and strikes, all of which maintain their importance even in contexts where the representativeness of unions may be questioned.[151] Rooted in its dual functions of struggle and negotiation, trade unionism generally follows two distinct trajectories: contestation unionism and participation unionism. These approaches reflect different forms of union democracy and embody two seemingly opposing political perspectives on social change: whether the role of unions is to civilise capitalism or to build a social alternative to it.[152]

---

145 Santos 1995a.
146 Harcourt and Wood 2004, pp. 4–5.
147 Santos 1995a, p. 136.
148 Santos 1995a.
149 Teague 1999, p. 55.
150 Offe and Wiesenthal 1980.
151 Costa 2011; Rogers and Streeck, 1995.
152 Santos 1995a.

3.2.1 Trade Unions and Social Movements

According to Santos, union democracy is strengthened through the transformation of the worker's identity into a citizen identity: in contemporary societies, unions can only fulfil their role as representatives of the *demos* through their involvement in broader struggles against alienation, such as consumer rights, ecological rights, cultural rights, etc.[153] During this process, unions need to work together with other progressive social movements, such as consumers, feminists, anti-racists, and environmentalists.

In the academic literature, this aspect of union democratisation is referred to as 'social movement unionism (SMU)'.[154] SMU is a union practice that goes beyond the politics of a specific company or sector and helps to build broader structures of resistance for common goals.[155] Or, as Turner and Hurd put it, SMU encompasses unions or labour organisations that orient their structures and members to 'building networks with different active groups and educate their rank-and-file members to prepare for and intervene in social movements'.[156]

Since the birth of the new social movements in the 1960s, these alliances have never been easy. The new social movements brought creative forms of activism, new discourses, and democratic forms of organisation against the 'old' bureaucratised movements and workers' parties. Unions have always looked with suspicion and scepticism at these movements that actively distanced themselves from the 'vanguard of the working class' and proposed new contours of social conflict.[157]

The crisis and austerity have strengthened competition between unions and social movements for the same social base, precarious workers in particular. The prospect of competition has worsened the traditionally very suspicious stance of Portuguese unions towards collaboration with other social movements.[158] Fonseca describes how union activists look at what they call 'inorganic movements' such as Platform 15O: they are unpredictable, lack identifiable organisational structures and accountability, have a lot of internal ideological heterogeneity, and are too radical.[159] For social movements, on the other hand, cooperation can also bring the threat of institutionalisation.[160]

153 Santos 1995a, p. 135.
154 Dibben 2004, p. 286; Engelhardt 2017b, p. 92.
155 Engelhardt 2017b, p. 93; Engeman 2015, p. 2.
156 Turner and Hurd 2001, p. 12.
157 Estanque 2008; Harcourt and Wood 2004.
158 Fonseca and Estanque 2018, pp. 219–20.
159 Fonseca 2016, p. 278.
160 Dibben 2004, p. 297.

For unions, the institutionalisation of struggles is fundamental to the realisation and defence of what they consider essential parts of democracy: public services, workers' rights, etc. Mário Nogueira, leader of FENPROF, one of the interviewees for this research, highlights this stark difference in approach:

> What really distinguishes the trade union movement from this type of movement is the fact that the trade union movement has an organization, is based on an organization and a structure that is successful and remains ... In the most difficult moments, the trade union movement becomes even more important. It is present and shows its face, goes to the fight and you have to go out in public and be able to denounce and demand ... In other moments, when these movements appear, things end up being easier. In these moments, people are more attentive, they are more easily available ... more available to protest .... Some arise from opportunism, in some contexts they can even mobilize, but they disappear as quickly as they appeared ... I value unions more, not only because I am a union leader, but because I think that the response that unions give is a permanent response, and people need that response all the time.[161]

According to Anne Engelhardt and Dora Fonseca, the anti-austerity protests, however, were marked by impressive examples of 'social movement unionism', with union structures deciding to approach social movement activists and support them.[162] As traditional democratic institutions have proven incapable of meeting the traditional demands of unions – for more jobs, decent work, greater social justice, combating precariousness, transparency, etc. – they came together in a common opposition to austerity.[163] Dora Fonseca uses the framework of Laclau and Mouffe to show how this identification in confronting a common opponent made them equivalent, accentuating their differentiation in relation to the system and creating an articulation between unions and social movements.[164] A divide was created between those who opposed austerity and the institutions that were responsible for it. The conflict between capital and labour has become strongly intertwined with demands for more and better democracy, which were transversal to all protests.[165] Social movement unionism developed links between union militants and social activists that still remain and could be valuable for future protest movements in Portugal.[166]

161 M. Nogueira, personal communication, 28 September 2020.
162 Engelhardt 2017b; Fonseca 2016.
163 Fonseca 2016.
164 Fonseca 2016, p. 183.
165 Fonseca 2016, p. 184.
166 Engelhardt 2017b.

3.2.2 The Example of the Dockworkers

The Union of Dockworkers, Traffic Controllers, and Shipmasters of the Centre and South of Portugal (SETC) played a vanguard role during the wave of protests against austerity. Being independent from the two main trade union confederations, CGTP and UGT, gave them more freedom. The union conflict at the time was not so much a protest against austerity: it had very specific objectives around working conditions in Portuguese ports.[167] They have been involved in four years of conflict over labour standards and collective bargaining agreements with the government and private port companies, as well as against the privatisation of port management.[168] The SETC not only mobilised its affiliates for prolonged strike actions over a long period. To combat the media campaign against them, they followed a strategy of broadening support for their struggle through alliances with social movements: they participated in and supported demonstrations against austerity organised by social movement activists, as well as on issues of housing and precariousness. Anne Engelhardt explains how, in doing so, Lisbon's dockworkers became the most visible example of social movement unionism in Portugal.[169]

On 15 September 2012, the dockworkers began to present themselves as a bloc at the *Que Se Lixe a Troika* demonstration. From that day on, the SETC was active almost every week in almost all the demonstrations that took place until 14 November, where it also had a strong bloc in the general strike demonstration. In addition, dockworkers began to support protests for social housing and organised a national demonstration against precarious working conditions in Portugal.

The Portuguese dockworkers had few resources and worked under the adverse political and economic circumstances of the Troika memorandum. But according to Fox-Hodess, they were ultimately successful because of the structure of the union and the orientation of its leadership, which allowed them to gain power in the ports. The outcome of their struggles – the reinstatement of laid-off precarious workers and the recognition of collective bargaining – was not only a victory for the workers immediately involved, it was also an important boost for national and international labour movements more broadly.[170]

---

167 Fox-Hodess 2017.
168 Engelhardt 2017b.
169 Engelhardt 2017a, p. 46.
170 Fox-Hodess 2017.

SETC-SEAL president António Mariano was one of the key players in the austerity struggles we interviewed for this research.[171] According to him, 'there is no democracy in Portugal'. Since economic interest groups have taken power and government policies have nothing to do with electoral programmes and promises, representative democracy ends on the day the votes are counted. Parliament and the president are reduced to pure 'decoration'. Elections lead to flawed results, which cannot be controlled later. At the same time, unions need to fight attempts to take away union and organisational rights.

Mariano understands democracy as 'government of the people and for the people'.[172] More specifically, he understands democracy as the possibility for workers to organise, discuss, and work for their future, their job security, and financial conditions to sustain their lives. For the dockworkers, there seems to be no separation between internal and external democracy; their own democratic and participatory practice is the way they want to see society. There are some parallels with the prefigurative practices of the *acampadas* movement, with the difference that the *acampadas* projected their practice as a utopian ideal for society, while for the unionists they are their daily material and work practices necessary for survival. Regarding the internal direct democracy of the *acampadas*, Mariano believes in it as a practical model for society:

> We practice democracy here, in our unionism. Among us, port workers, all important decisions are taken in assemblies, we work from the basis. We have power precisely because of our rank-and-file; This gives our union much more strength than relying solely on the mandate they gave us when they elected us. Democracy is the possibility for those affected by political decisions to participate in decision-making. In our own sphere, as dockworkers, internal democracy is both practical and required. The participation of workers through their class organization, with decisions taken in assemblies, as we advocate, is the only way.[173]

Even though the level of participation in Portuguese society has tended to decline again since the great demonstrations of 2011–12, the work needs to continue: Mariano believes that, just like the prefigurative politics of the *acampadas*, it is necessary to spread ideas through the example of actions and behaviours that obtain results:

171 A. Mariano, personal communication, 26 February 2015.
172 Ibid.
173 A. Mariano, personal communication, 26 February 2015.

> Through these methods we guarantee worker participation and a 100% unionization rate – while the average in Portugal is close to a shameful 10 percent of workers. Our workers are a cross-section of society, from the far right to the far left. We don't care about people's party or religious choices. These aspects are left out. Here we gather and collectively discuss our future.[174]

Mariano recognises that there is a union tradition in Portugal of keeping its distance from social movements, but the SETC acted differently when approaching these movements. The aim was not only to strengthen these movements with union support and give them more visibility, but also because it allowed the dockworkers to assert their own demands more efficiently. Mariano stated:

> Maybe we are not so radically anti-party and anti-parliament as these movements, but we believe that power must be continually pressured – and here we are aligned in terms of our struggles and objectives, whether in terms of the environment, layoffs, housing, unemployment, and precariousness. Our struggle for job security, for collective wage agreements, against the differentiation of contracts between workers and for the integration of precarious workers is very much in line with the fight of the movements against precariousness and unemployment.[175]

We can conclude that, although unions have lost their monopoly on social protest, they still have a central role and, through it, define citizens' perspectives on democracy. The aspect of participation and democracy as an ongoing practice is a very important aspect of trade union democracy as an alternative. Instead of the prefigurative utopian version of the *acampadas*, the practices of the unions are more a form of everyday work, the alliances with parties and social movements – social movement unionism – are not just a political ideal, but a matter of strategic survival.

3.3 The Party Alternative

Political parties have, since the nineteenth century, been seen as central institutions in parliamentary representative democracies.[176] For Bryce, parties are indispensable to representative government, Max Weber describes them as

174 A. Mariano, personal communication, 26 February 2015.
175 Ibid.
176 Dalton, Farrell and McAllister 2011, p. 3.

the main products of democracy and mass political participation, and Schattschneider goes so far as to claim that modern democracy is inconceivable without political parties.[177] Parties simplify political choices, educate and mobilise citizens, and thus ensure the stability of the political system.[178] Competition between parties forms the basis of the minimalist – hegemonic – model of democracy, as described by Schumpeter and Przeworski.

Can parties be an alternative to the crisis of liberal democracy, which is also a crisis of political parties? Research indicates a decline in citizens' identification and affiliation with political parties in recent decades.[179] The crisis led, as it did in the 1930s in France and the Weimar Republic,[180] to the rejection of party representation itself, exemplified not only by the success of non-partisan social movements such as the *acampadas*, but also by high dissatisfaction with intra-party democracy among party members.[181] In response, parties such as *5 Stelle* in Italy and *Podemos* in Spain have adapted by empowering their members and by opening up their internal decision-making processes to external citizens, seeking to increase participation and legitimacy by directly involving society in shaping party policies and directions.[182]

The notion that parties are the cornerstones of democracy presupposes a parliamentary and representative form of democracy and an electoral model of political parties. These assumptions should not be taken for granted. First, there are alternative forms of democracy: neither the Greek polis nor the first European parliaments had modern parties, and even in democratic theory, parties are a relatively recent phenomenon. David Hume described them as 'the most extraordinary and unaccountable phenomenon that has yet appeared in human affairs'.[183] Second, parties do not inherently conform to a democratic consensus. While they play a crucial role in shaping and representing society's opinions, this representation does not necessarily result from electoral legitimacy; parties may pursue antidemocratic, extra-parliamentary, or revolutionary goals. In this context, left-wing parties, particularly anti-capitalist ones, have long struggled to balance defending the concept of parties and rejecting liberal representative democracy.

177 Bryce 1921; Schattschneider 1977; Weber 1990.
178 Dalton et al. 2011, p. 6.
179 Dalton et al. 2011.
180 Daalder 2002.
181 Lisi 2019, p. 152.
182 Gianolla 2017.
183 Hume 1999, p. 161, cited in Daalder 2002, p. 39.

3.3.1 Parties and Portuguese Democracy

The parties played an important role in the establishment and consolidation of Portuguese democracy after the 1974 revolution. The PCP was instrumental in the anti-fascist resistance, while the PS guided the revolutionary process towards liberal democracy. In most European countries, parties have historically been in a legal grey area due to non-interventionist liberal principles.[184] However, in Portugal, parties have been strictly regulated since democratisation in 1974, making it one of the first European countries with strong party regulation. Portuguese law governs almost all aspects of party activity, organisation, and behaviour.[185] Consequently, Portuguese parties are legally and constitutionally organised, with regulations overseeing their recognition, internal structures, and finances. This legal framework guarantees political rights to parties, but also institutionalises them and increases their state dependence compared to other countries. Van Biezen and Casal Bértoa note that changes in party laws aimed to 'democratize' left-wing parties in Portugal.[186] However, until 2015, left-wing parties did not participate in any government agreement due to their orthodoxy and unwillingness to reach agreements, as well as the PS's reluctance to collaborate with them.[187] The party scenario has shown long-term stability,[188] marked by pragmatism, moderation, and dominance of parties covered by the so-called 'arc of governance' (PSD, PS, and CDS-PP), which fall within a relatively narrow band between centre-left and right.[189] These three parties supported the Memorandum of Understanding that imposed austerity. Given the insignificant presence of the radical right before the crisis, the focus here is on left-wing parties as a potential basis for a party-focused democratic alternative.

In parliament, PCP and BE were the main opposition to austerity and the Memorandum of Understanding. Both parties rejected the Troika's invitation to discuss the MoU in April 2011, questioning the legitimacy of international institutions to impose political conditions on the country. Their strategy involved principled opposition both in parliament and on the streets. Consequently, these left-wing parties were the closest link between anti-austerity

184 Rashkova and Van Biezen 2014, pp. 266–70.
185 Van Biezen and Casal Bértoa 2014, p. 76.
186 Van Biezen and Casal Bértoa 2014, p. 79.
187 Freire 2019, p. 62.
188 Jalali 2019, p. 82.
189 Gunther 2005, p. 270.

movements and representative democracy. They were prominent in most anti-austerity protests and acted as the main parliamentary voice for the movements' demands.

According to the prominent MPs of the PCP and BE, Miguel Tiago and José Soeiro, Portuguese democracy is 'formally intact', but 'disfigured' by four decades of liberalisation and the subsequent international blackmail that deeply eroded its social, economic, and cultural foundations and restricted democratic choices. In theory, both assume that capitalism cannot cope with real democracy: the 'phase' of liberal, parliamentary democracy should, at some point, be overcome. Contrary to this logic of a bright democratic future, the substantive and socialist dimensions of democracy – land occupation, workers' control of factories, trade union democracy, neighbourhood committees – seem to function as a utopia of the past: democracy as a conquest of the April Revolution, which gained formal dimension through the emphasis on constitutional rights and the courts to safeguard the threatened democracy. The crisis brought some radicalisation. For Miguel Tiago, the 'structural crisis of capitalist accumulation ... serves as a pretext to crush popular rights ... to destroy democracy ... without political sovereignty, we are a colonized people'. But the crisis also brings hope, because it is precisely in 'dead ends' that revolutions are made.

3.3.2 Parties and Social Movements

Since the 1990s, 'third way' politics, inspired by Tony Blair's New Labour, have left the 'masses' in most northern European countries without their mass, class-based social democratic parties. Meanwhile, on the European periphery, these parties often already had weaker roots in the working class, due to historical repression by right-wing dictatorships and the continued presence of cadre Communist parties guided by Moscow. These Communist parties survived through clandestine activities and centralised structures and quickly gained a mass base in the working class after the democratic transitions. In Greece and Portugal, these Communist parties maintained an anti-capitalist discourse. Their closed political structure made them able to survive the neoliberal hegemony of the 1990s but made them quite factional in relation to other left-wing organisations. In other countries, these Communist organisations adopted a Eurocommunist line. Eurocommunism emerged as a response to growing opposition among Western European Communists to the fierce political repression perpetrated by the Soviet Union, particularly after the Prague Spring of 1968. Eurocommunists, which included the PCF, the PCI/PD, the PCE, but also splits from the Portuguese and Greek Communist parties, accepted liberal democracy as their political horizon. These Eurocommunist organisations would serve as an important base for the formation of 'new left' formations, such as the Left Bloc, *Izquierda Unida* (IU), Syriza and, eventually, indirectly, *Podemos* as well.

Some of these parties emerged from struggles against austerity and are in line with what Kitschelt defined as movement parties: 'coalitions of political activists that emanate from social movements and try to apply the organizational and strategic practices of social movements in the arena of party competition'.[190] According to Della Porta, Fernández, Kouki, and Mosca, these movement parties attempted to fill the gap between protest movements and the political party form, a gap left by social democracy. The deliberate blurring of relations between parties and movements has led to some electoral success.[191] However, they never transformed into mass parties nor presented an anti-systemic alternative to the crisis of capitalism or liberal democracy.

The movement party par excellence, *Podemos* in Spain, emerged from the 15M movement, whose distrust of politicians prevented it from leading this process.[192] *Podemos* adopted many of 15M's political and organisational principles, such as prioritising democracy over class antagonism, direct participation, and focusing on citizens rather than ideological notions of left and right. The party quickly personalised itself around Pablo Iglesias, who, influenced by Essex School discourse theory, led the party towards Laclau-style left-wing populism. This approach emphasised individual leadership similar to Latin American left-wing populism, reinforcing vertical and centralising tendencies.[193] Starting as an anti-establishment force, *Podemos* was fully institutionalised in 2016, sharing governmental responsibilities within a liberal parliamentary model, to the point where it can no longer be considered a movement party.[194] Portugal did not see new movement parties like *Podemos*, so anti-austerity movements did not institutionalise through them. Instead, institutionalisation occurred through engagement with existing parties such as the PCP, the *Bloco de Esquerda*, and through depoliticisation and marginalisation.

The Left Bloc had a naturally closer connection with more recent social movements due to its historical links with groups such as the feminist UMAR, *Precários Inflexíveis*, and *SOS-Racismo*. These groups participated in the pro-

190 Kitschelt 2006, p. 280.
191 Della Porta et al. 2017.
192 Muñoz-Sánchez and Pérez-Flores 2016, p. 198.
193 Della Porta et al. 2017; Kioupkiolis and Katsambekis 2018, pp. 202, 215.
194 Vittori 2017.

tests against austerity, while the PCP always approached them with suspicion or enmity. The movements play a fundamental role in the Left Bloc's conceptualisation of democratic legitimacy, beyond strict formal procedures. In our interview, José Soeiro highlighted that parliamentary action only makes sense in deep connection with what happens outside parliament, which essentially functions as a sphere of expression and deliberation. The diversity of the movements functioned as a party guideline. Similar to the proposal by Laclau and Mouffe, the role of the party is to articulate its different perspectives with the class struggle, based on power relations constructed outside parliament, ranging from social democrats aspiring to institutional justice to autonomist micro-resistances and prefigurative policies.

For decades, the PCP was the main mass party of the organised working class and civil society in Portugal, closely linked to the country's main trade union confederation, the CGTP. Maintaining some official distance, the PCP has acted as the political voice of traditional social movements, cooperatives and professional associations, with its members in key positions. The PCP has been suspicious of the new emerging movements against austerity, often accusing them of being confused, petty-bourgeois, radical, and divisive. Miguel Tiago dismissed these new movements as a historical regression to utopian socialism, stating, 'Camping out in public places, voting on motions, growing our own food, organising theatre and workshops, all of this is very beautiful, romantic and exciting, but it neglects the fundamental issue of taking power. The working class has progressed for centuries to organise itself, to have unions, a party and revolutionary theory and practice, and now we are going back in time'. Anti-party sentiment favours the far right more than the left, creating the illusion that society would be better without parties, which supposedly divide people and harm democracy.

To align the defence of party parliamentary democracy with the communist ideal of direct worker participation – or a system like Cuba's, where parliament is elected without direct interference from the communist party – Miguel Tiago approaches Portuguese democracy as a specific 'stage'. The approach follows the teleological evolution of stages to which some Marxists have adhered, particularly in the context of popular front politics. Basically, liberal capitalist democracy is a phase of evolution before society is ripe for socialism. At this stage, liberal democracy must be defended against attacks from the conservative right and the far right, as a class compromise and a guarantee that communists themselves can do open political work, in opposition to feudal or fascist systems.

In the current 'stage', according to Miguel Tiago, we need to value 'parties' as large organisations of people in the fight for power: 'The existence of parties is a prerequisite for political choices'.[195] 'Even those who do not identify with parties', continues Miguel Tiago, 'must defend them due to the essence of the "party"'. In the current state of humanity, movements should not 'divide', 'nor distract', but rather 'aggregate'. 'What we need is for a class to organise and dispute power'.

In practice, and at least temporarily, both the PCP and the Left Bloc accepted the liberal-democratic order and the rules of the game. Until 2015, both parties remained anti-establishment. However, they had party structures and a political programme, participated in parliamentary discussions, proposed and voted on laws. Still, they had never held executive positions and have always been opposition parties, at least at the national level. Later, we will focus on how pressure for greater institutionalisation of these parties occurred after the crisis, through the strengthening of their parliamentary positions and the consequent responsibilities in government policies.

Many anti-austerity activists viewed political parties, including left-wing ones, with suspicion and hostility. Some were suspicious for ideological reasons – many activists had anarchist and libertarian backgrounds – but this also reflected a general anti-political and anti-party sentiment in society. Many were also suspicious for practical reasons. Activists feared that party structures that 'controlled' many activists together would influence decision-making processes in the movement and undermine its basic democratic character. The alleged revelation by the right-wing newspaper *jornal i*, which 'discovered' and disclosed that four of the six members of the QSLT coordination were in some way linked to the BE and the PCP, played on these feelings.[196] The suspicions raised many discussions within the movements, not only about internal decision-making procedures, but also about the acceptance of people affiliated with parties and the desirability of cooperating with parties in concrete actions and mobilisations.

The dismissive approach of the PCP and CGTP towards emerging social movements, especially in the early stages, further hampered efforts to bridge the gap between traditional and new forms of activism. The PCP and CGTP frequently excluded non-members from their mobilisations, repeatedly banning independent flags or banners at demonstrations. Party officials relegated non-aligned activists to the back of the demonstrations, behind a security corridor, justifying these measures as necessary to maintain security and prevent 'provocateurs'. Although there is no evidence of any secret agreements between the

195 M. Tiago, personal communication, 25 March 2015.
196 Costa 2019, p. 119.

PCP and the police regarding the demonstrations, trust between the parties and the movements deteriorated after two demonstrations were attacked by the police shortly after the PCP delegations had officially left the site. This fuelled suspicions among some activists, who began to spread the belief that the PCP had betrayed them and was cooperating with the state. The fact that the PCP and *Bloco de Esquerda* increasingly focused on electoral strategies, while many of the new social movements against austerity, often influenced by anarchist sympathies, framed their actions around a critique of the electoral democratic model, created further divergences that made cooperation between the traditional left and the newer movements particularly difficult.

3.3.3 Portugal's Party Configuration

Against the background of a profound crisis of democratic legitimacy, in which Prime Minister Pedro Passos Coelho proclaimed his famous phrase 'To hell with the elections!' and came into direct conflict with the Constitutional Court, and the anti-austerity protest movements, aligned with international movements such as the *Indignados* and Occupy Wall Street, united around the demands of 'Real Democracy Now!', we will analyse the electoral moments of 2013, 2014 and 2015, exploring how they contributed to the re-articulation of a renewed democratic hegemony.

Joseph Schumpeter, along with other proponents of the minimalist perspective such as Adam Przeworski, argued that the fundamental flaw of classical democratic theory lies in its reliance on the notion of a unified 'will of the people', which, they argued, cannot exist independently of political actors and institutions to represent and shape it. While much critical literature has highlighted the limitations of this formalist perspective, which approaches voters as consumers who select their preferred 'product', this analysis adopts Schumpeter's approach in a descriptive way. It examines how elections shape and rearticulate democratic discourses, effectively constructing a 'will of the people' within the framework of liberal democracy. Based on Laclau and Mouffe's concepts of hegemony and political articulation inspired by Gramsci, this study explores how the electoral processes in Portugal between 2011 and 2015 redefined a political universality through contingent articulations, highlighting the ongoing negotiation of hegemonic power at local, European, and national levels. We will try to show how elections fulfil the role of institutionalising the 'wills' of the people and thus formalise and institutionalise the hegemony of liberal democracy.

A significant part of this section engages in critical dialogue with the 2017 book *Para lá da 'Geringonça'* (Beyond '*Geringonça*'), by the late Portuguese political scientist André Freire.[197] The word *geringonça*, which literally means contraption or strange mechanism, became the popular nickname for the left-wing government led by António Costa, which came into being in 2015. Freire's book, one of the first important analyses of the *Geringonça* phenomenon, defended a position fundamentally opposed to the thesis presented here. Although we argue that the elections and the subsequent formation of the *Geringonça* government served to institutionalise and therefore deradicalise the anti-austerity protest movements, Freire defended the agreement as a genuine 'democratic revolution'. The question we must ask is: did the post-crisis elections really lead to a revolution? And what kind of democracy filled its content?

We saw how the eruption of the crisis in 2011 coincided with the emergence of a wide range of new social movements in which disorganised and precarious youth played the leading role. Immediately after the crisis that began in 2011, these protest movements, or at least the people active in them, moved in two distinct directions. One part was a movement that radically retracted from society as we know it. The other movement was the institutionalisation and politicisation of protest movements into broad mobilisation platforms around organised left-wing groups and parties. This happened in particular through the QSLT, the 15th of October Platform, and the *Precários Inflexíveis*. Over time, radical left parties became the political representatives of these movements.

The three main traditional parties of the 'arc of governance' – the Socialist Party (PS), the Social Democratic Party (PSD), and the Democratic and Social Centre-Popular Party (CDS-PP) – have dominated government politics in Portugal since 1976. In analysing the sources of democratic reconfiguration, our focus will be mainly on the left opposition, which suffered significant fragmentation during the crisis.[198] Due to its ideological and practical involvement in the protests of this period, the left-wing opposition played a central role in the reconfiguration of Portuguese democracy.

At the height of the crisis, there were two main parliamentary parties to the left of the pro-austerity parties: the Portuguese Communist Party and the Left Bloc. The PCP has been the main party of the Portuguese left since the 1974 revolution. It has a broad membership and strong links with the traditional working class and trade unions. Over the last three decades, there have been several attempts at internal change within the PCP and a process of pro-

197 Professor André Freire, who was part of the jury that evaluated the doctoral thesis that served as the basis for this monograph, passed away on 30 October 2024.

198 Freire 2017, p. 189.

found deradicalisation has taken place.[199] However, the party remains one of the most orthodox Communist parties in Europe.[200] The PCP usually participates in elections through an electoral front called CDU (Unitary Democratic Coalition), with the Ecologist Party The Greens (PEV) and independents. Over the years, the party had had a very stable electorate, around 10 percent.

In 1999, three radical left-wing organisations – the Trotskyist Revolutionary Socialist Party (*Partido Socialista Revolucionário*, PSR), the Maoist Popular Democratic Union (*União Democrática Popular*, UDP) and the Communist reformist movement *Política XXI*, founded a new party. *Bloco de Esquerda* – Left Bloc, also referred to as BE or *Bloco* – had a relatively unstable electorate before the crisis, mainly an urban and young electorate. While the PCP has always had its strongest base in the traditionally organised and older working class, the *Bloco de Esquerda* has tended to focus on the younger and 'precarious' generation.

Based on its supportive attitude towards the USSR and its theoretical criticism of liberal democracy, the PCP could be characterised more as 'extreme' left by André Freire.[201] The Left Bloc is more critical of the historical experience of the USSR and should therefore be considered more 'radical left'. Over time, the PCP has given less importance to the ideas of 'revolution' and 'utopia' as immediate political objectives, although references to 'fidelity' and 'deepening' of the April Revolution continue to be a recurring theme in the party's discourse. The main difference between both parties in the pre-crisis period would be their approach to governance. The PCP theoretically defended a classical Marxist-Leninist approach to democracy. It accepts liberal democracy and defends the 1976 constitution as a transitional phase, but rejects it as an ultimate political goal because 'true democracy' cannot be based on a free market economy. Due to its internal divisions between different political currents, the Left Bloc tends to be less clear on this point. While certain internal currents defend a perspective similar, or even more radical, to that of the PCP, in practice the BE tends to propose reforms in order to expand democracy without a necessary rupture with liberal institutions. The BE tends to be more alter-globalist and the PCP more patriotic. In its relations with the European Union, at least until the beginning of the crisis and the imposition of austerity measures, this translated into a Left Bloc that intended to reform the EU and a more radically Eurosceptic PCP.[202]

---

199 Freire 2017, p. 40.
200 Freire 2017, p. 199.
201 Freire 2017, p. 40.
202 Freire 2017, pp. 190–92.

The crisis radicalised the left and allowed a clear rapprochement between BE and PCP. The PCP associated the crisis with 40 years of right-wing governance, increased its Euroscepticism, and emphasised the need to nationalise strategic sectors of the economy, as well as to renegotiate the debt. The BE also advocated the nationalisation of the banking sector and the privatisation of public services, as well as a partial rejection of the debt, and adopted a much more critical position towards the EU.[203]

Freire argued that most of the programmatic proposals of both the BE and the PCP were not radical, since they mainly defended the programme of the 'old' social democracy.[204] Instead of promising a social revolution and the expropriation of capital, both parties focused mainly on the need for decent wages, pensions and working conditions, as well as defending past social achievements such as the national health service and public education. The change in the 'radicality' of the same concrete programmatic proposals is a consequence of the change in the historical political context.

The old social-democratic programme – defended by the reformist leadership of the historical labour movement in twentieth-century Europe, including the Socialist Party during Portugal's revolutionary period (PREC) – played a pragmatic, reformist, and deradicalising role in a context marked by revolutionary upheavals and perceived Communist threats. Over the last three decades, as former social-democratic parties have increasingly capitulated to neoliberalism – and more recently, its radicalised form of austerity – their earlier Keynesian proposals for state intervention have been taken up by radical parties and paradoxically acquired a radical connotation. In addition to this shift, the supposed or perceived radicalism of parties such as the PCP and the BE is also shaped by their historical criticism of representative governments and their long-standing reluctance to reach an agreement with other political protagonists.

These defining elements of Portugal's party configuration were affected by the various elections that the country has gone through since the implementation of austerity measures and the peak of the street protests: the 2013 local elections, the 2014 European elections and, most importantly, the 2015 legislative elections.

---

203 Freire 2017, pp. 193–95.

204 Freire 2017, p. 40.

3.3.4 Elections during the Portuguese Crisis

While many local particularities influenced the results, the local elections of 29 September 2013 stood out for their 'nationalised campaign', in which the opposition called for a vote against the government.[205] This first electoral moment since the application of the troika memorandum marked a historic defeat for the PSD/CDS-PP coalition in power, which lost around 700,000 votes and reduced its number of mayors from 140 to 106. However, the left did not exactly win either.[206] The PCP slightly increased its vote share from 9.8 percent to 11.1 percent and its number of mayors from 28 to 34. The PS saw its number of votes decrease from 2.1 million to 1.8 million, but its number of mayors rose from 132 to 149. The Left Bloc saw its vote share decrease from 3 percent to 2.4 percent, losing its only mayor. Part of this apparent decrease can be explained by the relative success of independent and locally supported candidacies. Widespread dissatisfaction with government policies was accompanied by a feeling that there were no credible alternatives. Although citizens were dissatisfied with government policies, 61 percent of respondents believed that opposition parties would not do better.[207] Freire argued that polarised discontent was channelled into citizens' lists rather than left-wing political parties.[208] Abstention increased dramatically, as did blank and invalid votes. Citizens' groups almost doubled their elected representatives and mayors between 2009 and 2013. The success of joint participation in citizens' lists in these elections served as a first test of the electoral articulation between social movements and parties.

A similar pattern can be observed in the 2014 European elections. The crisis reinforced Euroscepticism, transforming Portugal from one of the most pro-European member states into one of the most Eurosceptic.[209] This led to the lowest participation ever recorded: 33.7 percent.[210] The two government parties jointly participated in a unified list, *Aliança Portugal*, as a strategy to reduce the electoral damage caused by austerity and save the minority partner (CDS-PP) from electoral devastation. Its votes fell from 39.1 percent to 27.7 percent, and the number of MEPs fell from ten to seven. The PS barely managed to profit, adding just one more MEP in a narrow victory over *Aliança Portugal*, while

205 Freire 2017, pp. 49–50.
206 Freire 2017, p. 50.
207 Freire 2017, p. 54.
208 Freire 2017, p. 51.
209 Freire 2017, p. 122.
210 Freire and Santana-Pereira 2015.

losing a huge share of its votes – 22.7 percent, compared to the 2011 legislative elections. It failed to capitalise on the government's unpopularity due to its inclusion in the Memorandum of Understanding with the Troika.[211] The PS's inability to differentiate itself from the right led to a Pyrrhic victory that triggered a leadership dispute with António Costa, who, as mayor of Lisbon, had managed to forge alliances on the left, creating hope at a national level. Protests against the European Union, the government, and austerity measures were mainly channelled towards the PCP, whose number of MEPs increased from two to three, and the MPT.[212]

The campaign of the Left Bloc, led by Marisa Matias, had disastrous results, losing more than half of its votes and two of its three MEPs. This could be partially explained by strong divisions on the left and reasonable results of new micro-parties with populist and anti-institutionalist orientations, and of social movements, such as PAN, Livre, and MPT.[213] The Left Bloc also suffered from unclear political positions regarding the EU – combining an anti-austerity programme with a very pro-European perspective – and a crisis in the party leadership after the departure of its former leader, Francisco Louçã.[214] However, none of the Left Bloc's splits managed to elect MEPs. The 2014 campaign was marked by left weakness, lack of cooperation, and credible political alternatives to the crisis, leading to cynicism and abstention. The MPT, *Movimento Partido da Terra*, a 'conservative environmentalist party'[215] would benefit greatly from the discontent.[216] Its first candidate, Marinho Pinto, would be the first TV commentator projected by the private media to become an agenda-setting populist politician. With slogans against corruption and the establishment comparable to the *5 Stelle* movement in Italy led by Beppe Grillo, it would be the big surprise of the elections, electing two MEPs[217] A series of internal conflicts and political scandals affected the party's credibility, which eventually disappeared, but its success would pave the way for the far-right populism of Chega.

In the 2015 parliamentary elections, the right-wing governing coalition, now called *Portugal à Frente* (PàF), remained the largest political formation. It lost a large number of votes, voting percentages, and seats, as well as its parliamentary majority. It obtained 38.5 percent of the votes, which, through the D'Hondt

211 Ibid.
212 Freire and Santana-Pereira 2015.
213 Freire 2017, p. 123.
214 Freire and Santana-Pereira 2015, pp. 102–3.
215 Freire and Santana-Pereira 2015.
216 Salgado 2019b.
217 Salgado 2019b, p. 57.

method of seat distribution, translated into 46.5 percent of the seats in parliament.[218] Given the ongoing demonstrations against austerity policies, this 'victory' came as a surprise.[219] Freire attributed this to international pressure from the EU and financial markets, the idea that there was no alternative and that 'the worst was already done', and to the media's support for what Freire called the 'Syriza antidote' – the notion that even if the people elected an anti-austerity government, it would achieve nothing.

The left-wing opposition parties combined still obtained 61.4 percent of the votes and had an absolute majority.[220] The real 'winners' were the radical left parties, which obtained almost 20 percent, breaking the system of 'alternation' between the two 'regime parties' that had lasted for 40 years.[221] The PCP won 17 seats, compared to 16 in 2011. The biggest electoral gains went to the Left Bloc, which after two electoral defeats and a series of internal divisions, presented a coherent anti-austerity narrative and rose from eight to 19 seats, emerging as the third largest party in parliament. At the start of the campaign, the Left Bloc distanced itself from the about-face of its Greek sister party, Syriza, which, after failed negotiations with the EU continued the austerity policies of previous governments. The absence of new anti-system forces in Portugal, similar to *Podemos*, Syriza, or M5S – parties that have associated themselves with anti-austerity movements – can be attributed to several factors.[222] First, the PS left the government before the Troika agreement came into force, which allowed it to oppose the harshest austerity measures and thus limit the space for the radical left. Furthermore, the pre-existing radical left forces, which consistently won more than 10 percent of the vote, made it difficult for a new party to gain popularity among the same disaffected electorate. Instead, there was a push for collaboration among the left, including the PS.

With a disappointing 32.4 percent, the Socialist Party won 11 more seats, for a total of 85.[223] The party was squeezed between its traditional role, faithful to the interests of Portuguese capital, economic stability and compliance with European agreements, and social pressure against austerity, but it would not suffer the losses of its sister parties in Greece, Spain, or France. With its small electoral progress, the PS was presented by the media as the real loser of the elections, and the internal right-wing opposition demanded the resignation of

218 Freire 2017, p. 199.
219 Freire 2017, p. 160.
220 Freire 2017, p. 168.
221 Freire 2017, p. 161.
222 Della Porta et al. 2017.
223 Freire 2017, pp. 161–62.

its leader, António Costa. Some, further to the left, feared a left-wing overtaking and a 'pasokisation' in the future, and pressed for collaboration with the anti-budget cuts agenda of the BE and the PCP.[224]

3.4 The Road to *Geringonça*

Negotiations for a government coalition after the 2015 elections played an important role in restructuring the prospects for democracy in Portugal. The loss of the absolute majority of the PàF government coalition opened the way for a series of parliamentary alternatives, along with the reconnection of parliamentary and extra-parliamentary perspectives. The new balance of power ensured that a parliamentary majority would only be possible through a coalition between the two main parties of the regime or an agreement between the PS and the parties of the 'radical' left.

At first glance, the government participation of the Left Bloc and the Communist Party seemed highly unlikely. Radical left parties had never participated in governments in the 40 years of democracy after the approval of the 1976 constitution and the PS had never made agreements with partners to its left at the national level. The left has always been excluded from the so-called 'arc of governance' which refers to the three parties that have formed governments over the last 40 years: PS, PSD, and CDS-PP. During the Cold War, this exclusion of the radical left was the general rule in most European states. But in the years following the fall of the Berlin Wall, when left-wing forces, like the PCF, PCI and others, entered governments in France, Italy, Scandinavian countries and elsewhere, the Portuguese case became an exception.[225]

Freire and Estanque list three main reasons for the historical lack of convergence on the left.[226] First, there was the historical enmity surrounding the *Processo Revolucionário em curso* (PREC), the revolutionary period between the fall of the authoritarian regime on 25 April 1974, and 'democratic normalisation'. After this period, the left classified the PS as a 'traitor' to the revolution, since it intended to keep Portugal in a liberal democratic and European sphere. The PCP and the radical left, on the other hand, were labelled as authoritarian forces that wanted to implement a USSR-style dictatorship. A second reason, according to Freire and Estanque, is the way in which Portuguese unions are

224 'Pasokisation' refers to the electoral disaster of the social democratic PASOK party, punished for what was described as 'responsible governance' – the continuation of austerity policies during the Greek crisis.

225 Freire 2017, p. 107.

226 Freire and Estanque 2013.

organised. While a unified trade union movement could have fostered left-wing collaboration, its division along party lines in Portugal instead deepened political sectarianism. A third factor is the political differences between the left-wing parties, with the PS traditionally aligned to the right and more pro-European, while the 'radical' left, and in particular the PCP, has a much more Eurosceptic position. Before the elections, radical left parties declared that they would continue to resist any government coalition that pursued austerity policies. It seemed unlikely that the PS would agree to a series of crucial conditions to this end, including debt renegotiation, reassessment of European fiscal rules, and an end to austerity policies.

The parties that signed the Memorandum of Understanding with the troika – PS, PSD, and CDS-PP – won more than two-thirds of the seats in parliament. Historically and politically, these parties have agreed on important topics such as fidelity to international agreements, the fiscal pact, the Maastricht criteria, and the euro. The most likely scenarios for the process of forming a government, according to Freire, were therefore based on a partnership between the PàF government coalition in power, or part of it, with the PS: a PSD/PS/CDS-PP coalition or a continuation of the PàF government with parliamentary support from the PS.[227]

Nevertheless, PS and PSD are also each other's biggest opponents, especially regarding the petty politics of distributing political positions and influence in the deep state. A grand coalition – a 'central bloc' type coalition, in Portuguese terms – between the regime parties would also offer a monopoly over the opposition to the radical left and could pose the risk of delegitimising all the regime parties. Such a scenario would also put the CDS-PP in a difficult position. The main reason it remained in the unpopular PSD-led austerity government was to push through a conservative ethical agenda – blocking abortion law and gay rights, for example. In the newly elected parliament, with a progressive ethical majority, this could easily be overlooked.

The PàF alliance formed by PSD and CDS-PP therefore preferred the continuation of its government, now a minority one. Their political strategy consisted of framing it as a question of 'democracy', since they had 'won' the elections. They also sought to legitimise this solution based on the tradition of the 'arc of governance', the historic cordon sanitaire around the radical left that has existed since 1975. Less than two days after the elections, without any consultation with a view to a parliamentary majority, the PSD and CDS-PP announced a coalition agreement for the continuation of Passos Coelho's government. To

227 Freire 2015.

make it possible, they relied on the right-wing president in power, Cavaco Silva, with the idea of 'political stability' and with the parliamentary support of a divided PS, in the form of abstentions or disloyalty, as a 'responsible' opposition.

Several factors obstructed this solution. One is that a minority government led by the PSD would extend its monopoly right to positions in the deep state. Another was the ideological inflexibility of the right. Despite the negative economic results in terms of public debt and deficit, Passos Coelho persisted with policies that the PS had framed as 'more Troika-like than the Troika'. The continuation of these policies was contested by historical figures from the PSD itself, including Manuela Ferreira Leite and José Pacheco Pereira. Furthermore, the PSD/CDS-PP coalition government has continually legitimised its unpopular austerity policies as being a consequence of the 'excesses' of the previous PS government led by former Prime Minister José Sócrates.

Furthermore, António Costa had no interest in facilitating collaboration between the PS and the PàF.[228] By doing so, he would have immediately broken his main electoral promise not to support a new austerity budget by the government parties. Another factor was the internal divisions within the PS. Several PS figures demanded Costa's resignation after the elections. Costa probably would not have saved his position as secretary general of the PS if the party had remained in the opposition. The post of prime minister and access to the government after four years of exclusion had all the ingredients for the reunification of the party under his leadership, while at the same time saving his position.

Relations between PSD and PS worsened with the controversial decision by President Cavaco Silva to reappoint Passos Coelho. The president invoked the tradition of inviting the leader of the largest electoral formation to form a government, despite having proclaimed before the elections that he was in favour of a government with a large majority and a stable coalition.[229] The president's controversial speech openly attacked the left-wing parliamentary majority. In his statement, Cavaco Silva attempted to impose a cordon sanitaire on the left-wing parties BE and PCP due to their Eurosceptic and anti-NATO positions that would harm Portugal's image and interests before the European Union and financial markets.[230] He openly appealed to PS parliamentarians to ignore party discipline in the vote of confidence.

---

228 Freire 2017, p. 205.
229 Freire 2017, pp. 167–68.
230 Freire 2017, p. 167.

Allowing the PS, BE, and PCP to respond to the unilateral decision of the President of the Republic would only represent a waste of time that would only harm the country's financial situation and its credibility in international markets. The speech was framed as unacceptable and unconstitutional behaviour from an authoritarian president. According to Freire, the speech revealed incoherence, parochialism, and a lack of democratic political culture.[231] It had the opposite effect to that intended. Instead of dividing the left, it led to greater unity, both within the PS – where the internal opposition would support Costa almost unanimously and give him a mandate to negotiate with the BE and the PCP – and between the PS and the left-wing parties. Even the employers' federation CIP (*Confederação Industrial de Portugal*) criticised the President's 'unnecessarily polarising speech'.

The departure of the PSD and Passos Coelho became the opposition's main priority. After Cavaco Silva's speech, the PS announced that it would present a motion of no confidence, a possibility that, until then and during the electoral campaign, it had firmly rejected, defending instead an alternative agreement for a parliamentary majority. In the newly constituted parliament, the new balance of forces immediately crystallised with the election of the PS MP, Ferro Rodrigues, as president of the *Assembleia da República*.[232]

By the time the government was announced, it was already clear that the presidential initiative to form a minority government was doomed. Eleven days after his appointment, a motion of no confidence was passed and the newly formed twentieth constitutional government led by Passos Coelho resigned. At that time, António Costa already had a political agreement for a parliamentary majority with the BE, the PCP, and the PEV to support a PS government.

Initially, President Aníbal Cavaco Silva – who was also approaching the end of his term and therefore had reduced powers – refused to appoint António Costa. Some even hoped that he could keep Passos Coelho's government in charge of current affairs, with a national budget in twelfths, until new parliamentary elections could be called after the presidential elections.

The danger of a regime crisis, with power divided between parliament and government, a government without a budget and unable to meet its European obligations, combined with the potential for social mobilisation supported by a parliamentary majority – all of this would eventually lead the president to accept the PS government. The *Geringonça* solution was born, putting an end

231 Ibid.

232 Equivalent to the Speaker in the British House of Commons.

to the 27 days of the shortest government in the history of Portuguese democracy after 25 April 1974.

The word *geringonça* can be vaguely defined as 'something poorly constructed', a 'fragile structure that functions dangerously',[233] a 'contraption or device' or a 'poorly conceived plan'.[234] The term *geringonça* was used by critical opinion makers to name the agreement for the formation of Portugal's twenty-first constitutional government. The term, previously used to belittle the new coalition, would end up being recovered by the government and its supporters. It would be chosen as the Portuguese word of the year in 2016.

The *geringonça* would thus consist of a minority government formed by the PS, led by António Costa, with the parliamentary support of the PCP, BE, and PEV. The deal would signify a major shift in Portuguese parliamentary tradition, particularly the unwritten rule of the 'arc of governance', which excluded the left from participating in government. Protest movements against austerity were an important precondition for these political developments. The protest not only gave greater electoral weight to the left-wing parties BE and PCP, which had been the main parliamentary voice in the struggle against the cuts during the previous government, it also gave stronger social legitimacy to the demands of these parties among the general public, forcing the PS to take them seriously. Social pressure to form a governmental alternative to the continuation of the PàF government also led to an unexpected turnaround in the attitude of the left-wing parties, forcing them into a constructive position of dialogue with the PS. During the election campaign, Catarina Martins, spokesperson for the Left Bloc, presented three minimum conditions for dialogue with the PS: abandoning the plan to save an additional 1.6 billion euros in pensions, abandoning the new labour regime that would facilitate dismissals, and giving up plans to reduce corporate taxes.

Immediately after the elections, both leaders of the PCP and BE expressed their willingness to collaborate with the PS to avoid a government led by Passos Coelho. Both the general secretary of the PCP, Jerónimo de Sousa, and the spokesperson for the Left Bloc, Catarina Martins, stated that they would present a motion of no confidence against the right-wing government of Passos Coelho and that its survival would depend solely on the PS. As a regime party 'in bed' with potential coalition partners on both the left and the right, the PS suddenly found itself in a relatively comfortable position, despite the party's disappointing election results.

---

233 Houaiss 2001, p. 353. Our translation. In the original: '*o que é malfeito, com estrutura frágil e funcionamento precário*'.

234 Geringonça 2018, p. 532.

Responding to the intentions expressed by the BE and the PCP during the first week after the elections – while Cavaco Silva tried to support the PàF solution – the negotiators of the three parties began talks for a possible coalition. During the government formation process, António Costa met independently with the leaders of the radical left parliamentary forces. These negotiations did not occur without their fair share of problems.

Many attributed to Catarina Martins a brilliant strategy that would unmask the socialists or pave the way for a progressive coalition. There was also internal criticism of this strategy – a tension that revealed the difficulties of building an alliance involving people who led previous protest movements. The tension was expressed in the form of opposition to the three themes of the negotiations that did not address any of the structural problems behind the crisis; after all, Catarina Martins had not mentioned the debt renegotiation and the budget agreements. This was also expressed in the accusation of a lack of open internal democratic consultation on these issues. In the end, however, none of the representatives of the national leadership of the Left Bloc voted against the negotiations with the PS.

Greater difficulties were expected in the negotiations with the PCP. Although the communists had made it clear that they were open to cooperation with the left and that the failure to form a government led by Costa on the basis of a left majority in parliament would be the sole responsibility of the PS itself, the PCP still seemed very reluctant to give guarantees for the legislature. To the horror of the Europeanists of the PS and the anti-communist opinion-makers of the Portuguese media, during the negotiations the MEPs of the PCP also proposed a bill that would allow countries to leave the eurozone.

Separate agreements were eventually signed with the BE, PCP, and PEV that would guide the government's political principles in exchange for a vote of confidence and support for the government's proposal for the national budget. These agreements, among others, included: an increase in the minimum wage from 485 to 600 euros over the four-year legislative term; the recovery of pensions that had been frozen by the Passos Coelho government; the recovery of wages in the public sector; combating precarious contracts, with special attention to contracts of 'false' independent workers; a reduction in VAT for restaurants; and to stop the ongoing privatisations of public transport and public services.

This agreement was met with surprise and horror by both commentators and politicians on the Portuguese right, who claimed that Costa's solution was undemocratic.[235] Manuela Ferreira Leite, former president of the PSD, accused

235 Freire 2017, p. 163.

Costa of deceiving the people and organising a coup d'état.[236] Marco António Costa, another prominent figure in the PSD, described the new left-wing government solution as 'democratically illegitimate'.[237] In turn, right-wing opinion leader Rui Ramos spoke of 'post-election fraud'. If the party or alliance that won the election is unable to form a governing coalition because it obtained only a 'relative majority', the possibility of doing so should be given to the second largest party. This is common practice in most European parliamentary systems and is also in line with the Portuguese constitution. But in 40 years of democracy, it had never been practiced before.[238]

For many on the left, both in Portugal and in the European Union, the agreement was greeted with hope and enthusiasm. *Geringonça* was presented as a democratic alternative to neoliberalism and as an example of the success of left-wing policies in Europe.

3.4.1 Democratic Revolution or Thermidor?

What exactly was the impact of the *Geringonça* solution on democracy in Portugal? In his book *Para lá da 'Geringonça'*, Freire makes a positive assessment of the first years of the *Geringonça*, focusing on the fact that the agreement allows the Portuguese government to implement the necessary political changes, while always remaining in compliance with EU laws.[239] It is a satisfactory solution for the electorate, evidenced by the growing approval ratings in electoral polls during 2016 and 2017. For Freire, the *Geringonça* is a 'true democratic revolution' for three reasons:

1) The inclusion of 18 percent of the population (who voted for the PCP or BE) who were previously marginalised restored the principle of one person, one vote.[240] At the institutional level, the participation of the radical parliamentary left of the PCP, PEV, and *Bloco de Esquerda* in the government solution democratised representative institutions. Electoral democracy was expanded as more political parties and political programmes became available to voters again, with the reasonable expectation that they could participate in forming coalitions, thus expanding the 'useful vote' and the 'arc of governance';

236 Antena 1, 2016.
237 Sá 2015.
238 Freire 2017, p. 163.
239 Freire 2017, pp. 218–20.
240 Freire 2017, p. 165.

2) The improvement of the quality of representation on two levels, since finally the left-wing political elites are doing what their electorate expects them to do. Recent surveys show that the constituencies of the PS, BE and PCP prefer collaboration between left-wing parties rather than the traditional collaboration of the PS with the right. The government formation process also clarified different political options and increased political choice, taking the PS to the left.[241] This produced a break with the 'there is no alternative' discourse used by Pedro Passos Coelho and the Troika. Under pressure from the PCP and BE, the government pushed for limited reforms that broke with the idea of the inevitability of austerity policies, such as increasing the minimum wage to 557 euros in 2017, reintroducing previously eliminated holidays and ending the privatisation of the transport sector. All of this served to question the idea that economic recovery would only be possible through new cuts in wages and working conditions;
3) Freire believes that the government can have a positive effect in Europe, perhaps even becoming an inspiration for other countries on the continent, playing an important role in ending the neoliberal status quo at an international level.[242] The *Geringonça*, therefore, could mean a true democratic revolution.

Nonetheless, some problems remain. Given that government policies have remained fiscally conservative, the fact is that they have not ended austerity altogether. Even Freire points out that the accusations that 'the government and radical left parties lied to the electorate when they promised to end austerity'[243] are partially true. This is partly explained by the restrictions imposed by the EU. Since the government is not inclined to radically change the macroeconomic and macropolitical environment, the origins of the crisis remain.

Meanwhile, due to political pressure from left-wing parties, the burden of austerity has been distributed more evenly between capital and labour, but structural responses have not yet been provided.[244] No solution is given to the structural imbalances in the eurozone, the structural disadvantage of peripheral areas, the lack of democratic legitimacy of EU institutions, the pro-

241 Freire 2017, pp. 218–20.

242 Freire 2017, pp. 21–22.

243 Freire 2017, p. 214. Our translation. In the original: '*o governo e os PER são acusados de terem mentido aos eleitores – prometeram acabar com a austeridade, mas têm sido muito conservadores em termos fiscais e, na prática, não puseram fim à austeridade. Isso é parcialmente verdade*'.

244 Freire 2017.

market/pro-capital bias of the EU structure, nor to the problem of unsustainable public and private debt.

In a context of economic growth, albeit precarious in nature, driven essentially by tourism, a sector with many underlying problems such as precarious wages and working conditions, external dependence, and seasonality, the electorate, according to surveys, approves the government's policies.[245] While these more 'equitable' austerity policies are democratically legitimate, at the same time, the *Geringonça* solution has diminished the available parliamentary political options. As a result, the PCP and the BE partially lost their anti-system character and softened their political discourses and radical criticisms.

This is a particularly important consideration given that these parties previously functioned as the parliamentary voice behind many of the demands of the extra-parliamentary protest movements in the early phases of the crisis. Through the *Geringonça*, some of these demands were incorporated into government policy. However, at the same time, the adherence of BE and PCP to the government solutions affected their ability to represent and dynamise these movements. As a result, there was no credible opposition voice with social and political representation that clearly defended debt cancellation, nationalisation of the banking sector, or the exit from the eurozone, for example.

Portuguese socialists have not so far been confronted with a so-called 'pasokisation', a catastrophic electoral disaster of social democratic parties, such as their Greek sister organisation PASOK, the PSOE, or, more recently, the Dutch PVDA and the French PS. The *Geringonça* solution not only gave social democracy the opportunity to remain in power without being decimated by the application of harsh austerity measures, but also kept it alive as a legitimate electoral option, preventing a more polarised political scenario. The situation could prove electorally dangerous for the PCP and in particular for the Left Bloc, which traditionally has a more unstable electorate. The 2017 local elections were the first test of this theory. Although local dynamics, particularly outside large urban areas, are relatively independent of what happens at the national level, the trend is illustrative. The PCP suffered considerable losses, losing a third of its positions. At the same time, the Left Bloc failed to consolidate locally the electoral progress it had made at the national level during the legislative and presidential elections of 2015 and 2016.

This could be a consequence of another factor that, according to Freire, contributes to the positive trend towards democratic revolution: the *Geringonça* forced the radical left to assume its political proposals in adverse con-

245 Freire 2017, p. 214.

ditions. Research showed that the PS and Costa were the ones who profited most from that government solution. The *Geringonça* also reinforced the trend of social peace that began the year before the elections.[246] The massive non-partisan street protests, demonstrations, and *acampadas* against austerity have lost momentum due to a lack of organisation and perspective. Those that were better organised, namely around *Que Se Lixe a Toika* (QSLT), were institutionalised through the integration of their leaderships into the forces and dynamics of the left-wing parties, which, over time, would shift their focus to electoral and parliamentary struggles.

After the confrontation lost by the CGTP leadership to the government over the *Ponte-a-pé* demonstration in the autumn of 2013, there were no new large-scale demonstrations or strikes. Furthermore, the confederation's hope for political change would be channelled into the electoral terrain instead of street mobilisations. If social struggles and mobilisations are considered an essential part of democracy and democratisation, particularly in their participatory dimensions, it seems that the increase in 'representative quality' has seriously affected the participatory and popular character of Portuguese democracy.

All these aspects should raise at least some concern about the contradictions of the so-called 'democratic revolution'. Comparing the concept of 'revolution' with that of 'Thermidor' can perhaps provide a more enlightening perspective. Thermidor was the name given to the process of reaction after the French Revolution, the moment when Robespierre would be overthrown and the revolutionary process would return to normal, signifying a retreat from the most radical objectives of the revolution. The term Thermidor was later popularised by Leon Trotsky in his book *The Revolution Betrayed* to characterise how the bureaucracy put an end to the Russian revolutionary process and the participation of the masses in forms of participatory democracy – the Soviet system – that emerged from the Russian Revolution of 1917. Thermidor put an end to this revolutionary and emancipatory process, taking the initiative away from the revolutionary movements of the working class and institutionalising a new normality led by the Stalinist bureaucracy, rolling back not only formally but also in many of the substantive dimensions of Soviet democracy, such as access to social and equal rights for women and the LGBT community.

Of course, the concepts of 'revolution' and 'Thermidor' are used purely metaphorically here. Just as the concept of 'revolution' in Freire's work can only be

246 Martins 2016.

compared metaphorically with the October Revolution of 1917, the *Geringonça* policy is not equivalent to a policy of Stalinist reaction. Still, it is essential to ask: would the electoral process, within the limits of bourgeois democracy, not be playing the same role as Thermidor when compared to the emergence of protests, social movements, and alternative discourses on democracy in the face of the crisis?

In many ways, the *Geringonça* represents a return to a situation of 'normality', appeasing the radical elements that emerged during the crisis through a relatively stable government that respects the rules of the eurozone and the European Union. Is this situation really that different from Greece? Ranabir Samaddar described how Syriza, as the political representative of the anti-austerity struggles in Greece, betrayed its electoral programme and then neglected the result of the referendum on EU-imposed austerity, leading the author to conclude that institutionalised democracy would henceforth be the path from which the passive revolution would begin.[247] The 'radical' left, which during the protests constituted the political expression of the social movements, abandoned (albeit temporarily) its radical positions in the direction of a radical social transformation. Protests against austerity and the prospect of a radically different democracy have disappeared. At least for now.

4 Contemporary Socialist Perspectives

An analysis of Portugal's electoral cycles since the 2011 protests and the formation of the *Geringonça* government reveals how the protest movement eventually faded away and how its energy and hopes were channelled into electoral processes. The process did not culminate in a radical change, neither in terms of electoral representation nor in terms of policies. This leads us to the question: is this form of pacification and co-optation of social movement leaders inevitable in liberal representative democracy? Was Michels right in his 'Iron Law of Oligarchy' when he proclaimed that:

> History seems to teach us that no popular movement, however energetic and vigorous, is capable of producing profound and permanent changes in the social organism of the civilized world. The preponderant elements of the movement, the men who lead and nourish it, end by undergoing a gradual detachment from the masses, and are attracted within the orbit of the 'political class'. They per-

247 Samaddar 2016.

> haps contribute to this class a certain number of 'new ideas', but they also endow it with more creative energy and enhanced practical intelligence, thus providing for the ruling class an ever-renewed youth.[248]

While the practical conclusions of the crisis in Portugal point in the direction of such co-optation, our case also provides some elements of hope. The crisis also opened space for criticism of the electoral system as such. Many of the protesters involved in the *acampadas* and the *Indignados* were at the centre of criticism of liberal democracy. These groups were originally made up largely of highly qualified and precariously employed young people – the so-called *Geração à Rasca* (Generation on the Edge) – and were the main voice behind the call for 'Real Democracy Now!'. During the crisis, they were the standard-bearers of alternative forms of democracy, prefigurative democratic politics and council-based democracy.

In the post-crisis period, the tactics of the opposition to austerity mainly followed the logic of the popular front. The danger of the continuation of the ultra-austerity policy of the Passos Coelho government played the unifying role that the danger of fascism played in the unification of an inter-class alliance that this time involved the most 'progressive' forces of the bourgeoisie – in the first instance the PS, but also some right-wing intellectuals critical of austerity – and the parliamentary left, which had the support of working class organisations. The political horizon of this alliance never went beyond the logic of parliamentary negotiations, nor did it question the systemic characteristics of capitalism that were at the root of the crisis, while at the same time promising fidelity to the international agreements that formed the straitjacket of austerity. The co-optation of social movements and the integration of the radical left only brought structural responses to many of their social demands.

What could an alternative socialist tactic have looked like in relation to the democratic crisis? While anti-austerity movements have had historic proportions, they have never reached the levels of political engagement that similar movements have had in the Arab world. Class consciousness has not overcome the levels of political confusion and depoliticisation that were the result of 30 years of working-class defeats and neoliberal hegemony. Despite some experiences of popular participation in assembly movements, they remained on the fringes of society, even within the protest movement. Although some theorists have made theoretical comparisons between the *acampadas* movement and historical experiences of direct participation, such as the Paris Com-

248 Michels 1968, p. 355.

mune or the Russian soviets, nowhere did this phenomenon reach significant levels of dual power, let alone increase the possibilities of a popular uprising. In this political situation, some of the alternative historical tactics embodied in the democratic socialist strategies we highlighted earlier could have served as inspiration for alternative outcomes to the restoration of liberal parliamentary democracy accompanied by a lighter version of austerity.

Due to the uneven and combined development of capitalism, the Portuguese bourgeoisie was never able to establish a truly sovereign bourgeois democracy, modelled on the systems of countries such as France, the United Kingdom, or Germany, due to its peripheral and dependent political-economic position. As Portuguese capital has always remained extremely dependent on its main peers, its policy would always remain tied to these interests. The transition to a relatively stable parliamentary democracy was only possible through integration into the European Union. The concomitant loss of political and economic instruments fundamentally limited the parliament's capabilities to respond to the social and economic needs of the population. In the context of the revolutionary period of 1974–5, only a socialist transformation led by the interests of the working class, independent and against the interests of Portuguese capital, could have established true popular sovereignty. This is a lesson that should have been learned by the Portuguese left in the democratic crisis that erupted in 2011. Instead of being guided by the popular front tactic, the socialist opposition in Portugal could have developed an alternative strategy based on the united front tactic. As we have seen, the united front tactic was also developed to face a situation of major defeats for the socialist forces in Europe and unfavourable conditions for a socialist transformation of society. The tactic advised a broad collaboration of different organisations based on the interests of the working class and combined parliamentary methods and electoral alliances with extra-parliamentary class struggle. The idea was that this method would have a pedagogical effect on the consciousness of the working class and show the limits of any political alternatives within the framework of capitalism. How could such a tactic have been applied in this specific situation?

The left should have created a united front ahead of the 2015 elections, based on a clear anti-austerity programme, with the minimum objective of reversing all the neoliberal measures of the Passos Coelho government, including cuts in benefits and social rights, cuts in the education and health sectors, privatisations, and defending the cancellation of public debt and a socialist plan to recover the economy. This unity should have avoided the possibility of the PS leadership negotiating separately with the different forces to its left.

It could have guaranteed the inauguration of the PS government without guaranteeing the approval of the national budgets for four years. Instead of secret negotiations, it could have proposed open negotiations, in which any agreements would need the final approval of unions and social movements. It could have used its influence in unions and social movements and called for popular mobilisations to pressure government concessions. The PS could, of course, always make deals with the right to approve new austerity budgets. But this would weaken the government, show the limits of the fiscal framework within the European Union, and strengthen the left opposition with a clear democratic alternative.

In the end, the *Geringonça* did not bring any structural solution to the problems of the European economy that were at the root of the crisis. While softening austerity and creating some concessions for the working class, it demobilised the left opposition. This has created a situation that could serve as fertile ground for other reactionary forms of expressing social anger. The election of the first far-right MP since the revolution, in the 2019 elections – following four years of relative stability under the *Geringonça* – was an early warning sign. At the time, most of Portugal's left-wing bureaucracies and academics were still arrogantly dismissing the phenomenon, approaching it – Marie-Antoinette-style – from a moral high ground rather than recognising it as a dangerous threat that demanded militant action, political organisation, and credible alternatives.

Far-right populism still seemed like a distant threat, confined to the 'uncivilised' Americas in the form of Bolsonaro and Trump. Within Portugal's stable democracy, grounded in the constitutional ideals of April, the extreme right was largely perceived as capable of convincing only a small, misinformed minority duped by 'fake news'. Little attention was paid to the structural problems underlying the crisis, which remain fundamentally unresolved. While one might have expected democratic alternatives to re-emerge – and only time will tell if and how they do – political developments since then have demonstrated how a generalised dissatisfaction with the working of democracy can just as easily be captured by far-right populism.

We have seen that the hegemonic model of liberal democracy went through a serious crisis with the implementation of austerity policies starting in 2011. Record numbers of people mobilised in strikes, demonstrations, and other forms of protest between 2011 and 2013 – among the most emblematic are the *Geração à Rasca* demonstration, the general strikes, the *Que Se Lixe a Troika* demonstrations, and the Occupy movement of the *indignados*. Overall, we found that people who participated in these protests seemed to have a very negative view of the state of democracy in those years; almost all of our respondents considered democracy to be non-existent or in a bad state. Dissatisfaction with government policies was directly projected onto the very idea of democracy. People complained about the lack of social rights, the lack of accountability, the lack of legitimacy, the lack of freedom of expression and information, the lack of national sovereignty, the lack of participation, and the lack of respect for the constitution.

The vast majority of respondents were convinced that democracy had deteriorated because of the crisis and austerity. The crisis created a huge disparity between what people thought democracy should be and what it actually was, effectively creating a crisis of hegemony around democracy. While people rejected the current state of democracy, there was not necessarily a clear idea of how it should or could be different, and even if it did exist, democracy is often imagined as an ideal disconnected from its reality. At the same time, the absolute majority of respondents defined democracy in terms of the power of 'us', 'the people', 'citizens', or 'the population'.

Different social actors in the protests, activists from new social movements, union activists, and party members had different discourses on what the democratic alternative would be. Alongside the opposition to the persistence of the liberal-democratic model, this is a situation that could be empirically described by Boaventura de Sousa Santos' concept of demodiversity, which we referred to earlier as 'the peaceful or conflictual coexistence of different democratic models and practices'.[249] The democratic discourse of trade unions is linked to traditional working and everyday living conditions. Democracy, for trade unionists, means guaranteeing decent wages, pensions, contracts, and safety in the workplace. It also means direct and unconditional solidarity between co-workers, collective action and direct participation in union decisions. The democratic discourse of social movements was more utopian. It focused on systemic change, direct citizen participation in assemblies, horizontality, the values of internationalism and solidarity, as well as prefiguration practices. The parties' discourse, on the other hand, remains more institutionalist, focused on organisation, power, and the state. It focuses on social and constitutional rights, elections, history, ideology, and strategy.

We addressed the attempts and strategies of cooperation between these different actors, as well as the difficulties and prejudices that each of them encountered. Cooperation strategies included social movement forms such as trade unionism, joint mobilisation in general strikes, and cooperation in mobilisation platforms such as the 15O platform and the QSLT, as well as the

249 Santos and Mendes 2017, p. 70.

Congresso Democrático das Alternativas. Many recent analyses of the crisis of democracy have referred to Laclau and Mouffe's approach to hegemonic articulation as a framework for understanding collaboration between protest movements in Portugal.[250]

'Back to the hegemonic struggle' was the motto with which Laclau and Mouffe concluded their introduction to the second edition of *Hegemony and Socialist Strategy*. As we mentioned, Laclau and Mouffe's transition to a post-Marxist analysis privileges the ideas of 'political articulation' and 'hegemony' over what they call the 'Hegelian/naturalist' categories of traditional Marxism, such as the Hegelian notion of universal class or the Marxist notion of the proletariat as a universal class.[251] They claimed that their focus on 'contingent articulation' foreshadows the true central dimension of 'politics'. Transitions of hegemony are therefore entirely dependent on political articulation and not on pre-constituted entities outside the political field – they refer specifically to class interests. A political solution to the crisis therefore depends entirely on the communication capabilities and strategies of trade unions, social movements, and parties to produce a contingent narrative that replaces the hegemony of austerity.

We proposed Marxism as the ultimate political science to solve this problem in the context of crisis. Marxism argues that the crisis reveals the fundamental contradictions of capitalism – that is, between capital and labour – and that socialism/communism, based on class interests, is the way to overcome this contradiction. In *Hegemony and Socialist Strategy*, Laclau and Mouffe rejected this approach; for them, 'there is no logical and necessary relation between socialist objectives and the positions of social agents in the relations of production'.[252] According to Laclau and Mouffe, the constitutive character of the political, in Leninism, does not attribute any important role to superstructures such as ideology, institutions, and discourse, because it is based on a 'scientific monopoly enjoyed by a given class perspective' instead of the 'the efficacy of the political level in constructing social relations'.[253] Even though, since Kautsky, Marxism knew that the socialist determination of the working class did not arise spontaneously, but depended on the political mediation of intellectuals or the revolutionary party. Such mediation 'was not conceived as articulation – that is to say, as a political construction from dissimilar elements. It had an epi-

250 Brito 2016; Costa 2019; Fonseca 2016.
251 Laclau and Mouffe 2001, pp. x–xii.
252 Laclau and Mouffe 2001, p. 86.
253 Laclau and Mouffe 2001, p. 60.

stemological basis: socialist intellectuals read in the working class its objective destiny'.[254] Laclau and Mouffe write:

> Leninism evidently makes no attempt to construct, through struggle, a mass identity not predetermined by any necessary law of history. On the contrary, it maintains that there is a for itself of the class accessible only to the enlightened vanguard – whose attitude towards the working class is therefore purely pedagogical. The roots of authoritarian politics lie in this interweaving of science and politics. Once every political relation is conceived as a relation of representation, a progressive substitutionism moves from class to party (representation of the objective interests of the proletariat) and from party to Soviet State (representation of the world interests of the Communist movement). A martial conception of class struggle thus concludes in an eschatological epic.[255]

They adopted a rather analytical notion of class – in contrast to the dialectical Marxist notion – to repeat Bernstein's argument that 'the very unity and homogeneity of class subjects has split into a set of precariously integrated positions'.[256] This led to the final stronghold of class reductionism and a situation in which 'the logic of hegemony, as a logic of articulation and contingency, has come to determine the very identity of the hegemonic subjects'.[257] Laclau and Mouffe thus defend their theory of hegemony based on "structural undecidability" and the 'construction of a hegemonic subject articulation of those particularities in a situation of antagonism' against those who defended the return to the working class.[258] These critics argued that the left failed to listen to the working class and instead focused only on cultural and identity struggles. Although Laclau and Mouffe acknowledged that the left has abandoned the working class and focused on the middle classes, they blamed this on the lack of left alternatives to neoliberalism rather than a passion for identity issues. Instead, they argue that these are not opposing issues: struggles against sexism, racism, sexual discrimination, and environmental struggles must be articulated with those of workers in a new left-wing hegemonic project that they have called radical and plural democracy.[259]

254 Laclau and Mouffe 2001, p. 85.
255 Laclau and Mouffe 2001, p. 59.
256 Laclau and Mouffe 2001, p. 85.
257 Bernstein 1909 *apud* Laclau and Mouffe 2001, p. 85.
258 Laclau and Mouffe 2001, p. XIII.
259 Laclau and Mouffe 2001, p. XVIII.

Equivalence occurs through the articulation of particular demands within a context of antagonism. To transcend this antagonism, a political subject must come to represent universality. Yet, is this logic of hegemony not already embedded in Marx's conceptualisation of class – as discussed above (chapter 2, section 4.3)? Marx argued that a particular class can claim general dominance only by invoking the general rights of society. Its emancipatory potential stems from its ability to persuade the broader social body that the flaws of the system are concentrated in another class: for one class to position itself as the agent of liberation, another must be cast as the embodiment of oppression. Apparently this hegemonic relation occurs without abandoning the central role of the concept of a universal class.

In the terms of Laclau and Mouffe, exploitation – and the differentiation between capital and labour, as revealed by the 'enabling paradox' of crisis – is an effect of capitalist relations.[260] These conditions induce atomised individuals to act collectively. Within this antagonism, the worker's particular position comes to signify the universal, thereby encompassing other forms of oppressed identities and challenging, even potentially displacing, the existing capitalist hegemony.

Let us now return to the different discourses from the perspective of Marxist political science: considering the discourses of democracy as part of the ideological superstructure that is in a dialectical relationship with the infrastructure of production relations. This political approach to the crisis, in Schmittean terms, understands these discourses as a moment in which the 'real' appears. A crisis is not just a moment of knowledge creation and transcendental decision. At the same time, it is an affirmation of the essential antagonism between the classes.

If we look at the different democratic alternatives, we observe that there is a 'void' that covers the three different discourses we studied. Even if there are certain antagonisms between the different protest movements – such as the distrust between parties, unions, and social movements – in one way or another, all three discourses of democratic opposition, the union discourse, the party discourse, and that of the social movements, reflect some aspects of what in the past would have been called socialism or socialist democracy based on class interests. Isn't the historical ideology of socialism the unification of all these aspects: decent distribution of wealth, control of the workplace, solidarity, participation, internationalism, strategy, collective action, and praxis between daily needs and the utopia of a better society to come? On the oppos-

260 Roitman 2011.

ite side, the democratic void ends up being the absence of socialist democracy as the hegemonic opposite of the dominant elitist liberal democratic discourse. What was missing, however, was the unification or articulation of these ideas.

As we have already mentioned, Santos argues that the condition of emptiness only exists because the substantive contents were intentionally emptied by capitalism, colonialism, and patriarchy.[261] After the collapse of the Soviet Union and the success of the neoliberal doctrine that there is no alternative, socialism definitively disappeared from the available political alternatives. The old socialist parties adapted to third way politics, focused on other progressive issues such as ecology, feminism, or immigration rights, a retreat from class issues became widespread among intellectuals, even among those who claimed to be (post-)Marxists.[262] Even the radical left adopted a reformist horizon. At the same time, during the crisis, material interests, reflecting class interests, appeared like a wandering spectre over all democratic discourses. The task of a real *political* science under capitalism is to fill the void again with its socialist content.

261 Santos 2016b, p. 259; Santos and Mendes 2017, p. 32.

262 Wood 1998.

CHAPTER 6

Summary and Final Remarks

Portugal's transition to democracy was marked by significant contradictions. Until 25 April 1974, the country had the longest-lasting dictatorship and colonial power in Europe, seeming anachronistic in the modern era. However, within weeks of the Carnation Revolution, Portugal became a global epicentre of democratic, revolutionary, and socialist experimentation, characterised by nationalisations, agrarian reform, and citizen participation. The European integration project proved fundamental to the consolidation of a stable liberal parliamentary democracy, prevailing over the alternative democratic models that emerged during the revolution. Meanwhile, the Constitution enshrined many of the social achievements of the revolution, including free education and health care. However, Portugal's aspiration to build a social-democratic welfare state coincided with the neoliberal wave that swept Europe. European integration soon carried a neoliberal agenda of privatisation and liberalisation, rebuilding the country's financial and economic elites while restricting social and economic democracy.

As a peripheral economy within the European Union, Portugal has suffered significant deindustrialisation and a loss of political and economic sovereignty. By transferring substantial legal and political powers to the EU and giving up essential economic instruments such as monetary policy, the country has become increasingly dependent on debt, financing, subsidies, emigration, and tourism. Portuguese democracy, like its European counterparts, has faced persistent legitimacy challenges. Voter turnout has declined and trust in political parties, the judiciary, and other institutions has diminished, driven by depoliticisation, corruption, and inequality. The crisis of the European project and the imposition of austerity policies have further undermined social rights, public services, and living standards, intensifying the crisis of legitimacy of liberal parliamentary democracy.

Crises mean a breakdown of hegemony, where antagonistic political conflicts interrupt the post-political consensus. Crises expose these contradictions, serving as crucial moments of choice. Rather than seeing contradiction as a limitation, crises can function as a bridge between history and politics, reconciling specific historical contexts with universal truths and enabling transformative political change. Carl Schmitt's concepts of exception and politics – critiques of the technocratic void of liberalism that influenced thinkers such as Habermas, Mouffe, and Laclau – are valuable for understanding these

 | HTTPS://DOI.ORG/10.1163/9789004766235-008

moments of crisis. However, as Gramsci observed, crises are ambiguous periods in which 'the old is dying and the new cannot yet be born', creating space for 'morbid symptoms' and often enabling reactionary policies.

Crises force scholars and societies to take sides. While Schmitt equated liberalism with modernity and ruled out the possibility of a genuinely political science, Marx offers an alternative to such obscurantism. By politicising the economy and placing class struggle at the centre of his critique of capitalism, Marx historicises its dynamics and challenges Schmitt's mythical structure. A Marxist political science, based on the opposition between capital and labour, redefines political truth as a practical and strategic question. Thus crises reveal not only the limitations of neoliberal hegemony, but also the potential for transformative political action.

Democracy has been an inherently contested concept throughout modern history. For centuries, theorists have engaged with democracy both as an ideal and as a material reality, as utopia or dystopia, resulting in a wide range of theories and approaches. These include classical republicanism, utilitarianism, elitism, constitutionalism, anti-colonialism, empiricism, liberalism, deliberative and participatory models, agonism, and socialism.

Democracy, ultimately, is an ideological construct – an interpretative framework through which individuals make sense of their own and others' actions.[1] This means that democratic legitimacy ultimately depends on a hegemonic consensus on the meaning of democracy. During crises, when fundamental social contradictions come to the surface, this consensus dissolves. Dissent arises, especially under 'TINA' neoliberalism, where democracy has often become an empty substitute for genuine political alternatives, a dissent expressed in competing interpretations of democracy. Today, the struggle for democracy revolves around what it means. Žižek and Santos and Avritzer argue that democratisation is a dispute over its definition.[2]

Ellen Meiksins Wood reminds us that the struggle between capitalism and socialism can also be seen as a dispute between different forms of democracy.[3] We have seen how the relationship between capital and labour has long been mediated by democracy. Representative democracy, with its separation of political and economic spheres, has often served the oligarchic interests of capital. The composition of individual liberal citizenship reflects the alienation of the worker. After 30 years of neoliberal hegemony and amid the crisis of capitalism, Marxist literature on democracy gains renewed relevance. Contemporary

1 Therborn 1999, p. 2.
2 Žižek 2006, p. 37; Santos and Avritzer 2005, p. xlv.
3 Wood 1998, p. 134.

democratic crises challenge us to reinterpret democracy through the lens of the opposition between capital and labour and between capitalism and socialism.

Since the mid-1980s, the concept of 'discourse' has become central to democratic theory and social movement studies, particularly since Laclau and Mouffe, in *Hegemony and Socialist Strategy*, proposed their influential post-Marxist perspective that conceived of the social as a discursive space. Their approach privileges 'political articulation' and 'hegemony' over traditional Marxist categories, such as the proletariat as a universal class. From the beginning, Ellen Meiksins Wood criticised this linguistic turn, emphasising that democratic analysis and strategy go far beyond discourse. She argues that the task of the theorist is not to abstract democracy from its specific ideological and historical contexts, but to expose how specific class interests have been universalised within the framework of capitalist democracy.

She argued that the diversity of meanings attributed to democracy highlights the differences between bourgeois democracy and other forms. Capitalist democracy is based on the fusion of its particular interests with universal principles. For Meiksins Wood, the line separating different forms of democracy runs through where fundamental class interests diverge. To construct an alternative universal notion of democracy, it is essential to critically analyse the historical conditions that allowed the generalisation of specific class interests. This approach avoids the pitfalls of ideological co-optation and confusion.

This book addressed several other historical debates that provided a basis for examining the relationship between socialism, strategy, and democracy. Meiksins Wood's analysis reminds us that opposition to political dictatorship in liberalism emerged as an aristocratic reaction against the absolutism and centralisation of early modernity. Other important issues include the usefulness of the concept of 'dictatorship of the proletariat', the choice between reformism and revolution, the dynamics of imperialism and the periphery, parliamentarism, and the tactical debate between popular front and united front.

The 2011–15 crisis in Portugal served as a backdrop to illustrate these dynamics. Austerity measures were implemented under the guise of democratic legitimacy, with policymakers feeling obliged to frame these policies within a 'democratic discourse of austerity'. Policymakers interviewed for this research, such as IMF representative Selassie and former Finance Minister Maria Luís Albuquerque, legitimised austerity through depoliticisation, the culturalisation of political problems, and a neoliberal discourse of inevitability.

Depoliticisation was present in technocratic arguments, in economic determinism, and in the definition of the crisis as an 'exceptionality'. Responsibility for decisions was often transferred to external actors, while alternative policies were dismissed as irrational. Democratic legitimacy was invoked through formal procedures such as laws, elections, parliamentary majorities, treaties, and constitutional decisions, while substantive democratic elements such as broad public participation and social accountability were largely absent, dismissed as impractical given the crisis conditions.

This 'austerity model' of low-intensity, post-political democracy reflected the liberal-democratic paradigm that has dominated since the 1990s. In this context, the political spectrum is restricted by the constraints of financial markets, presenting democracy as universal and non-ideological.

Challenging this perspective on democracy, mass protests against austerity between 2011 and 2013 mobilised record numbers in Portugal, including the *Geração à Rasca* demonstration, general strikes, and protests driven by *Que Se Lixe a Troika*. Dissatisfaction with current democracy was widespread, with 89 percent of protesters we interviewed describing it as non-existent or in poor condition. This disillusionment exposed the crisis of hegemony. However, there was no clear consensus on how to reinvent it, reflecting diverse democratic ideals among social movements, unions, and political parties. While unions emphasised the importance of fair wages, workplace safety, and collective action, social movements advocated broader systemic changes, horizontality, and prefigurative practices, and political parties focused on constitutional rights and ideological strategy.

Overall, the anti-austerity movements in Portugal represented a politicising element, involving thousands of people in debates and fostering political awareness. As the assembly movements waned, the protests diverged in two directions: post-protest movements focused on individual and local change, while others, like *Que Se Lixe a Troika*, aligned with the organised left, unions, and parties to articulate an anti-neoliberal agenda.

Disillusioned with existing organisations and parties, some activists and collectives turned to alternative forms of political practice, adopting so-called post-protest practices or what Hardt and Negri called the post-*operaista* 'exodus' strategy. These activists prioritised immediate and tangible actions in their daily lives over traditional methods of protest, which they considered ineffective. But eventually it became clear that artistic and symbolic activism alone cannot dismantle neoliberal hegemony or trigger systemic transformation. While it can play a vital role in mobilisation, it must be complemented by broader political articulation. Otherwise, it becomes isolated romanticism. Another challenge of post-political and post-democratic discourses is that they often focus on the side effects of capitalism, such as corruption, without addressing its systemic roots. This tends to depoliticise struggles through ambiguous rhetoric, emphasising participation without clear political or economic alternatives.

Despite the antagonisms among protest movements, the democratic opposition discourses of unions, social movements, and parties reflect some facets of what has historically been called socialism or socialist democracy. Decent distribution of wealth, control of the workplace, solidarity, internationalism, collective action, and the integration of everyday needs with utopian aspirations were central to this ideology. What seemed missing, however, was a unifying articulation of these ideas to form a hegemonic counter-narrative to the liberal democratic and dominant elite discourse. Overcoming distrust within and between left-wing groups remains a critical challenge to building a unified opposition to neoliberal and technocratic policies in Europe.

The void left by this absence of unification was exacerbated by capitalism, colonialism, and patriarchy. Since the collapse of the Soviet Union and the rise of neoliberalism, socialism has largely disappeared from the mainstream political alternatives. Former socialist parties adopted third-way politics, focusing on issues such as ecology, feminism, and migrant rights, while moving away from class-based politics. However, during the crisis, class interests resurfaced, haunting democratic discourses like a 'wandering spectre'. The challenge for critical political science is to reintroduce the substantive content of socialism into democratic discourse, avoiding traps such as co-optation into the hegemonic model of democracy that legitimises capitalism.

The most significant attempt to articulate opposition to 'austerity democracy' occurred paradoxically within the liberal-democratic framework itself. The left-wing opposition, made up of the Left Bloc (BE) and the Communist Party (PCP), firmly opposed the austerity measures, which ended up promoting convergences between the two. However, this occurred in a context in which both parties gradually deradicalised, accepting liberal democracy as a transitory but apparently permanent stage, while retaining some elements of classical Marxist ideology. The crisis amplified the radicalism of their social democratic demands, which gained popular support in the context of austerity.

The subsequent elections offered opportunities for an electoral backlash against pro-austerity parties. Although the right-wing government suffered losses, the left-wing opposition failed to make a decisive breakthrough. Unlike Spain and Greece, Portugal did not see the emergence of a new and important left-wing formation. Instead, smaller parties such as PAN, Livre, and the MPT – an anti-establishment ecological party similar to Italy's 5 Star Movement – made modest gains, with the MPT securing two seats in the European Parliament.

In the 2015 general election, amid beliefs that 'the worst was over' and fears of a 'Syriza scenario', the right-wing PàF alliance ironically emerged as the strongest force, despite losing 700,000 votes and its parliamentary majority. Meanwhile, the left, BE, and PCP grew, collectively winning almost 20 percent of the votes. This marked an interruption in the 40-year alternation of power between the dominant Socialist Party (PS) and the Social Democratic Party (PSD). Initially, collaboration between the BE, the PCP and the PS seemed unlikely due to historical rivalries and different visions of Europe. However, shared opposition to a right-wing government and external pressure from social movements led to the formation of the '*Geringonça*', a minority PS government supported by the BE, PCP, and PEV.

The *Geringonça* introduced progressive measures such as increasing the minimum wage, restoring pensions, increasing public sector salaries, combating precarious employment, reducing VAT on restaurants, and suspending privatisations. Hailed as a democratic alternative to neoliberalism, it has become a model of left-wing governance in Europe. However, this arrangement also marked a shift to the radical left. Once a voice for social movements, the BE and the PCP increasingly prioritised parliamentary influence, leaving aside participatory democracy driven by mobilisation. What André Freire called a 'democratic revolution' can also be seen as a Thermidor – the channelling of the energy of the social movement towards a pacified normality within the framework of the eurozone.

Portugal's electoral cycles since 2011 illustrate how the energy of popular protests has been absorbed by institutional politics, failing to achieve radical systemic change. Some see this co-optation as an inevitable feature of liberal democracy, while others argue that it reveals missed opportunities that pose risks to democracy itself.

A socialist united front in 2015, based on working class organisations and combining parliamentary action with popular mobilisation, could have offered a more transformative path. Public negotiations with the PS, bolstered by the supervision of trade unions and movements, could have put pressure on the government while exposing the austerity constraints imposed by the EU. Such a strategy could have deepened working class consciousness and kept alive the possibility of radical change.

Throughout this investigation, we proposed and developed a theoretical framework that recovered a Marxist political ontology for analysis and explanation. This has several advantages, not only compared to traditional empiricist and comparative methods in political science, but also compared to some of the more popular traditional critical approaches. The historical materialist methodology of Marxism allows us to understand the present in the context of past and present struggles and power relations and integrates the struggle for democracy into a universal theory that accounts for the logics of class, periphery, legitimacy, political economy, and crisis. Marxism continues to be the theory par excellence for analysing social phenomena in the context of capitalist political economy. It is indispensable in the global context of depoliticisation that has marked the last thirty years of neoliberal hegemony. As a theory of the crisis of capitalism, this is even more true when this political economy is confronted with a deep crisis.

The politicisation offered by Marxism – in contrast to the original conservative-nationalist politicisation found in Carl Schmitt – provides a perspective of universal social emancipation. It also provides a historicising perspective that allows us to look beyond the state of being – in this case, the consensual interpretation of democracy in Portugal, based on a cross-class agreement that combined some of the social achievements of the revolutionary period of 1974–5 with European integration and economic development. Marxism inherently links scientific analysis with historical and political practice, paving the way for social and political emancipation. Our examination of democracy integrated scientific debate with the tactical and strategic questions necessary for transformative change. This tactical lens goes beyond the mere description of social injustices, challenging the notion that agency belongs only to the victors of political processes. This research provided empirical material on the perspectives of democracy from different sides of the social conflict in Portugal. In addition to confirming that the vast majority of protesters interviewed rejected the liberal democratic framework advocated by political decision-makers, we explored several alternative democratic practices and resistance strategies, identifying potential elements for democratic renewal and how these movements could have been articulated and coordinated to achieve significant and lasting victories.

In addition to developing and explaining the particularities of democracy in Portugal, its history, and its most recent complexity and contradictions, this book represents an important contribution to understanding how democracy works and is perceived in periods of crisis in many other circumstances, times, and places. Furthermore, approaching a crisis of hegemony as a divergence of perspectives on democracy allows us to understand the apparently contradictory situation in which an institution can be considered democratic on the one hand and antidemocratic on the other, providing levels of legitimacy for democracy to be overthrown or neglected, even in the absence of widespread public support for a democratic ideal.

At the theoretical level, this thesis provides a general framework for understanding different democratic theories. It provides a defence of historical materialism as a method of democratic analysis and action. It highlights some of the limits of the main critical democratic theories. For socialists and opponents of austerity, this thesis exposes some of the pitfalls of the struggles for democracy so far. It also provides some possible guidelines for democratic tactics. Even for those who do not follow the general theoretical framework of this thesis – which is the argument of crisis as object/subject to reestablish a Marxist political-scientific approach to democracy – our investigation has provided new and vital empirical materials on the discourses and perspectives of democracy, based on interviews with key protagonists in the political confrontation.

POSTSCRIPT

From Pandemic to the Rise of the Global Right

Since the global financial crisis, world capitalism has been experiencing new and profound political and economic crises. The global Covid-19 pandemic has led the world to unprecedented measures and economic recession. The pandemic crisis has shown us, once again, the weaknesses of capitalism and the neoliberal truths that we have been taught over the last 30 years. The crisis demonstrated the market's inability to respond. Apart from Bolsonaro and some lunatic libertarians, few defended the state's inaction in the face of crises like this one. Public health services have regained some prominence for the common good, while private ones have been unmasked for what they are: speculators who do not care about health. The fight against the disease required an almost complete paralysis of the capitalist economy. The quarantines functioned practically as a social strike, often imposed by the state, which affected all sectors of society. This paralysis and subsequent economic collapse reminded us of the fact that wealth is produced primarily by workers: men and women. Invested capital, 'creative entrepreneurship', managers, advertising – all of this is completely useless without the exploitation of labour. The pandemic has also shown us who performs the essential tasks in society: those who cannot stop and have had to take an unknown risk to their lives for the common good – food producers, supermarket workers, cleaners, logistics and transportation personnel, and medical personnel. These essential workers are often the ones who suffer the most from exploitation, are subject to greater insecurity and the lowest wages. Often, it is also workers who suffer the greatest oppression: for example, women and racialised workers, in addition to normal exploitation, suffer from 'super-exploitation' through sexism and racism.

Their integration and their struggles are one of the greatest contemporary challenges of the labour movement. They are from sectors with less tradition of unionisation in traditional bureaucratised unions, due to the great precariousness. The old trade union organisations have, at least until now, had great difficulty in penetrating these sectors. But these are also strategic sectors in a capitalist economy increasingly focused on services and just-in-time production, and as such, these sectors have very great potential power. Some sectors have already discovered this power. Just remember the impact of the powerful struggles of dockers, hazardous materials drivers, and nurses in Portugal during the last years. It will be a pedagogical process with many contradictions and errors, due to the lack of traditions and organisation, but essential for everyone.

 | HTTPS://DOI.ORG/10.1163/9789004766235-009

Recognising the flaws of the free market has not necessarily brought us policies for the common good. It revived a 'socialism of the rich', primarily concerned with finding a breath of fresh air for the financial sector and big business. Furthermore, among the winners of this crisis will be the worst sectors of the capitalist economy: platform economies (such as Amazon, Uber, and Glovo), large supermarkets, and large food industries. The crisis and imposed quarantines have strengthened their positions. Instead of being disrupted, their capital accumulation has skyrocketed, while their small-scale alternatives, small local businesses dependent on direct interaction with customers and with limited access to new digital technologies, have enormous difficulties in surviving.

This raised a lot of questions around the idea of democracy. What is democratic in this crisis? What about the widespread imposition of the state of emergency? Can we limit civil rights, and in whose interests? Is private scientific knowledge sustainable? Is public health a democratic right or should the market govern its efficient management? How does ideology shape people's perceptions of the crisis? Should we bail out private companies and banks or prioritise the most vulnerable? The theoretical framework that I developed in this book serve as a good starting point for analysis.

Meanwhile, not unlike the trend observed in Europe and the world, there has been a significant rise in right-wing populist forces. Liberal political elites and representative democracy, which managed to hold onto power in the early post-austerity years, now face a major shift. Social media, which during the Occupy movement were still seen as instruments that could strengthen democracies through popular mobilisation and participation and involving broad public debates, have become concentrations of hate speech and reactionary ideas. They have revealed themselves as vehicles for their tech billionaire owners who have taken on much more prominent political roles around Trump, and who use them to control and direct public and political discourse through algorithms and policy changes that, for example, enable anti-LGBT and racist hate speech but censor publications that criticise the genocide in Gaza.

In Portugal, these years were characterised by fragile minority governments, many of which collapsed amid allegations of corruption. The political landscape has been marked by instability, with four parliamentary elections held in just six years – 2019, 2022, 2024, and 2025. In this context, the far-right Chega party, led by former PSD member André Ventura, surged from holding a single seat in parliament in 2019 to securing 58 seats in 2025 – representing nearly a quarter of Portuguese voters. This period effectively ended Portugal's nearly fifty-year exceptional status following the Carnation Revolution, during which the far-right had remained absent from parliament.

Meanwhile, left-wing organisations have faced near collapse. The Left Bloc suffered the most dramatic decline, shrinking from 19 parliamentary seats in 2019 to just one in 2025. The party failed to articulate a strong opposition or offer a credible political alternative in the aftermath of its agreements with the Socialist Party (PS). It made no meaningful effort to reconnect with mass social or labour movements. Instead, its collaboration with the PS became its de facto political horizon. This crisis was exacerbated by a series of internal scandals – including allegations of mistreatment of female employees after maternity leave, the use of illegal and precarious employment contracts, and incidents of internal censorship – all of which further eroded the party's credibility and public support. The Communist Party fared only slightly better, losing 14 of its 17 seats between 2019 and 2025, while the PS recorded its third worst result in history.

In response to growing democratic instability and the rising threat of the far-right, the left has, ironically, assumed the role of what Brazilian philosopher Vladimir Safatle calls the new 'Party of Order' – a term he uses in reference to Marx's famous description of the conservative-monarchist coalition in *The Eighteenth Brumaire of Louis Bonaparte*. Rather than positioning itself as the primary opposition to bourgeois liberal democracy and bourgeois law, the left has become their most ardent defender. Faced with the radical right, left-wing discourse has increasingly focused on upholding the rule of law, parliamentary procedure, and institutional propriety. In practice, the left acts as though it holds power – when it does not. Capitalism remains firmly in the hands of capital.

As in many other countries, these changes introduced a new political discourse into the public sphere in Portugal. Often labelled 'illiberal democracy' – a term first used to describe Viktor Orbán's government in Hungary and later applied to other right-wing populist movements – this model challenges Portugal's longstanding tendency toward left-wing democratic discourse. Despite right-wing economic practices rooted in a privatised and peripheral capitalist economy, Portugal has largely maintained a progressive democratic discourse. Meanwhile, this era has come to an end. Issues such as immigration, crime, Islamisation, and corruption have become dominant themes in public debate.

Some historical parallels can be drawn with the forms of Bonapartism that capitalism has resorted to in times of great crises: a policy of strong leaders who channel social and political discontent into reactionary movements, supported by a state apparatus that appears to be above class divisions. However, Bonapartism has always played a historical role in suppressing social struggles and ensuring the survival of capitalism. Ultimately, it was always directed against the working class. In *The Civil War in France*, Marx contrasted the Paris

Commune, the most famous experiment in direct democracy by the working masses, with the Bonapartist regime of Versailles, which represented an authoritarian bourgeois state in decline. Although Versailles paid homage to representative democracy through elections and sought social legitimacy through populist donations to the lumpenproletariat, its real function was to maintain bourgeois rule.

The thesis presented in this book suggests that the rise of the far right in Portugal was facilitated, in part, by the so-called *Geringonça* government agreement. This alliance led to the erosion of any anti-system stance or radical content, if it ever existed, within the Portuguese left-wing parties, the PCP, and the *Bloco de Esquerda*. The *Geringonça* exemplified a broader trend, in which the left under late liberalism is perceived, and acts, as a 'party of power', but fails to change the fundamental political economy of capitalism. Instead, it becomes a representative of the existing order, the last defender of capitalist liberalism, representative democracy, the rule of law, and rationality, precisely at a time when these institutions face their deepest crisis of legitimacy since the 1930s.

For the left to regain its position as a genuine systemic alternative, it must move beyond defending liberal-bourgeois institutions and instead advocate a politics rooted in proletarian democracy and a post-capitalist society.

Bibliography

Acampada Lisboa 27 May 2011, As ruas são nossas, Acampada Lisboa.

Accornero, Guya and Pedro R. Pinto 2015a, '"Brandos costumes?" Protesto e mobilização em Portugal sob a austeridade, 2010–2013', *Estudos Ibero-Americanos*, 41, 2: 393–421.

Accornero, Guya and Pedro R. Pinto 2015b, '"Mild mannered"? Protest and mobilisation in Portugal under Austerity, 2010–2013', *West European Politics*, 38, 3: 491–515.

Accornero, Guya and Pedro R. Pinto 5 June 2015c, 'Patterns of protest in Portugal show the relationship between the "old" politics of labour and "new" anti-austerity movements'. *Democratic Audit UK*.

Adam, Hussein M. 1993, 'Frantz Fanon as a Democratic Theorist', *African Affairs*, 92, 369: 499–518.

Adams, Guy B., Priscilla V. Bowerman et al. 1990, 'Joining purpose to practice: A democratic identity for the public service', in *Images and identities in public administration*, edited by Henry D. Kass and Bayard L. Catron, Newbury Park, California: Sage.

Agamben, Giorgio 2005. *State of Exception*, translated by Kevin Attell, Chicago: University of Chicago Press.

Albuquerque, Maria Luís 3 March 2017, Interview with Maria Luís Albuquerque [Personal communication].

Alcidi, Cinzia, Alessandro Giovannini et al. 23 May 2012, '"Grexit": Who would pay for it?', *CEPS Policy Brief*, 272.

Alfredo 14 November 2012, Greve geral, Piquete de greve, CTT Arroios [Personal communication].

Alípio, P., Norega, F. et al. 2013, 'Occupying Democracy – Acampada de Coimbra', *CES Contexto*, 2: 351–64.

Almeida, Maria A.D.F.P.D. 2016, *Grupos de cidadãos nas autarquias portuguesas: contributo para a prática da cidadania e para a qualidade da democracia?*, Lisboa: Escrytos.

Althusser, Louis 2006, *Lenin and philosophy and other essays*, New Delhi: Aakar Books.

Amorim Neto, Octavio and Marina C. Lobo 2009, 'Portugal's semi-presidentialism (re)considered: an assessment of the president's role in the policy process, 1976–2006', *European Journal of Political Research*, 48, 2: 234–55.

Ana 14 November 2012, Manifestação em São Bento, Greve Geral [Personal communication].

Anderson, Perry 1976, 'The antinomies of Antonio Gramsci', *New Left Review*, I, 100: 5–78.

Ango 2 March 2013, Manifestação Lisboa: Que se Lixe a Troika! O Povo É Quem Mais Ordena [Personal communication].

Antena 1 16 October 2015, "António Costa está a fazer um golpe de Estado", *RTP Notícias*.

Antonio, Robert J. 1981, 'Immanent critique as the core of critical theory: its origins and developments in Hegel, Marx and contemporary thought', *The British Journal of Sociology*, 32, 3: 330–45.

Antunes, Ernesto M. 1985, 'As Forças Armadas e o MFA: de 25 de abril de 1974 a 25 de novembro de 1975', *Revista Crítica de Ciências Sociais*, 15/16/17: 47–52.

Arendt, Hannah 1972, *Crises of the republic: lying in politics; civil disobedience; on violence; thoughts on politics and revolution*, Volume 219, Boston: Houghton Mifflin Harcourt.

Arendt, Hannah 1973. *The origins of totalitarianism*, San Diego; New York; London: Harcourt Brace Jovanovich.

Arendt, Hannah 2013, *The human condition*, Chicago: University of Chicago Press.

Arendt, Hannah 2016, *On revolution*, London: Faber & Faber.

Aristóteles 1998, *Política*, translated by António Campelo Amaral and Carlos de Carvalho Gomes, Lisboa: Vega.

Arnsperger, Christian and Yanis Varoufakis 2006, 'What is neoclassical economics? The three axioms responsible for its theoretical oeuvre, practical irrelevance and, thus, discursive power', *Panoeconomicus*, 53, 1: 5–18.

Assembleia Popular de Coimbra 26 May 2011, Manifesto da Acampada Coimbra.

Autárquicas 2013 – Resultados 29 September 2013, Território Nacional, Eleições Autárquicas.

Avritzer, Leonardo. 2002, *Democracy and the public space in Latin America*, Princeton: Princeton University Press.

Avritzer, Leonardo and Sérgio Costa 2004, 'Teoria crítica, democracia e esfera pública: concepções e usos na América Latina', *Dados – Revista de Ciências Sociais*, 47, 4: 703–28.

Azad, Amir 2005, *The Austrian school of economics*.

Bagnai, Alberto and Christian A.M. Ospina 2017, 'Neoclassical versus Kaldorian explanations of Southern Europe's productivity slowdown', *Acta Oeconomica*, 67, s1: 113–35.

Balibar, Etienne 1977, *On the dictatorship of the proletariat*, London: New Left Books.

Balibar, Etienne 19 May 2017, 'Lenin's three theoretical arguments about the dictatorship of the proletariat', *Verso Blog*.

Barrett, James R. 2009, 'Rethinking the popular front', *Rethinking Marxism*, 21, 4: 531–50.

Baumgarten, Britta 2013, '*Geração à Rasca* and beyond: mobilizations in Portugal after 12 March 2011', *Current Sociology*, 61, 4: 457–73.

Baumgarten, Britta and Rubén D. García 2017, 'More than a copy paste: the spread of Spanish frames and events to Portugal', *Journal of Civil Society*, 13, 3: 247–66.

Bello, Walden 2005, 'The crisis of the globalist project and the new economics of George W. Bush', *Critical globalization studies*, 101–9.

Benhabib, Seyla (ed.) 1996, *Democracy and difference: contesting the boundaries of the political*, Princeton: Princeton University Press.

Bernstein, Eduard 1909, *Evolutionary socialism: a criticism and affirmation*, translated by Edith C. Harvey, New York: B.W. Huebsch.

Black, Edwin 1978, *Rhetorical criticism: a study in method*, Madison: University of Wisconsin Press.

Blanchard, Olivier 2007, 'Adjustment within the Euro: the difficult case of Portugal', *Portuguese Economic Journal*, 6, 1: 1–21.

Blommaert, Jan 2005, *Discourse: a critical introduction*, Cambridge: Cambridge University Press.

Bobbio, Norberto 1997, *Democracy and dictatorship: the nature and limits of State Power*, Oxford: Polity Press.

Bodansky, Daniel 1999, 'The legitimacy of international governance: a coming challenge for international environmental law?', *The American Journal of International Law*, 93, 3: 596–624.

Bohle, Dorothee October 2010, 'The crisis of the Eurozone', EUDO – European Union Democracy Observatory, Italy.

Bonet, Antoni J.A. 2010, 'La democracia revolucionaria, un proyecto para el siglo XXI (Entrevista a Boaventura de Sousa Santos)', RIFP – *Revista Internacional de Filosofía Política*, Madrid, 35: 117–48.

Bordiga, A. 1977, *Theses on parliamentarism*, Second Congress of the Communist International, London.

Bordignon, Michela 2012, 'Contradiction or non-contradiction? Hegel's dialectic between Brandom and Priest', *Verifiche*, 41, 1/3: 221–45.

Borriello, Arthur 2017, '"There is no alternative": how Italian and Spanish leaders' discourse obscured the political nature of austerity', *Discourse & Society*, 28, 3: 241–61.

Bosco, Anna and Verney Susannah 2012, 'Electoral epidemic: the political cost of economic crisis in Southern Europe, 2010–11', *South European Society and Politics*, 17, 2: 129–54.

Box, Richard C., Gary S. Marshall et al. 2002, 'New public management and substantive democracy', *Public Administration Review*, 61, 5: 608–19.

Bratsis, Peter 2010, 'The Greek crisis', *Journal of Modern Greek Studies*, 28, 2: 301–2.

Brenner, Mary E. 2006, 'Interviewing in educational research', in *Handbook of complementary methods in education research*, edited by Judith L. Green, Gregory Camilli et al., Mahwah: Lawrence Erlbaum Associates.

Brito, Nuno M.C. 2016, *O movimento do protesto: discurso digital e manifestações de reivindicação de direitos sociais no espaço público – os casos de 'Rios ao Carmo' e 'Dentro de Ti Ó Cidade' durante as celebrações do 400 aniversário do 25 de Abril* [Doctoral thesis], Lisboa: ISCTE-IUL.

Brouwer, Roland 1995, '*Baldios* and common property resource management in Portugal', *Unasylva*, 46, 180: 37–43.

Brown, Nicholas and Imre Szeman 2005, 'What is the multitude? Questions for Michael Hardt and Antonio Negri', *Cultural Studies*, 19, 3: 372–87.

Brown, Wendy 2003, 'Neo-liberalism and the end of liberal democracy', *Theory & Event*, 7, 1.

Brown, Wendy 2006a, 'American nightmare: neoliberalism, neoconservatism, and de-democratization', *Political Theory*, 34, 6: 690–714.

Brown, Wendy 2006b, 'Tolerance as a discourse of depoliticization', in *Regulating aversion: tolerance in the age of identity and empire*, by Wendy Brown, Princeton: Princeton University Press.

Bryce, Viscount James 1921, *Modern democracies*, Volume 2, New York: Macmillan.

Bukharin, N. 1977, *Report on parliamentarianism*, Second Congress of the Communist International, London.

Burnham, Peter, Karin Lutz et al. (eds.) 2004, *Research methods in politics*, Basingstoke: Palgrave Macmillan.

Butler, J. 9 September 2011, 'Bodies in alliance and the politics of the street', *European Institute for Progressive Cultural Policies* [web journal].

Butler, Judith, Ernesto Laclau et al. 2000, *Contingency, hegemony, universality: contemporary dialogues on the left*, London; New York: Verso.

Cabral, Manuel V. 1997, *Cidadania política e equidade social em Portugal*, Oeiras: Celta.

Cabral, Manuel V. 2000, 'O exercício da cidadania política em Portugal', *Análise Social*, 35, 154/155: 85–113.

Caldas, José C. 2015, 'Desvalorização do trabalho: do Memorando à prática' *Cadernos do Observatório sobre Crises e Alternativas*, 6: 1–23.

Caldas, José C. and João R. Almeida 2016, 'Narrativas da crise no jornalismo económico', *Cadernos do Observatório sobre Crises e Alternativas*, 7: 1–31.

Callinicos, Alex 1982, 'Trotsky's theory of "Permanent Revolution" and its relevance to the third world today', *International Socialism*, 2, 16: 98–112.

Camargo, João 2014, 'No a la Troika en Portugal: movimiento y resistencias', *Kult-Ur*, 1, 2: 135–54.

Carlos 26 October 2013, Manifestação – QSLT – não há becos sem saída [Personal communication].

Carmo, Renato M. and José A.V. Simões (eds.) 2020, *Protest, youth and precariousness: the unfinished fight against austerity in Portugal*, New York; Oxford: Berghahn Books.

Carneiro, Anabela, Pedro Portugal et al. 2014, 'Catastrophic job destruction during the Portuguese economic crisis', *Journal of Macroeconomics*, 39: 444–57.

Castañeda, Ernesto 2012, 'The indignados of Spain: a precedent to Occupy Wall Street', *Social Movement Studies*, 11, 3/4: 309–19.

Catroga, Fernando 2010, 'O republicanismo português (Cultura, história e política)', *História* – Revista da Faculdade de Letras, Porto, 11, 3: 95–119.

Cheibub, José A., Jennifer Gandhi et al. 2010, 'Democracy and dictatorship revisited', *Public Choice*, 143, 1/2: 67–101.

Chilcote, Ronald 2010, *The Portuguese revolution: state and class in the transition to democracy*, Lanham: Rowman & Littlefield.

Chouliaraki, Lilie and Norman Fairclough 1999, *Discourse in late modernity: rethinking critical discourse analysis*, Edinburgh: Edinburgh University Press.

Citizenship Academy 2013, The citizenship academy manifesto.

Clara 27 November 2012, Protesto CGTP Budget, Lisboa São Bento [Personal communication].

Clarke, Nick 2012, 'Urban policy mobility, anti-politics, and histories of the transnational municipal movement', *Progress in Human Geography*, 36, 1: 25–43.

Collins, Adela Y. 1984, *Crisis and catharsis: the power of the apocalypse*, Louisville: Westminster John Knox Press.

'Congresso Democrático das Alternativas chega ao fim' 16 June 2016, *Público*.

Costa, Alexandre M.A.D.C. 2019, *Resgatar a democracia? A emergência e declínio de novas redes de ativismo nos protestos anti-austeritários em Portugal* [Doctoral thesis], Lisboa: Universidade Nova de Lisboa.

Costa, Ana and José C. Caldas 2014, 'A União Europeia e Portugal entre os resgates bancários e a austeridade: um mapa das políticas e das medidas', in *A economia política do retrocesso: crise, causas e objectivos*, coordinated by José Reis, Coimbra: Almedina.

Costa, Hermes A. 2011, 'O sindicalismo contemporâneo entre as tipologias e as formas de acção', *Estudos de Sociologia*, 16, 31: 447–74.

Costa, Jorge, Luís Fazenda et al. 2010, *Os donos de Portugal: cem anos de poder económico (1910–2010)*, Porto: Afrontamento.

Daalder, Hans 2002, 'Parties: denied, dismissed, or redundant? A critique', in *Political parties: old concepts and new challenges*, edited by Richard Gunther, José R. Montero et al., Oxford: Oxford University Press.

Dahl, Robert A. 1971, *Polyarchy: participation and opposition*, New Haven: Yale University Press.

Dahl, Robert A. 1999, *La democracia: una guía para los ciudadanos*, translated by Fernando Vallespín, Madrid: Taurus.

Dalton, Russell J., David M. Farrell et al. 2011, *Political parties and democratic linkage: how parties organize democracy*, Oxford: Oxford University Press.

Davidson, Mark 2018, 'Participatory budgeting, austerity and institutions of democracy', *City*, 22, 4: 551–67.

De Grauwe, Paul February 2010, 'Crisis in the eurozone and how to deal with it', *CEPS Policy Brief*, 204.

De Grauwe, Paul and Yuemei Ji 4 October 2013, 'The legacy of austerity in the Eurozone', *CEPS Commentary*, 1–6.

De Ridder, Eline, An Schrijvers et al. 2008, 'Civilian power Europe and Eastern enlargement: the more the merrier?', in *Europe's global role: external policies of the European Union*, edited by Jan Orbie, Farnham: Ashgate.

De Smet, Brecht and Koenraad Bogaert 2017, 'Resistance and passive revolution in Egypt and Morocco', in *States of discipline: authoritarian neoliberalism and the contested reproduction of capitalist order*, edited by Cemal B. Tansel, London: Rowman & Littlefield International.

'Declaração do Congresso Democrático das Alternativas' 11 October 2012, *Esquerda*.

Decreus, Thomas, Matthias Lievens et al. 2014, 'Building collective identities: how new social movements try to overcome post-politics', *Parallax*, 20, 2: 136–48.

Della Porta, Donatella, Joseba Fernández et al. 2017, *Movement parties against austerity*, New Jersey: John Wiley & Sons.

Devos, Carl, Manu Mus et al. (eds.) 2011, *De toekomst van het sociaal overleg*, Gent: Academia Press.

Diani, Mario 1992, 'The concept of social movement', *The Sociological Review*, 40, 1: 1–25.

Dias, C. 19 February 2015, Interview with an activist of the Acampada de Coimbra [Personal communication].

Dibben, Pauline 2004, 'Social movement unionism', in *Trade unions and democracy: strategies and perspectives*, edited by Mark Harcourt and Geoffrey E. Wood, Manchester: Manchester University Press.

Díez García, Rubén 2014, 'Does the Spanish 15M have an ideology? Issues of method and measurement', *Athenea Digital*, 14, 3: 199–217.

Díez García, Rubén 2017, 'The "Indignados" in space and time: transnational networks and historical roots', *Global Society*, 31, 1: 43–64.

Dinan, Desmond 2004, *Europe Recast: a history of European Union*, Basingstoke: Palgrave Macmillan.

Döbert, Rainer and Gertrud Nunner-Winkler 1973, 'Konflikt- und Rückzugspotentiale in spätkapitalistischen Gesellschaften', *Zeitschrift für Soziologie*, 2, 4: 301–25.

Douzinas, Costas and Petros Papaconstantinou, June 27 2011, 'Greece is standing up to EU neocolonialism', *The Guardian*.

Downs, Anthony 1957, An economic theory of political action in a democracy, *Journal of Political Economy*, 65, 2: 135–50.

Dryzek, John S. 2016, 'Can there be a human right to an essentially contested concept? The case of democracy', *The Journal of Politics*, 78, 2: 357–67.

Duncombe, Stephen 2016, 'Does it work?: the Æffect of activist art', *Social Research – An International Quarterly*, 83, 1: 115–34.

Duverger, Maurice 1980, 'A new political system model: semi-presidential government', *European Journal of Political Research*, 8, 2: 165–87.

Ebbinghaus, Bernhard and Jelle Visser 2000, *Trade unions in Western Europe since 1945*, Basingstoke: Palgrave Macmillan.

Engelhardt, Anne 2017a, 'Anti-austerity movements and authoritarian statism in Portugal: integrating social movement research into Poulantzas' theory of the capitalist state', *New Research in Global Political Economy*, 4.

Engelhardt, Anne 2017b, 'What belongs together will grow together? The anti-austerity movements in Portugal', in *Where have all the classes gone? A critical perspective on struggles and collective action*, edited by Oksana Balashova, Ismail D. Karatepe et al., München: Rainer Hampp Verlag.

Engels, Frederick 2010, *The origin of the family, private property and the state*, London: Penguin.

Engeman, Cassandra 2015, 'Social movement unionism in practice: organizational dimensions of union mobilization in the Los Angeles immigrant rights marches', *Work, Employment and Society*, 29, 3: 444–61.

Esping-Andersen, Gøsta 2013, *The three worlds of welfare capitalism*, New Jersey: John Wiley & Sons.

Essed, Philomena 1991, *Understanding everyday racism: an interdisciplinary theory*, Thousand Oaks: Sage.

Estanque, Elísio 2008, 'Sindicalismo e movimentos sociais', *Janus*.

Estanque, Elísio 2014, 'Rebeliões de classe média? Precariedade e movimentos sociais em Portugal e no Brasil (2011–2013)', *Revista Crítica de Ciências Sociais*, 103: 53–80.

Estanque, Elísio, Hermes A. Costa et al. 2013, 'The new global cycle of protest and the Portuguese case', *Journal of Social Science Education*, 12, 1: 31–40.

Eurostat 2020, Main tables.

Fairclough, Norman 1992, *Discourse and social change*, Cambridge, UK; Cambridge, MA: Polity Press.

Fairclough, Norman 1999, 'Global capitalism and critical awareness of language', *Language Awareness*, 8, 2: 71–83.

Fairclough, Norman 2001, *Language and power*, 2nd ed., London: Pearson Education.

Fanon, Frantz 2005, *The wretched of the Earth*, translated by Richard Philcox, New York: Grove Press.

Fanon, Frantz 2011, *Œuvres: Peau noire, masques blancs. L'An V de la révolution algérienne. Les Damnés de la terre. Pour la révolution africaine*, Paris: La Découverte.

Federici, Silvia 2004, *Caliban and the witch: women, the body and primitive accumulation*, New York: Autonomedia.

Fernandes-Jesus, Maria, Maria L. Lima at al. 2018, 'Changing identities to change the world: identity motives in lifestyle politics and its link to collective action', *Political Psychology*, 39, 5: 1031–47.

Ferreira, António C. 2004, 'Diálogo social: notas de reflexão a partir da experiência europeia e portuguesa', in *Relações laborais e sindicalismo em mudança: Portugal,*

Brasil e o contexto transnacional, organised by Elísio Estanque, Leonardo M. Silva et al., Coimbra: Quarteto.

Ferreira, António C. 2011, 'A sociedade de austeridade: poder, medo e direito do trabalho de exceção', *Revista Crítica de Ciências Sociais*, 95: 119–36.

Ferreira, António C. 2012, *Sociedade da austeridade e direito do trabalho de exceção*, Porto: Vida Económica.

Ferreira, António C. and José M. Pureza 2013, 'Estado de direito ou Estado de exceção: a justiça constitucional face ao questionamento do Estado Social', in *A anatomia da crise: identificar os problemas para construir as alternativas*, José Reis, João Rodrigues et al., Coimbra: CES/Observatório sobre Crises e Alternativas.

Fonseca, Dora J.M.C. 2016, *Movimentos sociais e sindicalismo em tempos de crise. O caso português: alianças ou tensões latentes?* [Doctoral thesis], Coimbra: Universidade de Coimbra.

Fonseca, Dona and Elísio Estanque 2018, 'Sindicalismo e lutas sociais em tempos de crise', *e-cadernos CES*, 29: 213–36.

Foucault, Michel 1997 'What is critique', in *The politics of truth*, Michel Foucault, edited by Sylvere Lotringer and John Rajchman, New York: Semiotext(e).

Fourcade-Gourinchas, Marion and Sarah L. Babb 2002, 'The rebirth of the liberal creed: paths to neoliberalism in four countries', *American Journal of Sociology*, 108, 3: 533–79.

Fox-Hodess, Katy 2017, '(Re-)Locating the local and national in the global: multi-scalar political alignment in transnational European Dockworker Union Campaigns', *British Journal of Industrial Relations*, 55, 3: 626–47.

Francisco 16 February 2013, Jornada Nacional de Ação e Luta, Coimbra [Personal communication].

Fraser, Duncan 2001, 'Long waves in economics – Waves of democracy', *Democratization*, 8, 4: 41–64.

Fraser, Nancy 2007, 'Re-framing justice in a globalizing world', in (*Mis*) *recognition, social inequality and social justice*, Nancy Fraser and Pierre Bourdieu, edited by Terry Lovell, London: Routledge.

Freire, André 2003, 'Desempenho da democracia e reformas políticas: o caso português em perspectiva comparada', *Sociologia, Problemas e Práticas*, 43: 133–60.

Freire, André 2006, 'The party system of Portugal', in *Die Parteiensysteme Westeuropas*, edited by Oskar Niedermayer, Richard Stöss et al., Wiesbaden: VS Verlag für Sozialwissenschaften.

Freire, André 16 October 2013, 'O arco constitucional e democrático', *Público*.

Freire, André 7 October 2015, 'O eleitorado unidimensional ou a derradeira hipótese das esquerdas', *Público*.

Freire, André 2016, 'The condition of Portuguese democracy during the Troika's intervention, 2011–15', *Portuguese Journal of Social Science*, 15, 2: 173–93.

Freire, André 2017, *Para lá da 'Geringonça': o governo de esquerdas em Portugal e na Europa*, Lisboa: Contraponto.

Freire, André 2019, 'Electoral systems and political reforms: Portugal in comparative perspective', in *Political institutions and democracy in Portugal: assessing the impact of the Eurocrisis*, edited by António C. Pinto and Conceição P. Teixeira, Cham: Springer.

Freire, André and Elísio Estanque 8 June 2013, 'Da reunião à convergência das esquerdas: porquê, como, para quê', *Público*.

Freire, André and Pedro Magalhães 2002, *A abstenção eleitoral em Portugal*, Lisboa: Imprensa de Ciências Sociais.

Freire, André and José Santana-Pereira 2015, 'More second-order than ever? The 2014 European Election in Portugal', *South European Society and Politics*, 20, 3: 381–401.

Freire, André, Emmanouil Tsatsanis et al. 2015, 'Crise económica, mudança de valores e representação política: um teste quasi-experimental para a teoria da representação em Portugal', in *Crise económica, políticas de austeridade e representação política*, organised by André Freire, Marco Lisi et al., Lisboa: Assembleia da República.

Friedman, Thomas L. 2000, *The Lexus and the olive tree: understanding globalization*, New York: Farrar, Straus and Giroux.

Frykman, Jonas 1999, 'Culturalization of the Mediterranean space', *Narodna Umjetnost – Croatian Journal of Ethnology and Folklore Research*, 36, 1: 283–86.

Fukuyama, Francis 1989, 'The end of history?', *The National Interest*, 16: 3–18.

Furner, James 2014, 'Carl Schmitt's "Hegel and Marx"', *Historical Materialism*, 22, 3/4: 371–87.

Gallie, Walter B. 1955/1956, 'Essentially contested concepts', *Proceedings of the Aristotelian Society*, 56: 167–98.

Geração à Rasca: nacionalistas vão à manifestação 12 March 2011, TVI24.

'Geringonça' 2018, in *Dicionário Português-Inglês*, 3rd ed., Porto: Porto Editora.

Gianolla, Cristiano 2017, *Gandhian democratisation: an account against political colonisation* [Doctoral thesis], Coimbra: Universidade de Coimbra.

Gianolla, Cristiano 2018, *5 stelle: Chi decide, come decide: centralismo e partecipazione all'interno del MoVimento*, Roma: Castelvecchi.

Gibson, Morgan R. 2013, 'The anarchism of the occupy movement', *Australian Journal of Political Science*, 48, 3: 335–48.

Giddens, Anthony 2013, *The third way: the renewal of social democracy*, New Jersey: John Wiley & Sons.

Gills, Barry and Joel Rocamora 1992, 'Low intensity democracy', *Third World Quarterly*, 13, 3: 501–23.

Giner, Salvador 1986, 'Political economy, legitimation, and the State in Southern Europe', in *Transitions from authoritarian rule: Southern Europe*, edited by Guillermo O'Donnell, Philippe C. Schmitter et al., Baltimore: Johns Hopkins University Press.

Goldberg, David T. 1993, 'Modernity, race, and morality', *Cultural Critique*, 24: 193–227.

Gorbunova, Ekaterina and Filipa Raimundo 2013, 'Direitos e liberdades e qualidade da democracia em Portugal', in *A qualidade da democracia em Portugal: a visão dos cidadãos*, organised by António C. Pinto, Luís de Sousa et al., Lisboa: Imprensa de Ciências Sociais.

Gorz, André 2004, 'Économie de la connaissance, exploitation des savoirs: entretien avec Carlo Vercelone et Yann Moulier Boutang', *Multitudes*, 1, 15: 205–16.

'Governo reafirmou aos parceiros sociais que não há alternativa à austeridade' 12 October 2012, *TSF Rádio Notícias*.

'Governo reitera que não há alternativa à austeridade', November 24 2011, *TSF Rádio Notícias*.

Graeber, David 2012, *Debt: the first 5000 years*, London: Penguin.

Gramsci, Antonio 1978, *Introdução à filosofia da práxis*, translated by S. Ferreira, Lisboa: Antídoto.

Gramsci, Antonio 1992, *Prison notebooks*, translated by Joseph A. Buttigieg and Antonio Callari, Volume 2, New York: Columbia University Press.

Gramsci, Antonio 2011, *Prison notebooks*, translated by Joseph A. Buttigieg and Antonio Callari, Volume 1, New York: Columbia University Press.

Gunaratne, Shelton A. 2006, 'Public sphere and communicative rationality: interrogating Habermas's Eurocentrism', *Journalism & Communication Monographs*, 8, 2: 93–156.

Gunn, Christopher 2011, '"Workers" participation in management, workers' control of production: Worlds apart', *Review of Radical Political Economics*, 43, 3: 317–27.

Gunther, Richard 2005, 'Parties and electoral behavior in Southern Europe', *Comparative Politics*, 37, 3: 253–75.

Habermas, Jürgen 1975a, *Legitimation crisis*, translated by Thomas McCarthy, Boston: Beacon Press.

Habermas, Jürgen 1975b, 'Towards a reconstruction of historical materialism', *Theory and Society*, 2, 1: 287–300.

Habermas, Jürgen 1985, *The theory of communicative action*, translated by Thomas, Volume 2 – Lifeworld and system: a critique of functionalist reason, McCarthy, Boston: Beacon Press.

Habermas, Jürgen 1991, *The structural transformation of the public sphere: an inquiry into a category of bourgeois society*, translated by T. Burger, Cambridge: MIT Press.

Habermas, Jürgen 1998, *Between facts and norms: contributions to a discourse theory of law and democracy*, translated by William Rehg, Cambridge: MIT Press.

Hadjimichalis, Costis 2011, 'Uneven geographical development and socio-spatial justice and solidarity: European regions after the 2009 financial crisis', *European Urban and Regional Studies*, 18, 3: 254–74.

Harcourt, Mark and Geoffrey E. Wood (eds.) 2004, *Trade unions and democracy: strategies and perspectives*, Manchester: Manchester University Press.

Hardt, Michael and Antonio Negri 2003, *Empire*, Cambridge: Harvard University Press.

Hardt, Michael and Antonio Negri 2004, *Multitude: war and democracy in the age of Empire*, New York: Penguin.

Harvey, David 1991, *The condition of postmodernity: an enquiry into the origins of cultural change*, New Jersey: Wiley-Blackwell.

Harvey, David 2005, *The new imperialism*, Oxford: Oxford University Press.

Harvey, David 2007, *A brief history of neoliberalism*, Oxford: Oxford University Press.

Harvey, David 2011, *The enigma of capital and the crises of capitalism*, 2nd ed., London: Profile Books.

Hegel, Georg W.F. 2006, *The phenomenology of mind*, translated by James B. Baillie, New York: Cosimo.

Hegel, Georg W.F. 2010, *The science of logic*, translated by George Giovanni, Cambridge, UK; Cambridge, MA: Cambridge University Press.

Held, David 2006, *Models of democracy*, Malden: Polity Press.

Held, David 2013, *Introduction to critical theory: Horkheimer to Habermas*, New York: John Wiley & Sons.

Herzfeld, Michael 1984, 'The horns of the Mediterraneanist dilemma', *American Ethnologist*, 11, 3: 439–54.

Hespanha, Pedro and Jorge Caleiras 2017, 'O labirinto das políticas de emprego', *Cadernos do Observatório sobre Crises e Alternativas*, 10: 1–62.

Heylen, Freddy 2004, *Macro-economie*, Antwerpen: Garant.

Heylen, Freddy 2014, *Macro-economie. Derde, herziene uitgave*, Nederlands: Maklu.

Hilferding, Rudolph 2019, *Finance capital: a study in the latest phase of capitalist development*, London: Routledge.

Hobsbawm, Eric J. 1994, *Age of extremes: the short twentieth century, 1914–1991*, London: Michael Joseph.

Horkheimer, Max 1976 [1937], 'Traditional and critical theory', in *Critical sociology: selected readings*, edited by Paul Connerton, Harmondsworth: Penguin.

Horkheimer, Max 1978, *Dawn & decline: notes 1926–1931 and 1950–1969*, translated by Michael Shaw, New York: Seabury Press.

Horkheimer, Max 1993, 'The present situation of Social Philosophy and the tasks of an Institute for Social Research', in *Between Philosophy and Social Science: selected early writings*, Max Horkheimer, translated by G. Frederick Hunter, Matthew Kramer et al., Cambridge: MIT Press.

Horkheimer, Max and Theodor W. Adorno 2002, *Dialectic of enlightenment: philosophical fragments*, translated by Edmund Jephcott, edited by Gunzelin S. Noerr, Stanford: Stanford University Press.

Houaiss, Antônio (ed.) 2001, 'Geringonça', in *Dicionário Houaiss da Língua Portuguesa*, Rio de Janeiro: Objetiva.

Huntington, Samuel P. 1991, *The third wave: democratization in the late twentieth century*, Norman: University of Oklahoma Press.

Indignados Lisboa 2011, Manifesto aberto dos Indignados Lisboa, Facebook.

Jacobs, Lawrence R. and Robert Y. Shapiro 1994, 'Studying substantive democracy', *PS – Political Science & Politics*, 27, 1: 9–17.

Jalali, Carlos 2019, 'The Portuguese party system: evolution in continuity?', *Political institutions and democracy in Portugal: assessing the Impact of the Eurocrisis*, edited by in António C. Pinto and Conceição Teixeira, London: Palgrave Macmillan.

Jessop, Bob and Charlie Malcolm-Brown (eds.) 1990, *Karl Marx's social and political thought: critical assessments*, London: Routledge.

João 1 25 April 2013, Manifestação, Lisboa [Personal communication].

João 2 26 October 2013, Manifestação Lisboa – QSLT – não há becos sem saída [Personal communication].

João 3 31 October 2012, Anti-Austerity budget demonstration, São Bento Lisbon [Personal communication].

Jorge 27 November 2012, Protesto CNA Budget, Lisboa São Bento [Personal communication].

Kalyvas, Andreas 2008, *Democracy and the politics of the extraordinary*, New York: Cambridge University Press.

Keniston, Kenneth 1968, *Young radicals: notes on committed youth*, New York: Harcourt, Brace & World.

Keynes, John M. 1997, *The general theory of employment, interest, and money*, Amherst: Prometheus.

Khaldun, Ibn 1987, *The Muqaddimah: an introduction to history*, edited by Nessim J. Dawood, translated by Franz Rosenthal, London: Routledge and Kegan Paul.

Kioupkiolis, Alexandros and Giorgos Katsambekis 2018, 'Radical left populism from the margins to the mainstream: a comparison of Syriza and Podemos', in *Podemos and the new political cycle: left-wing populism and anti-establishment politics*, edited by Óscar G. Agustín and Marco Briziarelli, London: Palgrave Macmillan.

Kirchheimer, Otto 1966, 'The transformation of the Western European party systems', in *Political parties and political development*, edited by Joseph Lapalombara and Myron Weiner, Princeton: Princeton University Press.

Kitschelt, Herbert 2006, 'Movement parties', in *Handbook of Party Politics*, edited by William Crotty and Richard Katz, New York: Sage.

Kivotidis, Dimitrios 11 December 2019, 'Marxist legal theory: dictatorship of the proletariat', *Critical Legal Thinking – Law and the Political*.

Klein, Naomi 2008, *The shock doctrine: the rise of disaster capitalism*, New York: Picador.

Koselleck, Reinhart 2002, *The practice of conceptual history: timing history, spacing concepts*, translated by Todd S. Presner, Kerstin Behnke, et al., Stanford: Stanford University Press.

Koselleck, Reinhart and Michaela W. Richter 2006, 'Crisis', *Journal of the History of Ideas*, 67, 2: 357–400.

Krugman, Paul 30 January 2012a, 'The conscience of a liberal: Eurozone problems', *The New York Times*.

Krugman, Paul 24 June 2012b, 'The conscience of a liberal: revenge of the optimum currency area', *The New York Times*.

Krugman, Paul 29 April 2015, 'The case for cuts was a lie. Why does Britain still believe it? The austerity delusion', *The Guardian*, 29: 31–3.

Kuhn, Thomas S. 1996, *The structure of scientific revolutions*, 3rd ed., Chicago: University of Chicago Press.

Labrincha, João 7 March 2012, 'Manifesto do 12 de março de 2012', *5dias.net*.

Laclau, Ernesto 1986, 'Os novos movimentos sociais e a pluralidade do social', *Revista Brasileira de Ciências Sociais*, 1, 2: 41–7.

Laclau, Ernesto 2005, *On populist reason*, London; New York: Verso.

Laclau, Ernesto and Chantal Mouffe 2001, *Hegemony and socialist strategy: towards a radical democratic politics*, London; New York: Verso.

Lapavitsas, Costas 2010, 'The Greek crisis – politics, economics, ethics: a debate held at the Birkbeck Institute for the Humanities, Birkbeck College, University of London, 5 May 2010', *Journal of Modern Greek Studies*, 28, 2: 293–310.

Laranjeiro, A. 13 February 2012, 'Vitor Bento: "Não há alternativa à austeridade"', *Sábado*.

Laurentino 14 November 2012, Piquete STML Lisboa [Personal communication].

Lenin, Vladimir I. 1966 [1920], *Lenin: collected works*, translated by Julius Katzer, Volume 31, Moscow: Progress.

Lenin, Vladimir I. 1977, Discourse on parliamentarianism, Second Congress of the Communist International, London.

Lenin, Vladimir I. 1999, *Imperialism: the highest stage of capitalism*, Australia: Resistance.

Lenin, Vladimir I. 2015, *State and revolution*, edited by Todd Chretien, Chicago: Haymarket.

Lijphart, Arend 1984, *Democracies: patterns of majoritarian and consensus government in twenty-one countries*, New Haven: Yale University Press.

Lijphart, Arend 1994, *Electoral systems and party systems: a study of twenty-seven democracies, 1945–1990*, New York: Oxford University Press.

Lijphart, Arend 2012, *Patterns of democracy: government forms and performance in thirty-six countries*, 2nd ed., New Haven; London: Yale University Press.

Campos Lima, Maria da Paz et al. 2011, 'Crisis and trade union challenges in Portugal and Spain: Between general strikes and social pacts', *Transfer: European Review of Labour and Research*, 17, 3: 387–402.

Lipset, Seymour M. 1959, 'Some social requisites of democracy: economic development and political legitimacy', *American Political Science Review*, 53, 1: 69–105.

Lisi, Marco 2019, 'New challenges, old parties: party change in Portugal after the European crisis', in *Political institutions and democracy in Portugal: assessing the impact of the Eurocrisis*, edited by António C. Pinto and Conceição Teixeira, London: Palgrave Macmillan.

Lisi, Marco, Riccardo Marchi et al. 2013, 'Participação política e qualidade da democracia', in *A qualidade da democracia em Portugal: a visão dos cidadãos*, organised by António C. Pinto, Luís de Sousa et al., Lisboa: Imprensa de Ciências Sociais.

Lobo, Marina Costa and Pedro C. Magalhães 2011, 'Room for Manoeuvre: Euroscepticism in the Portuguese parties and electorate 1976–2005', *South European Society and Politics*, 16, 1: 81–104.

Lopreite, Milena 2011, 'The Portugal situation during the financial crisis', *Advances in Management & Applied Economics*, 1, 1: 111–24.

Louçã, Francisco 1985, 'A "Vertigem Insurreccional": teoria e política do PCP na viragem de agosto de 1975', *Revista Crítica de Ciências Sociais*, 15/16/17: 149–62.

Louçã, Francisco and Michael Ash 2017, *Sombras: a desordem financeira na era da globalização*, Lisboa: Bertrand.

Lourenço, Nuno S. 17 March 2011, 'Passos Coelho: PEC IV é um "típico pedido de ajuda externa"', *Público*.

Löwy, Michael 1978a, *Método dialético e teoria política*, translated by R. Piero, Rio de Janeiro: Paz e Terra.

Löwy, Michael 1978b, 'Objetividade e ponto de vista de classe nas ciências sociais', in *Método dialético e teoria política*, Michael Löwy, translated by Reginaldo Di Piero, Rio de Janeiro: Paz e Terra.

Löwy, Michael 2010, *The politics of combined and uneven development: the theory of permanent revolution*, Chicago: Haymarket.

Lukács, Georg 1971, *History and class consciousness: studies in Marxist dialectics*, translated by Rodney Livingstone, Cambridge: MIT Press.

Lusa 18 November 2008, 'Ferreira Leite pergunta se "não seria bom haver seis meses sem democracia" para pôr "tudo na ordem"', *Público*.

Lusa 14 December 2011, 'Relvas: "tempos difíceis" mas "não há alternativa"', *Diário de Notícias*.

Lusa 13 March 2012, '"Não há alternativa" a trajeto de consolidação orçamental', *Diário de Notícias*.

Lusa and Sol 7 April 2013, 'CDS apela ao "arco da governabilidade"', *Sol*.

Luxemburg, Rosa 2004a, 'The Junius Pamphlet', in *The Rosa Luxemburg reader*, edited by Peter Hudis and Kevin Anderson, New York: Monthly Review Press.

Luxemburg, Rosa 2004b, 'The Russian Revolution', in *The Rosa Luxemburg reader*, edited by Peter Hudis and Kevin Anderson, New York: Monthly Review Press.

Luxemburg, Rosa 2007, *The essential Rosa Luxemburg: reform or revolution and the mass strike*, edited by Helen Scott, Chicago: Haymarket.

Luxemburg, Rosa 2014, *The complete works of Rosa Luxemburg*, edited by Peter Hudis, Volume 1 – Economic Writings 1, London; New York: Verso.

Luxemburg, Rosa 2016, *The complete works of Rosa Luxemburg*, edited by Peter Hudis and Paul Le Blanc, Volume 2 – Economic Writings 2, London; New York: Verso.

Macpherson, Crawford B. 1977, *The life and times of liberal democracy*, New York: Oxford University Press.

Maeckelbergh, Marianne 2009, *The will of the many: how the alterglobalisation movement is changing the face of democracy*, London: Pluto Press.

Magalhães, Pedro C. 2005, 'Disaffected democrats: political attitudes and political action in Portugal', *West European Politics*, 28, 5: 973–91.

Magalhães, Pedro C. 2014, 'The elections of the great recession in Portugal: performance voting under a blurred responsibility for the economy', *Journal of Elections, Public Opinion and Parties*, 24, 2: 180–202.

Magnette, Paul 2003, 'European governance and civic participation: beyond elitist citizenship?', *Political Studies*, 51, 1: 144–60.

Malcolm X 1966, *Malcolm X Speaks: selected speeches and statements*, edited by George Breitman, London: Secker et Warburg.

Malcolm X 1992, *By any means necessary: speeches, interviews, and a letter*, edited by George Breitman, New York: Pathfinder.

Maley, Terry 2011, *Democracy and the political in Max Weber's thought*, Toronto: University of Toronto Press.

Mamdani, Mahmood 2004, *Good Muslim, bad Muslim: America, the Cold War, and the roots of terror*, New York: Three Leaves Press.

Mandel, Ernest (ed.) 1973, *Contrôle ouvrier, conseils ouvriers, autogestion*, Volumes 1–2, Paris: François Maspero.

Mandel, Ernest 1982, 'Introduction to Capital. In K. Marx', *Capital: a critique of political economy*, translated by Ben Fowkes, Volume 1, Harmondsworth, UK: Penguin/New Left Review.

'Manifestação: Que se Lixe a Troika! Queremos as nossas Vidas!' 28 August 2012, Esquerda.

Manifesto 2011, Protesto da Geração à Rasca.

Manifesto Primavera Global 2012, Facebook.

Manifiesto Plural 18 May 2011, Puntos de acuerdo del manifiesto plural redactado durante la madrugada del 18 de mayo en la Puerta del Sol, Manifiesto Plural.

Manin, Bernard 1987, 'On legitimacy and political deliberation', *Political Theory*, 15, 3: 338–68.

Manuel 1 31 October 2012, Anti-Austerity budget demonstration, São Bento Lisbon [Personal communication].

Manuel 2 14 November 2012, Greve geral Piquete de greve, CTT Arroios [Personal communication].

'Marcelo Rebelo de Sousa: não há alternativa à austeridade' 14 October 2011, *Expresso*.
Margarida 26 October 2013, Manifestação – QSLT – não há becos sem saída [Personal communication].
Maria 16 February 2013, Jornada Nacional de Ação e Luta, Coimbra [Personal communication].
Mariano, A. 26 February 2015, Interview with the secretary general of SEAL [Personal communication].
Marta 2 March 2013, Manifestação Lisboa: Que se Lixe a Troika! O Povo É Quem Mais Ordena [Personal communication].
Martin, Andrew and George Ross 1999, 'European unions face the millennium', in *The brave new world of European labor: European trade unions at the millennium*, edited by Andrew Martin and George Ross, New York: Berghahn.
Martins, R. 5 December 2016, 'Greves caem para menos de metade em cinco anos', *Público*.
Marx, Karl 1873, 'Afterword', in *Capital: a critique of political economy*, translated by Samuel Moore and Edward Aveling, 2nd German ed., Volume 1, Moscow: Progress.
Marx, Karl 1968, *Theories of surplus value*, translated by Emile Burns, edited by S. Ryazanskaya, Volume IV – Capital, Moscow: Progress.
Marx, Karl 1976, *The German ideology: including Theses on Feuerbach and introduction to The critique of political economy*, 3rd rev. ed., Moscow: Progress.
Marx, Karl 1977, *Critique of Hegel's 'Philosophy of Right'*, edited by Joseph O'Malley, Cambridge: Cambridge University Press.
Marx, Karl 1982, *Capital: a critique of political economy*, translated by Ben Fowkes, Volume 1, Harmondsworth: Penguin/New Left Review.
Marx, Karl 1998, *The German ideology: including Theses on Feuerbach and introduction to the critique of political economy*, Amherst: Prometheus.
Marx, Karl 2010, 'The philosophical manifesto of the historical school of law', in *Collected works*, Karl Marx and Friedrich Engels, Volume 1 – Karl Marx 1835–43, London: Lawrence & Wishart.
Marx, Karl 2012a, *Economic and philosophic manuscripts of 1844*, North Chelmsford: Courier Corporation.
Marx, Karl 2012b, *The civil war in France*, London: Dodo Press.
Marx, Karl 2013, *The communist manifesto*, New York: Simon and Schuster.
Marx, Karl and Lenin Vladimir I. 1988, *The Civil War in France: the Paris Commune*, New York: International.
Maxwell, Kenneth 1986, 'Regime overthrow and the prospects for democratic transition in Portugal', in *Transitions from authoritarian rule: Southern Europe*, edited by Guillermo O'Donnell, Philippe C. Schmitter et al., Baltimore: Johns Hopkins University Press.
Maxwell, Kenneth 1997, *The making of Portuguese democracy*, Cambridge: Cambridge University Press.

McCormick, John P. 1999, *Carl Schmitt's critique of liberalism: against politics as technology*, Cambridge: Cambridge University Press.

McGiffen, Steve 2011, 'Bloodless coup d'Etat: the European Union's response to the Eurozone crisis', *Socialism and Democracy*, 25, 2: 25–43.

McIntyre, Alice 2008, *Participatory action research*, London: Sage.

McLean, Iain and Alistair McMillan 2003, 'Hegemony', in *The concise Oxford dictionary of politics*, edited by Iain McLean and Alistair McMillan, 2nd ed., New York: Oxford University Press.

Medearis, John 2005, 'Social movements and deliberative democratic theory', *British Journal of Political Science*, 35, 1: 53–75.

Merton, Robert K. 1938, 'Social structure and anomie', *American Sociological Review*, 3, 5: 672–82.

Meyer, Michel 1980, 'Dialectic and questioning: Socrates and Plato', *American Philosophical Quarterly*, 17, 4: 281–89.

Michels, Robert 1968, *Political parties: a sociological study of the oligarchical tendencies of modern democracy*, New York: Simon and Schuster.

Mies, Maria 1994, *Patriarchy and accumulation on a world scale: women in the international division of labour*, 5th ed., London: Zed Press.

Miguel 14 November 2012, Manifestação em São Bento, Greve Geral [Personal communication].

Monedero, Juan C. 2017, 'Populismo crítico o pós-democracia? Problemas políticos do governo representativo', *Abya-Yala – Revista Sobre Acesso à Justiça e Direitos Nas Américas*, 2, 3: 183–205.

Montesquieu 1989, *The spirit of the laws*, edited by Anne M. Cohler, Basia C. Miller et al., Cambridge; New York: Cambridge University Press.

Muñoz-Sánchez, Víctor M. and Antonio M. Pérez-Flores 2016, 'Podemos party origin: from social protest to Spanish parliament', *International Scholarly and Scientific Research & Innovation*, 10, 1: 195–201.

Moore, Jason W. 2011, 'Ecology, capital, and the nature of our times: accumulation & crisis in the capitalist world-ecology', *Journal of World-Systems Research*, 17, 1: 107–46.

Morrow, Raymond A. and David D. Brown 1994, *Critical theory and methodology*, London: Sage.

Mouffe, Chantal 1994, *Le politique et ses enjeux: pour une démocratie plurielle*, Paris: La Découverte.

Mouffe, Chantal 2000, *The democratic paradox*, London; New York: Verso.

Mouffe, Chantal 2005, *On the political*, London; New York: Routledge.

Mouffe, Chantal 2008, 'Art and democracy: art as an agnostic intervention in public space', *Open*, 14: 6–15.

Mouffe, Chantal 2013, *Agonistics: thinking the world politically*, London; New York: Verso.

Mouffe, Chantal 2014, *Artistic strategies in politics and political strategies in art*, Hemispheric Institute.

Mouffe, Chantal 2018, *For a left populism*, London; New York: Verso.

Moury, Catherine and Jorge M. Fernandes 2018, 'Minority governments and pledge fulfilment: evidence from Portugal', *Government and Opposition*, 53, 2: 335–55.

Müller-Jentsch, Walther 1995, 'Germany: from collective voice to co-management', in *Works councils: consultation, representation, and cooperation in industrial relations*, edited by Joel Rogers and Wolfgang Streeck, Chicago: University of Chicago Press.

Mylonas, Yiannis 2012, 'Media and the economic crisis of the EU: the "culturalization" of a systemic crisis and Bild-Zeitung's framing of Greece', *TripleC – Cognition, Communication, Co-Operation: Open Access Journal for a Global Sustainable Information Society*, 10, 2: 646–71.

Ness, Immanuel and Dario Azzellini 2011, *Ours to master and to own: Workers' control from the commune to the present*, Chicago: Haymarket Books.

Nkrumah, Kwame 1965, *Neo-colonialism, the last stage of imperialism*, London: Thomas Nelson & Sons.

Noela 16 February 2013, Jornada Nacional de Ação e Luta, Coimbra [Personal communication].

Nogueira, Mário 28 September 2020, Interview with Mário Nogueira [personal communication].

Nuno 1 14 November 2012, Piquete STML Lisboa [Personal communication].

Nuno 2 27 November 2012, Protesto CGTP Budget, Lisboa São Bento [Personal communication].

O'Connor, James R. 2002, *The fiscal crisis of the state*, New York: Transaction.

O'Donnell, Guillermo A. and Philippe C. Schmitter 1986, *Transitions from authoritarian rule: tentative conclusions about uncertain democracies*, Baltimore; London: Johns Hopkins University Press.

O'Donnell, Guillermo A., Philippe C. Schmitter et al. (eds.) 1986, *Transitions from authoritarian rule: prospects for democracy*, Baltimore; London: Johns Hopkins University Press.

Offe, Claus and Helmut Wiesenthal 1980, 'Two logics of collective action: theoretical notes on social class and organizational form', in *Political power and social theory*, edited by Maurice Zeitlin, Volume 1, Greenwich: JAI Press.

Ohanian, Lee E. 2010, 'The economic crisis from a neoclassical perspective', *Journal of Economic Perspectives*, 24, 4: 45–66.

Orbie, Jan (ed.) 2008, *Europe's global role: external policies of the European Union*, Aldershot: Ashgate.

O'Rourke, Brendan K. and John Hogan 2012, 'Neo-liberal discourse on an edge: communicating political economic crisis in post-2007 Ireland', SSRN – Social Science Research Network.

Palley, Thomas I. 2005, 'From keynesianism to neoliberalism: shifting paradigms in economics', in *Neoliberalism: a critical reader*, edited by Alfredo Saad and Deborah Johnston, London: Pluto Press.

Parvus 1907, *Die Kolonialpolitik und der Zusammenbruch*, Leipzig: Verlag der Leipziger Buchdruckerei Aktiengesellschaft.

Pateman, Carole 1970, *Participation and democratic theory*, Cambridge: Cambridge University Press.

Paterson, Matthew 2010, 'Legitimation and accumulation in climate change governance', *New Political Economy*, 15, 3: 345–68.

Perugorría, Ignacia and Benjamín Tejerina, 2013, 'Politics of the encounter: cognition, emotions, and networks in the Spanish 15M', *Current Sociology*, 61, 4: 424–42.

Pickerill, Jenny and John Krinsky 2012, 'Why does occupy matter?', *Social Movement Studies*, 11, 3/4: 279–87.

Piketty, Thomas 2014, *Capital in the twenty-first century*, translated by Arthur Goldhammer, Cambridge: Belknap Press of Harvard University Press.

Pinto, António C. and Luís de Sousa et al. (orgs.) 2013, *A qualidade da democracia em Portugal: a visão dos cidadãos*, Lisboa: Imprensa de Ciências Sociais.

Polanyi, Karl 2001, *The great transformation: the political and economic origins of our time*, 2nd ed., Boston: Beacon Press.

Poole, Michael 1979, 'Industrial democracy: A comparative analysis', *Industrial Relations*, 18, 3: 262–72.

Poole, Michael, Russell Lansbury et al. 2001, 'A comparative analysis of developments in industrial democracy', *Industrial Relations*, 40, 3: 490–525.

Popper, Karl 2002, *The poverty of historicism*, London: Psychology Press.

Popper, Karl 2005, *The logic of scientific discovery*, London: Routledge.

Pordata 2019, 'Eleitores nas eleições para a Assembleia da República: total, votantes e abstenção', *Pordata – Base de Dados Portugal Contemporâneo*.

Portugal 1976, Portugal's Constitution of 1976 with Amendments through 2005.

Przeworski, Adam 1985, *Capitalism and social democracy*, Cambridge: Cambridge University Press.

Przeworski, Adam 1991, *Democracy and the market: political and economic reforms in Eastern Europe and Latin America*, Cambridge: Cambridge University Press.

Przeworski, Adam 1999, 'Minimalist conception of democracy: a defense', in *Democracy's value*, edited by Ian Shapiro and Casiano Hacker-Cordón, Cambridge: Cambridge University Press.

Przeworski, Adam, Michael E. Alvarez et al. 2000, *Democracy and development: political institutions and well-being in the world, 1950–1990*, Cambridge: Cambridge University Press.

Público and Lusa 28 February 2013, 'Passos Coelho ouve Grândola, Vila Morena e insultos', *Público*.

Purakayastha, Anindya S. 2014, 'Postcolonial agonistic demo-crazy: artivism and mestiza pluralism as the dissensual politics of the governed', *Parallax*, 20, 2: 49–60.

Pureza, José M. 2015a, *Desobedecer à União Europeia*, Porto: Deriva.

Pureza, José M. 2015b, *Linhas vermelhas: crítica da crise-como-política*, Amadora: Bertrand.

Purtill, Richard L. 1967, 'Kuhn on scientific revolutions', *Philosophy of Science*, 34, 1: 53–8.

Que se lixe a Troika 22 January 2013, Manifesto – 20/01/2013. Que se lixe a Troika 15 setembro.

Rabaka, Reiland 2002, 'Malcolm X and/as critical theory: philosophy, radical politics, and the African American search for social justice', *Journal of Black Studies*, 33, 2: 145–65.

Ramos, Rui 8 October 2015, 'A fraude pós-eleitoral', *Observador*.

Rancière, Jacques 2005, 'From politics to aesthetics?', *Paragraph*, 28, 1: 13–25.

Rancière, Jacques 2011, 'The thinking of dissensus: politics and aesthetics', in *Reading Rancière*, edited by Paul Bowman and Richard Stamp, London; New York: Continuum.

Rashkova, Ekaterina R. and Ingrid V. Biezen 2014, 'The legal regulation of political parties: contesting or promoting legitimacy?', *International Political Science Review*, 35, 3: 265–74.

Rawls, John 2009, *A theory of justice*, Cambridge: Belknap Press of Harvard University Press.

Raymond, Walter J. 1992, *Dictionary of politics: selected American and foreign political and legal terms*, Lawrenceville: Brunswick.

Redação/VC 8 November 2012, 'Teodora Cardoso: "Já atingimos limite de impostos"', *TVI24*.

Refudeen, Mohammed A. 1998, 'Phenomenology versus Historicism: the case of Imamate', *American Journal of Islamic Social Sciences*, 15, 2: 63–73.

Reinhart, Carmen M. and Kenneth S. Rogoff 2009, *This time is different: eight centuries of financial folly*, Princeton: Princeton University Press.

Reinhart, Carmen M. and Kenneth S. Rogoff 2010, *Growth in a time of debt*, National Bureau of Economic Research.

Reis, José, João Rodrigues et al. 2013, 'Compreender a crise: a economia portuguesa num quadro europeu desfavorável', in *A anatomia da crise: identificar os problemas para construir as alternativas*, Reis, José, João Rodrigues et al., Coimbra: CES/Observatório sobre Crises e Alternativas.

Riddell, John (ed.) 2011, *Toward the united front: proceedings of the Fourth Congress of the Communist International, 1922*, Leiden; Boston: Brill.

Roberts, Michael 26 July 2012, 'The rate of profit is key', *The Next Recession*.

Roberts, Michael 2 April 2018, 'Marx's law of value: a debate between David Harvey and Michael Roberts', *The Next Recession*.

Robinson, James A. 1968, 'Crisis', in *International Encyclopedia of the Social Sciences*, edited by David L. Sills and Robert K. Merton, New York: Thomson Gale.

Rodney, Walter 1975, "Marxism and African liberation", *Yes to Marxism*, People's Progressive Party, Georgetown, Guyana, 18–19.

Rogers, Joel and Wolfgang Streeck 1995, 'The study of works councils: concepts and problems', in *Works councils: consultation, representation, and cooperation in industrial relations*, edited by Joel Rogers and Wolfgang Streeck, Chicago: University of Chicago Press.

Rohgalf, Jan 2013, 'Democracy of the many? Occupy Wall Street and the dead end of prefiguration', *Distinktion – Journal of Social Theory*, 14, 2: 151–167.

Roitman, Janet 2011, 'Crisis: Political concepts: Issue one', *Political concepts: A critical lexicon*.

Rosanvallon, Pierre 2013, *La légitimité démocratique: impartialité, réflexivité, proximité*. Paris: Seuil.

Roth, Michael S. 2019, *Knowing and history: appropriations of Hegel in Twentieth-Century France*, Ithaca: Cornell University Press.

Rousseau, Jean-Jacques 2001, 'The social contract', in *Democracy: a reader*, edited by Ricardo Blaug and John Schwarzmantel, 2nd ed., New York: Columbia University Press.

Rustow, Dankwart A. 1970, 'Transitions to democracy: toward a dynamic model', *Comparative Politics*, 2, 3: 337–63.

Sá, P. 31 October 2015, 'Marco António Costa: se o PS se casar com o PCP e o BE "é para a vida"', *Diário de Notícias*.

Sabariego, Jesús and Ana R. Matos 2018, 'Entre a crise e a austeridade: potencialidades e desafios das novas formas de ativismo dos recentes movimentos sociais globais em Espanha e Portugal', in *Actas del II Congreso Internacional MOVE.net sobre Movimientos Sociales y TIC*, Seville: Universidad de Sevilla; Compolíticas.

Salgado, Susana 2019a, 'The 2015 election news coverage: beyond the populism paradox, the intrinsic negativity of political campaigns in Portugal', in *Mediated campaigns and populism in Europe: political campaigning and communication*, edited by Susana Salgado, Cham: Palgrave Macmillan.

Salgado, Susana 2019b, 'Where's populism? Online media and the diffusion of populist discourses and styles in Portugal', *European Political Science*, 18, 1: 53–65.

Samaddar, Ranabir 2016, *A post-colonial enquiry into Europe's debt and migration crisis*, Singapore: Springer.

Santana-Pereira, J. 2016, 'A esquerda radical no período pós-2009: nada de (muito) novo em Portugal?', *Oficina do Historiador*, 9, 1: 58–77.

Santos, Boaventura S. 1984, 'A crise e a reconstituição do Estado em Portugal (1974–1984)', *Revista Crítica de Ciências Sociais*, 14: 7–29.

Santos, Boaventura S. 1985, 'Os três tempos simbólicos da relação entre as Forças Armadas e a sociedade em Portugal', *Revista Crítica de Ciências Sociais*, 15/16/17: 11–45.

Santos, Boaventura S. 1995a, 'Teses para renovação do sindicalismo em Portugal, seguidas de um apelo', *Vértice*, 68: 132–9.

Santos, Boaventura S. 1995b, 'Three metaphors for a new conception of law: the Frontier, the Baroque, and the South', *Law & Society Review*, 29, 4: 569–84.

Santos, Boaventura S. 1995c, *Toward a new common sense: law, science and politics in the paradigmatic transition*, New York: Routledge.

Santos, Boaventura S. 1998, *Reinventar a democracia: entre o pré-contratualismo e o pós-contratualismo*, Coimbra: CES-FEUC.

Santos, Boaventura S. 2000, *Introdução a uma ciência pós-moderna*, 3rd ed., Rio de Janeiro: Graal.

Santos, Boaventura S. 2002, *Toward a new legal common sense: law, globalization, and emancipation*, New York: Cambridge University Press.

Santos, Boaventura S. 2003, 'Poderá o direito ser emancipatório?', *Revista Crítica de Ciências Sociais*, 65: 3–76.

Santos, Boaventura S. (ed.) 2005, *Democratizing democracy: beyond the liberal democratic canon*, London; New York: Verso.

Santos, Boaventura S. 2007, 'Para além do pensamento abissal: das linhas globais a uma ecologia de saberes', *Revista Crítica de Ciências Sociais*, 78: 3–46.

Santos, Boaventura S. 2012, *Portugal: ensaio contra a autoflagelação*, Coimbra: Almedina.

Santos, Boaventura S. 2016a, 'Epistemologies of the South and the future', *From the European South: A Transdisciplinary Journal of Postcolonial Humanities*, 1: 17–29.

Santos, Boaventura S. 2016b, *La difícil democracia: una mirada desde la periferia europea*, Madrid: Akal.

Santos, Boaventura S. and Leonardo Avritzer 2005, 'Introduction: opening up the canon of democracy', in *Democratizing democracy: beyond the liberal democratic canon*, edited by Boaventura S. Santos, London; New York: Verso.

Santos, Boaventura S. and José M. Mendes (orgs.) 2017, *Demodiversidade: imaginar novas possibilidades democráticas*, Lisboa: Edições 70.

Santos, Boaventura S. and Maria P. Meneses (eds.) 2019, *Knowledges born in the struggle: constructing the epistemologies of the global South*, New York: Routledge.

Santucci, Antonio A. 2010, *Antonio Gramsci*, New York: Monthly Review Press.

Scharpf, Fritz W. 2012, 'Legitimacy intermediation in the multilevel European polity and its collapse in the euro crisis', *MPIfG Discussion Paper*, 12/6, Max Planck Institute for the Study of Societies, Cologne.

Schattschneider, Elmer E. 1977, *Party government*, London; Westport: Greenwood.

Schmidt, Vivien A. 2013, 'Democracy and legitimacy in the European Union revisited: input, output and "throughput"', *Political Studies*, 61, 1: 2–22.

Schmitt, Carl 1986, *Political theology: four chapters on the concept of sovereignty*, translated by George Schwab, Cambridge: MIT Press.

Schmitt, Carl 1988, *The crisis of parliamentary democracy*, translated by Ellen Kennedy, Cambridge: MIT Press.

Schmitt, Carl 1996, *Roman Catholicism and political form*, translated by Gary L. Ulmen, London; Westport: Greenwood.

Schmitt, Carl 2008, *The concept of the political: expanded edition*, translated by George Schwab, Chicago: University of Chicago Press.

Schmitt, Carl 2014, 'Hegel and Marx', *Historical Materialism – Research in Critical Marxist Theory*, 22, 3/4: 388–93.

Schmitt, Carl (ed.) 2017, *Political romanticism*, New York: Routledge.

Schumpeter, Joseph A. 1976, *Capitalism, socialism, and democracy*, New York: Harper & Row.

Selassie, Abebe 2013, Interview with Abebe Selassie [Personal communication].

Serra, R. 2019, 'Baldio', in *Dicionário Alice*, coordinated by Boaventura S. Santos, Maria P. Meneses et al., Coimbra: Centro de Estudos Sociais.

Seymour, Richard 2014, *Against austerity: how we can fix the crisis they made*, London: Pluto Press.

Sharpe, Matthew and Geoff M. Boucher 2010, *Žižek and politics: a critical introduction*, Edinburgh: Edinburgh University Press.

Sloane, Thomas O. (ed.) 2001, *Encyclopedia of Rhetoric*, New York: Oxford University Press.

Smith, Adam 1976, *An inquiry into the nature and causes of the wealth of nations*, Chicago: University of Chicago Press.

Smith, Cyril 1996, *Marx at the millennium*, London: Pluto Press.

Soares, Mónica C. 2017, 'Prefigurative politics and emergent communitarian spaces: the case of Portugal', *Santiago*, 144: 519–33.

Soeiro, José 2014, 'Da Geração à Rasca ao Que se lixe a Troika: Portugal no novo ciclo internacional de protesto', *Sociologia – Revista da Faculdade de Letras da Universidade do Porto*, 28: 55–79.

Soeiro, José 15 July 2020, Interview with José Soeiro [Personal communication].

Soeiro, José, Miguel Cardina et al. (coords.) 2013, *Não acredite em tudo o que pensa: mitos do senso comum na era da austeridade*, Lisboa: Tinta da China.

Springer, Simon, Kean Birch et al. (eds.) 2016, *The handbook of neoliberalism*, New York: Routledge.

Starn, Randolph 2005, 'Crisis', in *New Dictionary of the History of Ideas*, Randolph Starn, The Gale Group.

Stiglitz, Joseph E. 2002, *Globalization and its discontents*, New York; London: W.W. Norton.

Stiglitz, Joseph E. 10 October 2013, 'After the financial crisis we were all Keynesians – but not for long enough', *The Guardian*.

Stiglitz, Joseph E. 26 September 2014, 'Europe's austerity zombies', Project Syndicate.

Stiglitz, Joseph E. 2017, 'The fundamental flaws in the euro zone framework', in *The Euro and the crisis: perspectives for the Eurozone as a monetary and budgetary union*, edited by Nazaré C. Cabral, José R. Gonçalves et al., Cham: Springer.

Stoleroff, Alan 2016, 'The Portuguese labour movement and industrial democracy: From workplace revolution to the European crisis', *Journal of Industrial Relations*, 58, 1: 26–44.

Suchting, Wallis A. 1972, 'Marx, Popper, and "historicism"', *Inquiry – An Interdisciplinary Journal of Philosophy*, 15, 1/4: 235–66.

Swyngedouw, Erik 2007, 'Impossible sustainability and the post-political condition', in *The sustainable development paradox: urban political economy in the United States and Europe*, edited by Rob Krueger and David Gibbs, London: Guildford.

Swyngedouw, Erik 2009, 'The antinomies of the postpolitical city: in search of a democratic politics of environmental production', *International Journal of Urban and Regional Research*, 33, 3: 601–20.

Swyngedouw, Erik 2011, 'Interrogating post-democratization: reclaiming egalitarian political spaces', *Political Geography*, 30, 7: 370–80.

Swyngedouw, Erik 2014, 'Where is the political? Insurgent mobilisations and the incipient "return of the political"', *Space and Polity*, 18, 2: 122–36.

Teague, Paul 1999, 'Reshaping employment regimes in Europe: policy shifts alongside boundary change', *Journal of Public Policy*, 19, 1: 33–62.

Temple, Luke, Maria T. Grasso et al. 2016, 'Neoliberal narrative in times of economic crisis: a political claims analysis of the U.K. Press, 2007–14', *Politics & Policy*, 44, 3: 553–76.

Therborn, Göran1977, 'The rule of capital and the rise of democracy', *New Left Review*, 103: 3–41.

Therborn, Göran 1999, *The ideology of power and the power of ideology*, London; New York: Verso.

Thomas, Peter 2009, *The Gramscian moment: philosophy, hegemony and Marxism*, Leiden; Boston: Brill.

Tiago 14 November 2012, Greve geral Piquete de greve, CTT Arroios [Personal communication].

Tiago, Miguel 25 March 2015, Interview with Miguel Tiago [Personal communication].

Tong, Shijun 2000, *The dialectics of modernization: Habermas and the Chinese discourse of modernization*, Sydney: Wild Peony.

Trotsky, Leon 1986, *Their morals and ours: the class foundations of moral practice*, 4th ed., New York: Pathfinder.

Trotsky, Leon 1991, *The revolution betrayed: what is the Soviet Union and where is it going?*, Oak Park: Mehring Books.

Trotsky, Leon 2001, *The history of the Russian Revolution*, 7th ed., New York: Pathfinder.

Trotsky, Leon 2007, *The first five years of the Communist International*, Volume 1, New York: Pathfinder.

Trotsky, Leon 2010, *The permanent revolution & Results and prospects*, Seattle: Red Letter.

Trotsky, Leon 2015, *Permanent revolution*, Andesite.

Tsatsanis, Emmanouil and Ana M. Belchior 2020, 'Democratic legitimacy and trust in political institutions in Portugal before and after the Great Recession: transitory or lasting effects?', in *Political representation and citizenship in Portugal: from crisis to renewal*, edited by Marco Lisi, André Freire et al., Lexington: Lexington Books.

Turner, Lowell and Richard W. Hurd 2001, 'Building social movement unionism: the transformation of the American labor movement', in *Rekindling the movement: labor's quest for relevance in the 21st Century*, edited by Richard W. Hurd, Harry C. Katz et al., Ithaca: Cornell University Press.

Udehn, Lars 2002, *Methodological individualism: background, history and meaning*, London; New York: Routledge.

Van Biezen, Ingrid and Fernando C. Bértoa 2014, 'Party regulation in post-authoritarian contexts: Southern Europe in comparative perspective', *South European Society and Politics*, 19, 1: 71–87.

Van Vossole, Jonas 2015a, 'De confrontatie tussen Belem en Sao Bento: een overzicht van de Portugese coalitie-gesprekken', *DeWereldMorgen.be*, 1.

Van Vossole, Jonas 2015b, 'Post-political articulations of democracy: a critical review of the anti-austerity protest discourses', in *Comunicambio: comunicación y sociedad civil para el cambio social*, organised by Eloísa Nos-Aldás, Alex Iván Arévalo Salinas et al., Madrid: Fragua.

Van Vossole, Jonas 2016a, 'Framing PIGS: patterns of racism and neocolonialism in the Euro crisis', *Patterns of Prejudice*, 50, 1: 1–20.

Van Vossole, Jonas 2016b, 'Historische Portugese verkiezingen openen perspectieven voor links', SPanning: Tijdschrijft van het Wetenschappelijk bureau an de SP, 1.

Van Vossole, Jonas 2018, '"Crisis" as a social-scientific and critical perspective on the question of democracy in Portugal 2011–2014', in *Plunging into Turmoil: social sciences and crises processes*, organised by Patrícia Oliveira, Newcastle upon Tyne: Cambridge Scholars.

Van Vossole, Jonas 2020, 'Reinstitutionalising democracy: the role of the Portuguese elections in temporally taming the democratic crisis', in *Protest, youth and precariousness: the unfinished fight against austerity in Portugal*, edited by Renato M. Carmo and José A.V. Simões, New York; Oxford: Berghahn Books.

Varela, Raquel C. 21 March 2013, 'Nasce a "Aliança Povo-MFA"', Raquel Varela – Historiadora Labour Historian.

Varela, Raquel C. 2010, *História da política do Partido Comunista Português durante a Revolução dos Cravos (1974–1975)* [Doctoral thesis], Lisboa: ISCTE-IUL.

Varela, Raquel C. and Roberto D. Santa 2023, *Breve História de Portugal. A era contemporânea (1807–2020)*, Lisboa: Bertrand Editora.

Vasconcelos, Álvaro 2019, *25 de abril no futuro da democracia*, Porto: Estratégias Criativas.

Vilas Boas, C. 26 February 2015, Interview with an activist of the Acampada de Coimbra [Personal communication].

Visser, Jelle 1995, 'Trade unions from a comparative perspective', in *Comparative industrial and employment relations*, organised by Joris V. Ruysseveldt, Rien Huiskamp et al., London: Sage.

Von Mises, Ludwig 1984, *The historical setting of the Austrian school of economics*, Auburn: Ludwig von Mises Institute.

Wahl, Jean 1982, *Le malheur de la conscience dans la philosophie de Hegel*, Paris: FeniXX.

Walker Jr., William O. 1986 [1984; 1985], 'Crisis and catharsis: the power of the apocalypse. By Adela Yarbro Collins, Philadelphia: Westminster, 1984, 180 pages. $11.95 (paper). – The book of revelation: justice and judgment. By Elisabeth Schüssler Fiorenza. Philadelphia: Fortress, 1985. xii + 211 pages. $11.95 (paper)', *Horizons*, 13, 1: 154.

Wallerstein, Immanuel 2002, 'The itinerary of world-systems analysis; or, how to resist becoming a theory?', in *New directions in contemporary sociological theory*, edited by Joseph Berger and Morris J. Zelditch, Lanham: Rowman & Littlefield.

Webb, Sidney and Beatrice Webb 2003, *History of trade unionism*, Barnes & Noble Digital.

Weber, Max 1990, 'The advent of plebiscitarian democracy', in *The West European Party System*, edited by Peter Mair, Oxford: Oxford University Press.

Wickham, James 2002, 'The end of the European social model: before it began?', in Irish Business and Employers' Confederation, Irish Congress of Trade Unions, Dublin: IBEC.

Willoughby, John 1995, 'Evaluating the Leninist theory of imperialism', *Science & Society*, 59, 3: 320–38.

Wodak, Ruth 2011, 'Critical linguistics and critical discourse analysis', in *Discursive Pragmatics*, edited by Jan Zienkowski, Jan-Ola Östman et al., Volume 8 – Handbook of pragmatics highlights, Amsterdam: John Benjamins.

Wood, Ellen M. 1998, *The retreat from class: a new "true" socialism*, London; New York: Verso.

Wood, Ellen M. 2016, *Democracy against capitalism: renewing historical materialism*, London; New York: Verso.

Wood, Geoffrey 2006, 'Trade unions and theories of democracy', in *Trade unions and democracy: strategies and perspectives*, edited by Mark Harcourt and Geoffrey Wood, Manchester: Manchester University Press.

Yin, Robert K. 2011, *Qualitative research from start to finish*, New York: Guilford Press.

Young, Iris M. 2011, 'Activist challenges to deliberative democracy', *Raisons Politiques*, 42, 2: 131–58.
Žižek, Slavoj 1989, *The sublime object of ideology*, London; New York: Verso.
Žižek, Slavoj 2000, *The ticklish subject: the absent centre of political ontology*, London; New York: Verso.
Žižek, Slavoj 2004, 'The lesson of Rancière', in *The politics of aesthetics: the distribution of the sensible*, Jacques Rancière, translated by Gabriel Rockhill, London: Continuum.
Žižek, Slavoj 2006, *The parallax view*, Cambridge; London: MIT Press.
Žižek, Slavoj 2009, *In defense of lost causes*, London; New York: Verso.
Žižek, Slavoj 2012, *Less than nothing: Hegel and the shadow of dialectical materialism*, London; New York: Verso.

Index

www.ingramcontent.com/pod-product-compliance
Ingram Content Group UK Ltd.
Pitfield, Milton Keynes, MK11 3LW, UK
UKHW022227051026
15624UKWH00002B/392

9 789004 766228